An Oneida Indian in Foreign Waters

The Iroquois and Their Neighbors

Christopher Vecsey, *Series Editor*

An ONEIDA INDIAN *in* FOREIGN WATERS

The Life of
CHIEF CHAPMAN SCANANDOAH,
1870 – 1953

Laurence M. Hauptman

Syracuse University Press

First Edition 2016
16 17 18 19 20 21   6 5 4 3 2 1

∞ The paper used in this publication meets the minimum requirements of the American
National Standard for Information Sciences—Permanence of Paper for Printed Library
Materials, ANSI Z39.48-1992.

For a listing of books published and distributed by Syracuse University Press,
visit www.SyracuseUniversityPress.syr.edu.

ISBN: 978-0-8156-3489-8 (hardcover)   978-0-8156-1079-3 (paperback)
978-0-8156-5387-5 (e-book)

Library of Congress Cataloging-in-Publication Data
Names: Hauptman, Laurence M., author.
Title: An Oneida Indian in foreign waters : the life of Chief Chapman Scanandoah,
    1870–1953 / Laurence M. Hauptman.
Other titles: Life of Chief Chapman Scanandoah, 1870-1953
Description: Syracuse, New York : Syracuse University Press, [2016] | Series: The Iroquois
    and their neighbors | Includes bibliographical references and index.
Identifiers: LCCN 2016030788 (print) | LCCN 2016032697 (ebook) | ISBN 9780815634898
    (hardcover : alk. paper) | ISBN 9780815610793 (pbk. : alk. paper) | ISBN 9780815653875
    (e-book)
Subjects: LCSH: Scanandoah, Chapman, 1870-1953. | Oneida Indians—Kings and rulers—
    Biography. | Oneida Indians—History. | Oneida Indians—Land tenure. | Inventors—
    New York (State)—Biography. | Mechanics—New York (State)—Biography. | United
    States. Navy—Machinist's mates—Biography. | Indians, Treatment of—New York
    (State) | Onondaga Indian Reservation (N.Y.)—Biography. | Lenox (N.Y.)—History, Local.
Classification: LCC E99.O45 H378 2016 (print) | LCC E99.O45 (ebook) | DDC
    974.700497/55430092 [B] —dc23
LC record available at https://lccn.loc.gov/2016030788

For my friends Gordy and Betty McLester who have done so much to preserve and disseminate their Oneida people's history

Contents

Illustrations

Figures

Maps

Table

Preface

This book had its beginnings in the early 1980s while I was on a research visit to the Rochester Museum and Science Center. Late in the afternoon, I met up with Keith Reitz, an Oneida Indian residing at the time in nearby Pittsford. I had been acquainted with Reitz for several years, largely through my friendship with the late Richard Chrisjohn, the noted Oneida artist, and had spoken to him before about Oneida history. However, on that hot summer July day, I had the opportunity to listen to Reitz's reflections about his own family history. We walked several blocks down East Avenue from the museum and sat on the steps of the Rochester Historical Society.[1]

For two and a half hours, I listened to this Oneida in his deep baritone voice proudly tell the history of his Hanyoust (Honyost, Hanyost, Honyoust) family and how he ended up residing in the suburbs of Rochester. Some of what he told me appeared to be far-fetched but later proved to be entirely accurate. He recounted how twenty-four of his relatives, going against all odds, had fought successfully to win a favorable decision in federal courts in 1919 and 1920. The case, *United States v. Boylan*, allowed his family to win back what he referred to as the "thirty-two acres" in the town of Lenox, Madison County, New York. Facing impossible roadblocks at nearly every turn and at a time when millions of acres were passing out of Native American hands under federal policies that began with the Dawes General Allotment Act in 1887, Reitz's small family was able to obtain justice. The courts not only recognized them as rightful owners of the thirty-two acres, but deemed them a federally recognized Indian tribe with treaty rights that put them outside the bounds of state jurisdiction.[2] Despite this landmark victory, for various reasons described in

Fig. 1. Chapman Scanandoah, 1907. After temporarily getting shore leave, Scanandoah was part of an Oneida delegation to the Office of Indian Affairs in Washington, DC, who were petitioning for federal help in an effort to retain their lands. Photograph by Delancey W. Gill. Courtesy of the National Anthropological Archives, Smithsonian Institution, Image NAA INV 06208200.

chapter 6, most Hanyousts, now threatened by local whites after this decision, stayed away from returning to the thirty-two acres. Many remained at the Onondaga Reservation where they had lived for decades; others, including Reitz's parents, left for Rochester, where George P. Decker, their attorney, found them employment.[3]

In 2013 I decided to revisit this story. I did so after spending the previous four decades researching and writing Seneca and Wisconsin Oneida history and doing applied work for several Native American communities. In investigating the history of this case that began with the ejectment of the Hanyousts in 1909, I was to uncover materials about the remarkable life of Chapman Scanandoah (also spelled "Schanandoah" or "Schenandoah"), an extraordinary New York Oneida who lived from 1870 to 1953. He was one of two dozen Hanyousts who had helped save the thirty-two acres. Chapman was a key figure in the case and was a vital member of this Native community over an eighty-year period. Indeed, the more I dug into the history of this case as well as into Oneida history in the last three decades of the nineteenth century through the first half of the twentieth century, the more I found about Scanandoah's exceptional life and how he contributed to tribal survival.

Scanandoah was truly a remarkable individual. He was a noted mechanic, a decorated navy veteran, a prizewinning agronomist, a historian, linguist, and philosopher, an early leader of the Oneida land-claims movement, and an elected chief of the Oneidas. However, his fame today among his Oneida people rests with his career as an inventor.[4] On March 1, 1926, a reporter wrote about Scanandoah's scientific accomplishments: "Chief Chapman Schanandoah, sachem, Oneida Tribe of Iroquois and a resident of the Onondaga Reservation at Nedrow, has won recognition from the Great White Father as an inventor in the realm of science which always has seemed the white man's realm. . . . He holds the confidence and the rapport of the dusky men and women in the midst of where he lives. They are glad he has won this honor in the world outside their valley and has proved the Indian of today knows tools, machines, and molecules."[5]

The present study emphasizes that without Chapman Scanandoah and his mother, Mary, as well as his brother Albert, his cousin William Hanyoust Rockwell, and their extended family, Oneida existence in New York might have been extinguished. Their success in defending the remaining thirty-two-acre Oneida land base in the first two decades of the twentieth century made it possible for the Oneidas' resurgence over the past few decades. Since the early 1990s, the Oneidas have extended their land base to well over thirty-five thousand acres in central New York, attained tremendous economic success by initiating casino gaming, and established other tribal enterprises, including the newspaper *Indian Country Today*, which has the largest circulation of any tribally published newspaper in North America. Visitors to the Oneida Nation's Turning Stone Resort and Casino in Verona, New York, are unaware of the difficult road these Native Americans traveled in the eight decades of Chapman Scanandoah's life. Instead, visitors are overwhelmed by seeing the glitz of a four-star resort and one of the larger casinos in North America, with its championship golf course, gourmet restaurants, and facilities for major billiards and boxing matches and world-class entertainment.

During Chapman Scanandoah's lifetime, Plains and Southwestern Indians were conquered by the US Army, federal allotment policies resulted in the loss of significant Indian natural resources and approximately ninety million acres of their lands, and governmental officials attempted to terminate Washington's treaty obligations. Consequently, much of the writings on Native American history have focused on loss and not on the great ability of Native peoples to adapt.

Scanandoah was heavily influenced by events transpiring in Indian Country, including what had befallen his Oneida people, namely, the loss of nearly six million acres of their land since 1785. However, he did not just look nostalgically back to the pre-Revolutionary greatness of the Iroquois League. Quite importantly, Scanandoah was part of a new generation of Hodinöhsö:ni´ who clearly were able to adapt to the rapid changes occurring around them in the new industrial order in America. At the same time, these same Hodinöhsö:ni´ were able to maintain their Oneida cultural identity and their larger sense of Six Nations nationalism. Not only was Scanandoah himself employed at General Electric's central operations in Schenectady, but his expertise as a mechanic led him to work in large firms from Massachusetts to Michigan as well as at the New York and Washington Naval Shipyards and at the Frankford Arsenal in Philadelphia.

In his thought-provoking book *Indians in Unexpected Places*, historian Philip Deloria has aptly pointed out that American Indian concepts of sovereignty have "always lived in the America context, in tension with the powerful idea of inclusion." That statement fits well into characterizing Scanandoah's extraordinary life, as he balanced being a proud Hanyoust, protecting his family's homestead and Oneida treaty rights, with the pursuit of several careers outside of his Native homeland. Deloria has also observed that, in the last years of the nineteenth and first part of the twentieth centuries, "a significant cohort of Native people engaged the same forces of modernization that were making non-Indians reevaluate their own expectations of themselves and their society."[6]

Indeed, during these decades, which corresponded to almost the exact years of Scanandoah's life, the Hodinöhsö:ni´ entered the building trades as ironworkers and transformed American cities in high steelwork by constructing bridges and skyscrapers. Thus, in undertaking these new occupational pursuits, Scanandoah and many of his Hodinöhsö:ni´ contemporaries challenged the stereotypes of the times, ones that too often presented Native Americans as primitive, pretechnological, and missing out on "modernity."

Despite his commitment to protect and later reclaim his family's small Oneida tribal land base, Scanandoah ironically lived and worked most of his life among others. Out of educational necessity, he went off for his schooling to Virginia. Out of economic necessity, he found himself securing employment away from Oneida territory. In the traditional Hodinöhsö:ni´ manner, after marrying Bertha Crouse, an Onondaga, he moved to her reservation. Yet as we will see, although he stayed at Onondaga for more than forty years, raising his five children there, he held on to his separate Oneida identity.

While residing in "foreign waters," he successfully managed to succeed in nearly everything he did. He was an outsider at the primarily African American Hampton (Normal and Agricultural) Institute in Virginia, where he was educated in the late 1880s and early 1890s; one of the very few Native Americans in the US Navy from 1897 to 1912; an Oneida with no land or political rights on the Onondaga Reservation, where he resided for much of his life; a litigant in the white man's court attempting to prevent the loss of the last remaining Oneida lands in the Empire State; a Native American inventor earning patents in the age of Thomas Edison; one of the founders of the Indian Village at the New York State Fair; and a valued employee and mechanic working for major companies in Schenectady and Syracuse. While he was traveling in all of these foreign waters, he was serving his Oneida people as the man behind the scenes, as advisor to his first cousin Chief William Hanyoust Rockwell. Chief Rockwell was a garrulous leader with a flair for storytelling, who often took credit for Oneida success in court. Chapman was far better educated and more worldly and was the man behind the scenes furthering his people's efforts.[7]

Unlike other Oneidas at the time, Scanandoah's life is, fortunately for us, well documented. Fifty-nine of his letters to Joseph Keppler Jr. (born

Udo J. Keppler) and to Harriet Maxwell Converse are in the Carl A. Kroch Library's Rare and Manuscript Division at Cornell University. Both saw themselves as reformers of Indian policies and used their influence to help the friends they made in Six Nations communities. From 1899 into the 1940s, the Oneida corresponded with Keppler, the prominent political cartoonist, editor, and publisher of *Puck*. Scanandoah's letters were often addressed to Keppler as "Brother Wolf," since the editor had been adopted by the Seneca Indians and given the name *Gy-ant-wa-ka*, the name once held by Chief Cornplanter. He was a reformer of Indian policy and an Indian lacrosse enthusiast, and he had advocated, among other things, that Native Americans be given discount railway passes. As a collector of Iroquoian art and folklore, he later served as the vice president of the board of trustees at the Heye Foundation that administered the Museum of the American Indian.[8] Keppler, a muckraking cartoonist, leading Progressive, and personal friend of President Theodore Roosevelt, was to serve as Scanandoah's advisor, benefactor, financier, and friend. He provided financial and political assistance and served as an intermediary between Scanandoah and his family and their attorneys.[9] Both Keppler and Converse saw themselves as defenders of the Hodinöhsö:ni´. Among the many causes that they jointly took up was the elaborate reburial ceremony of Lewis Bennett, popularly known as "Deerfoot," the internationally famous, world-class long-distance runner, alongside the graves of other prominent Senecas—Ely S. Parker, Red Jacket, Destroy Town, Little Billy, Young King, and Captain Pollard—at the Forest Lawn Cemetery in Buffalo.[10]

For a much briefer time, Scanandoah had a special friendship with Harriet Maxwell Converse, the noted woman of letters and writer on Iroquoian arts and traditions.[11] He corresponded with her from 1899 to her death in November 1903. After the Civil War, Converse had become a friend and confidante of Ely S. Parker, the Tonawanda sachem and first Native American to be appointed commissioner of Indian affairs. To Ely's descendants such as Arthur C. Parker, she became "Aunt Hattie."[12] Converse, whose family for two previous generations had befriended the Hodinöhsö:ni´. In the mid-1880s, she was adopted into the Snipe Clan by the Senecas and given the name *Ga-ya-nes-ha-oh*, or "Bearer of the Law."

Because her Maxwell family had long been involved in state and federal politics and had made acquaintances with influential congressmen on Capitol Hill, Converse helped the Senecas resist federal and state efforts to allot the Allegany and Cattaraugus Reservation lands. In the early 1890s, she was adopted and condoled as a chief by the Iroquois Confederacy and renamed *Ya-ie-wa-noh*, or "She Watches over You."[13] Much like Keppler, she was the Oneidas' advisor, benefactor, financier, and friend. Consequently, Scanandoah would refer to her as "Cousin Snipe." Whenever Scanandoah needed information, money, a recommendation for promotion, or assistance to get out of "hot water," she was the first non-Indian he contacted.[14]

Other materials that throw light on Scanandoah's extraordinary life have also survived. Several of his letters are reprinted in the *Southern Workman* and *Talks and Thoughts of the Hampton Indian Students*, two periodicals published by Hampton Institute, the school that the Oneida attended from 1888 to 1894. Valuable information about the Oneida are also found in Hampton publications from 1890 to 1921. An autobiographical account by Chief William Rockwell, who was born the same month and year as his first cousin Chapman Scanandoah, is housed at the Madison County Historical Society and provides information about their childhood in the 1870s and 1880s as well as the important relationship of the two men over seven decades. I have also made use of Scanandoah's testimony at major federal and state hearings that reveal his views on Hodinöhsö:ni´ sovereignty. Court records and the George Decker Papers at St. John Fisher College in East Rochester provide information about the Hanyousts' herculean legal efforts to win back their lands from 1909 to 1920.

Visits to the New York State Archives in Albany, the Federal Records Center in Manhattan, and the National Archives in Washington, DC, provided valuable information about Oneida land claims and Scanandoah's efforts to fight termination policies of the late 1940s and early 1950s. Scanandoah's naval service record was located at the National Personnel Records Center of the National Archives in St. Louis. It contained materials related to his naval assignments, conduct and disciplinary actions, medical history, and promotions. This extensive file also revealed information about the Oneida's postnaval career, including his work at the

New York Navy Yard at Brooklyn and his unsuccessful attempts to rejoin the US Navy years after his honorable discharge.

The massive William Beauchamp Collection at the New York State Library, central New York newspapers, and the vertical files at the Onondaga Historical Association in Syracuse helped fill in missing pieces in the life of Chapman Scanandoah. Hope E. Allen, the noted historian of the Middle Ages, collected folklore among the Oneidas from 1916 to 1945. Allen's field notes and interviews, which are at the Bird Library at Syracuse and at the Burke Library at Hamilton College, provide valuable information about Oneida beliefs and customs. These records focus on the Oneidas' Orchard more than Scanandoah's Windfall community, but reveal much about Oneida women, including Chapman's mother, Mary.

My fieldwork experiences and interviews, especially with the Senecas, have given me an awareness that Hodinöhsö:ni´ communities are diverse populations and that residents of their territories often include minorities of other Native American peoples and non-Indians as well. For example, numerous Cayugas from the early nineteenth century onward have lived with the Senecas and are a minority group, especially at the Cattaraugus Indian reservation. As outsiders, they were allowed to "spread their blanket," an important Iroquoian metaphor, as long as they followed the rules set by the Seneca Nation council. Numerous Oneidas, such as Chapman Scanandoah, lived as a minority at Onondaga. Remarkably, although there were times of tensions and even discrimination, they were able to maintain their separate identity within the boundaries of this reservation. Although married to an Onondaga, Bertha Crouse, and raising five children as Onondagas following Hodinöhsö:ni´ customs of matrilineage, Scanandoah identified himself, and in most cases was identified by others, as an Oneida throughout his nearly forty years of residency there.[15] Thus, despite the central New York focus of this book, the life of Chapman Scanandoah has wider relevance about maintaining tribal identity throughout Iroquoia and beyond, since similar situations exist throughout Indian Country.

My interest in writing biography is a long-standing one. Approximately twenty years ago, Chief William Tooshkenig of the "Three Fires People" (Odawa, Ojibwe, and Potawatomi) from Walpole Island Reserve encouraged me to write more biographical studies.[16] I took up the challenge with the assistance of my coauthor L. Gordon McLester III, an Oneida tribal historian. Consequently, in 2002 the University of Oklahoma Press published *Chief Daniel Bread and the Oneida Indians of Wisconsin*, a study of the most prominent Oneida political leader of the nineteenth century. In it we explained that the rationale for the project was that anthropologists and historians had produced too few biographies of prominent Hodinöhsö:ni´ leaders and that biographers had largely focused on Plains and Southwestern warriors of the nineteenth century, such as Sitting Bull and Geronimo. I followed up this project with a study, *Seven Generations of Iroquois Leadership: The Six Nations since 1800*, published by Syracuse University Press in 2008, an eleven-chapter book that dealt with male and female leadership that was mostly political. In it I noted that leadership was a major factor in cultural persistence and that it had to be examined from inside the community outwardly, not just from the far-off perspectives of officials in Albany and Washington.[17]

By focusing on the life of Chapman Scanandoah, this study builds on these previous two books. I have now broadened my writings away from merely focusing on political leadership. Scanandoah was not just a political leader who testified before official hearings on behalf of his Oneida people. Besides his role as a chief, his achievements were many and a source of pride for his people at times of crisis. Oneidas in New York had to contend with the foreclosure of their lands, both federal and state assimilationist policies, racial discrimination by whites and second-class status on another Indian reservation, extreme poverty and limited access to education, and internal divisions.

Several caveats are needed relating to spelling throughout this book. Scanandoah's surname is spelled at least five different ways from his birth records in 1870 to his tombstone in 1953. These included "Sconondoa," "Scanandoah," "Schanandoah," "Schenandoah," and "Shanandoah." This variation is also true of one of Chapman's inventions, an explosive known as "shanandite." Sometimes it was also spelled "schanadite" and "schenedite." In order to be consistent throughout the book, I spell the Oneida's surname "Scanandoah" and the explosive as "shanandite." Second, the family name Hanyoust was also spelled "Hanyost" or "Honyoust." Once again to be consistent, I have used "Hanyoust" more than other spellings of the family name. I have also used the word "Hodinöhsö:ni‴" for the Iroquois or Six Nations, "the people of the longhouse or extended lodge," throughout the book, although there are several different variations of the term.

New Paltz, New York
March 1, 2016

Acknowledgments

Through the kindness of anthropologist Dr. Jack Campisi, I was first introduced to Oneida community members in New York, Wisconsin, and Ontario, Canada, and became interested in the historical and contemporary concerns that these communities had and have. I owe him a great debt. Over the years, I have been fortunate to meet and learn from Oneidas in these communities. Keith Reitz and Ray Elm, two New York Oneidas, and Richard Chrisjohn, born at Southwold, Ontario, were especially helpful in my initial learning about their Oneida people. As early as 1972, I was motivated to do more research on the Oneidas after listening to an impassioned speech on their land-claims litigation delivered by Jake Thompson, a savvy Mohawk adopted by Oneida matron Delia (Dolly) Cornelius Waterman.

L. Gordon McLester III, a Wisconsin Oneida community historian and director of the Oneida Indian Historical Society, deserves special mention. Over a thirty-year period, we have worked on numerous history conferences and written and published four books on his people's history. He has frequently pointed out to me that Oneida politics and tribal decision making are not simply carbon copies of what are found in Albany, New York; Madison, Wisconsin; or Washington, DC. I thank him for his wise tutelage. Indeed, he has been a true friend, not merely a coresearcher, coauthor, or mentor.

For a dozen years in the 1970s and 1980s, I would make my way to the Seneca Nation's Cattaraugus Indian reservation to visit Pauline Lay Seneca, a beloved Cayuga elder, former schoolteacher, and wife of the late Seneca president Cornelius Seneca. Her people's presence among the Senecas was similar in many ways to what Chapman Scanandoah experienced at Onondaga. "Aunt Polly," as she was affectionately called by relatives and friends, was a descendant of several past Seneca presidents and major political and community leaders who had married Cayuga women. Retired and visually impaired, she had taught at state district schools and at the Thomas Indian School and had been among the first residents on the reservation to earn a master's degree. I would listen quite carefully to her remarks about "her Cayugies" living with the Senecas on the reservations as well as her views about her tribe's former existence along Cayuga Lake. Always realizing that her people were guests among the Senecas and that her people's homeland was far to the east, Pauline on occasions would make a casual reference to the well-known Hollywood film of the early 1940s *The Man Who Came to Dinner*, which had starred Monty Woolley. She would refer to her Cayugas living at Cattaraugus as "the tribe who came to dinner but stayed two hundred years." I could not have had a more generous mentor in learning about Cayugas and their minority existence among the Senecas. Unfortunately, she would pass away in the mid-1980s before I had a chance to fulfill a promise about taking her to visit her people's homeland along Cayuga Lake.

Several attorneys must be acknowledged for teaching me the convoluted legal history of the Oneidas. They include the two lead attorneys— George Shattuck (1974) and Arlinda Locklear (1985)—both of whom brought Oneida land-claims cases before the US Supreme Court. I also thank Gerald Hill, an Oneida and the former senior attorney of the Wisconsin Oneida law office, for his keen observations over the years about historical events that have shaped his people's history both in New York and in Wisconsin.

Others need to be acknowledged as well. Roger Joslyn, a nationally recognized genealogist, provided assistance that was invaluable at an early stage of this project. Anthony Wonderley, the director of Mansion House and former archivist for the Oneida Nation of New York, provided valuable insights about these Native Americans in his exquisite writings, in a personal interview, and in his helpful comments in reading an earlier version of this manuscript. Over the years, I have benefited by my conversations with Karim Tiro, professor of history at Xavier University, about numerous aspects of Oneida history. James

Folts, senior archivist at the New York State Archives, and Nancy Horan, senior reference law librarian at the New York State Library, have always answered my questions, thereby opening the door to new directions in my research. William Gorman and Andrew Arby of the New York State Archives and Vicki Weiss, manuscript librarian at the New York State Library, were always introducing me to the great holdings available at the Cultural Education Center. Valerie Lutz, manuscript librarian at the American Philosophical Society, aided me in searching the collections of leading Iroquoianists, while Christian Goodwillie, director of the Hamilton College Archives at the Burke Library, helped facilitate my research by providing a CD of the Hope E. Allen Oneida Folklore Collection. Dennis Connors of the Onondaga Historical Association helped me hunt down illustrations for this book and provided me with information about the industrial history of Syracuse. James Adams and Theresa Barbaro of the Smithsonian Institution's National Museum of the American Indian helped me secure the rights to reproduce the finest photographic portrait of Chapman Scanandoah in existence, one that appears at the beginning of the preface. Chris Hunter at the Museum of Innovation and Science in Schenectady helped guide my research through its extensive General Electric Collection. At St. John Fisher College in East Rochester, Michelle Price of the Lavery Library provided CDs of Oneida correspondence with George Decker, the brilliant attorney who represented the Six Nations both in the United States and in Canada for decades before and after World War I. I should also like to thank Donzella Maupin of the Hampton University Archives as well as the entire staff at the Kroch Rare Book and Manuscript Library of the Olin Library at Cornell University for their help as well. As a result of his work as a historical consultant on environmental issues related to Onondaga Lake, Michael Leroy Oberg, SUNY distinguished professor of history at the State University of New York–Geneseo, compiled a massive document, "Annotated Bibliography: The Onondagas and the Onondaga Lake Watershed." I thank him for providing me with this important source and for his helpful suggestions about improving an earlier version of this manuscript. Caleb Abrams, an accomplished photographer and filmmaker from the Allegany Territory of the Seneca Nation, provided an important image reproduced in this book. David Jaman, now of the Villages, Florida, once again provided technical assistance on the project.

Since 1979 I have had the good fortune to work with Syracuse University Press. I am indebted especially to the late Arpena Mesrobian, the founder and director of the press, who encouraged me and saw the value of publishing on the modern Hodinöhsö:ni´ when scholarly presses were still fixed on publishing only on American Indians in the colonial, Revolutionary, and removal eras or on the history of Native peoples in the trans-Mississippi West. She and Joyce Atwood, the press's former managing editor, taught me, a young aspiring academic who dared talk to living Native Americans about their past, the "ropes" of editing, proofing, and indexing. They both saw the value of publishing books that focused on nineteenth- and twentieth-century Hodinöhsö:ni´ history. I should also like to thank Alice R. Pfeiffer, the present director of Syracuse University Press, for her encouragement of my work by facilitating my online access to the vast collections held by Syracuse University's Bird Library. Moreover, the present work as well as past writings have benefited by many discussions with Christopher Vecsey, professor of religion at Colgate University and editor of the Iroquois and Their Neighbors series.

Most important, my wife, Ruth, has always encouraged my research and excused my many trips into Iroquoia as well as my obsession with deadlines. She has also tolerated my incessant chatter over the dinner table about Hodinöhsö:ni´ history and contemporary concerns. To her I owe everything good that has happened to me over the past half century.

An Oneida Indian in Foreign Waters

1

The Oneida World in New York in the Century after the American Revolution

C hapman Scanandoah came from an impressive lineage.[1] He was a descendant of the legendary orator and chief Skenando, the "Deer," hero of the American Revolution. His mother's kin included members of the Hanyoust (Hanyost, Honyoust, Honyost) family, prominent Oneidas who had served as officers for the Patriots in 1776 and again with distinction in the American Army in the War of 1812.[2] Chapman's great-grandmother was Polly Cooper, who, according to Oneida oral tradition, brought corn to feed General Washington's starving troops at Valley Forge and who in gratitude was given a black shawl and a bonnet by Martha Washington. Significantly, Chapman and his brother Albert as well as their Scanandoah-Hanyoust descendants were custodians of this shawl.[3]

Later, during the War of 1812, a company of Oneidas under the leadership of Adam Skenando, another of Chapman's ancestors, was to serve with distinction. On May 30, 1814, a company of Oneidas, several Stockbridges, and a few Onondagas destroyed three British gunboats armed with Congreve rockets at the Battle of Big Sandy (Sandy Creek), an American victory that helped lift the British blockade of Lake Ontario.[4]

To this day, Oneidas in New York and Wisconsin use stories of their ancestors' participation as allies of the United States. These stories generate pride in being Oneida, since they highlight their ancestors' important roles in the past. Second, the stories are cultural touchstones reinforcing their heritage, their collective memory, their national identity, one that is

1

not entirely exclusive from the American national identity. Third, during the struggle to regain their territory, described in chapter 5, and right through contemporary land-claims litigation, Oneidas recount these stories at state and federal hearings, in court briefs and testimony, and in newspaper interviews, to remind Albany and Washington officials that they had and have an obligation to rectify what befell their allies the Oneidas after the American Revolution. Both Chapman Scanandoah and his first cousin William Hanyoust Rockwell were to frequently make the point to non-Indians that their Oneida people had suffered immense losses and had made huge sacrifices in coming to the aid of the United States during times of war. It was a conscious effort by these and later Oneidas to regain part of their lands and protect their sovereignty as a separate indigenous nation.[5]

From the Revolution through much of the nineteenth century, those Oneidas who remained in central New York retained approximately one half of 1 percent of their landholdings that they had possessed in 1784! Close to 6 million acres had been alienated out of their hands. By the time of Chapman Scanandoah's birth in 1870, the Oneida Indians' continued existence in central New York was clearly in jeopardy. By then, Madison County had a white population of 43,124 and a nonwhite population of 398; the adjacent Oneida County had a white population totaling 109,358 and a nonwhite population of 650.[6] Twenty years later, the Oneidas in New York numbered fewer than 300 souls. What was left was Scanandoah's community at Windfall in the town of Lenox in Madison County, whose inhabitants lived on 742.66 acres, mostly allotted lands. The other Oneida Indian community, the Orchard, also known as Marble Hill, was in Oneida County, less than three miles down the road. It contained 190.70 acres, all allotted lands.[7]

The vast majority of Oneidas had served on the Patriot side in the American Revolution; however, a small group of British-allied Oneidas after the war had left to resettle with other member nations of the Iroquois Confederacy along the Grand River in Canada. In 1784 the United States recognized the boundaries of the Oneidas' vast territory in New York in the Treaty of Fort Stanwix. Oneida lands were defined as stretching from the St. Lawrence River valley to today's Pennsylvania line. At the heart of their territory was the short portage between the Mohawk River and Wood Creek known as the "Oneida Carrying Place," which was strategic for both the Hodinöhsö:ni´ as well as later for Euro-Americans. To the southeast was the headwaters of the Mohawk, which flows eastward until it joins the Hudson, connecting the Atlantic Ocean at New York City. On the north was Wood Creek, which, along with Fish Creek, Oneida Lake, and the Oswego River, is a major passageway to Lake Ontario and the rest of the Great Lakes. From Wood Creek, the boundary ran southeast along the Unadilla River to the Susquehanna and then to the second branch of the Delaware River. To the north, where great timber resources abounded in the western Adirondacks, the Oneida homeland went from East Canada Creek to West Canada Creek, near today's Poland, New York, and then west across the headwaters of the Black and Oswegatchie Rivers and northwest to the St. Lawrence River, following the shoreline of Lake Ontario southward to nearly the rift of the Onondaga River valley. It ran due south to a point five miles west of the outlet of Oneida Lake, one of the great fisheries of eastern North America in the eighteenth century, and then southeast to Chittenango Falls, on Chittenango Creek and Cazenovia Lake. The boundary line then returned to its starting point via the headwaters of the Oswego River and the course of the Susquehanna.[8] Yet despite the promises made to the Oneidas in this federal treaty, the Oneidas were to be dispossessed of more than 5 million acres of their lands in three state treaties from 1785 to 1795.[9]

Oneida lands were quite fertile for farming and rich in timber resources. These same lands were attractive because of the great fishery of Oneida Lake. Land speculators could also see that the huge Oneida territory offered a water-access route to Lake Ontario and the western Great Lakes. Thus, any and all east–west and north–south development in central New York required the extinguishment of Oneida title to their lands. As a consequence, Indian dispossession continued unabated until the majority of Oneidas had left New York State by the mid-1840s. More than twenty-five state treaties were concluded between 1785 and 1842, most of which were not held with a federal commissioner present or ratified by the US Senate, as required by the federal Indian Trade and Intercourse Acts.[10]

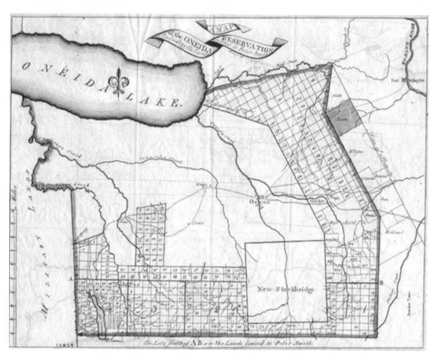

Map 1. Oneida lands and non-Indian settlement in central New York, ca. mid- to late 1790s. The map clearly shows the pressures the Oneidas faced from non-Indians desiring their lands. *Source*: Franklin B. Hough, comp., *Notice of Peter Penet and His Operations among the Oneida Indians* (1868). From the collections of the New York State Library, Manuscripts and Special Collections, Albany, New York.

One of the features of early-nineteenth-century America is what historians have labeled the "market revolution," a dynamic chapter in the growth and expansion of capitalism as a result of active government promotion of the economy. Public officials promoted road building as well as canal building to construct an economic infrastructure in the Empire State. Among those benefiting were the agents and investors of the Holland Land Company and later the Ogden Land Company, some of whose agents were members of the New York State Board of Canal Commissioners. These companies chipped away at Oneida territory, seeking lands to acquire cheaply and sell off dear to a fast-growing population of non-Indians pouring into central New York.[11]

Land companies' efforts to secure title to these attractive lands were helped by the divided nature of the Oneida polity. Historian Karim Tiro has indicated that the bitter infighting was not just over religious differences between Oneidas in the so-called Christian Party and their rivals known as the "Pagan" Party. Tensions were exacerbated by the ambitions of two men, namely, Cornelius Dockstader (Doxtator), a member of the "Pagan" Party, and Angel de Ferrière, a non-Indian land speculator of French ancestry. On March 21, 1805, twenty-five Oneidas signed an agreement to divide their reservation. The partition led to assigning Oneida lands along Fish Creek and territory west of Oneida Creek and north of the Genesee Turnpike to the Christian Party, while the "Pagan" Party was assigned a smaller tract south of the Genesee Turnpike. As payment for his services, Dockstader was given a one-hundred-acre tract for his personal use. Thus, the partition resulted in the creation of two separate Oneida legal entities, with separate community leaders negotiating with state officials about land sales.[12] Not surprisingly under these weakened conditions, the Oneidas were to cede more of their territory in state treaties from 1807 to 1837.[13]

The development of major modes of transportation in central New York led to an expanding white population and increased land values at the key junctions of rivers or along the routes of roads and canals.[14] It also led directly to the rise of metropolitan areas in central New York—Utica, Rome, and Syracuse—all within thirty-five miles of Oneida Indian lands. With improved transportation, these cities became centers for salt processing, for the transporting of agricultural products produced on central New York farms, for textile manufacturing, and later for the building of carriages.[15]

The construction of the first great state road (now Route 5) from Albany to Buffalo, known at various times as the Genesee Turnpike, Seneca Trail, the Seneca Turnpike, or the Great Western Turnpike, ran through historic Oneida territory at New Hartford and the southern end of Oneida Castle westward to Canandaigua. Other roads soon abounded, including the Hamilton and Skaneateles Pike, the Plainfield Pike, and the Cherry Valley Pike. Canals, including the Western Inland Lock Navigation Company and later the Erie Canal and three of its branch canals—the Black

River, Chenango, and Oneida Lake Canal—also crisscrossed Oneida territory. The result was that these non-Indian emigrants flooded into the region, establishing their farms and towns around the two Oneida Indian communities.[16]

One of the most important influences on Scanandoah's childhood at Windfall was the expansion of railroad lines through central New York. Scanandoah's fascination with these "iron horses" was to spur his interest in mechanics.[17] However, with the coming of railroad lines, especially after 1840, more and more non-Indians poured into upstate New York. Starting in 1850s, Cornelius Vanderbilt began consolidating several of these lines into what became the New York Central Railroad system. In Scanandoah's youth in the 1870s and 1880s, central New York was crisscrossed by several different railroads, including the New York and Ontario Midland Railroad (later the New York Ontario and Western Railroad in 1879); the Syracuse and Utica Railroad and its leased subsidiary the West Shore, the Chenango Branch of the West Shore; and the Lehigh Valley, Delaware, Lackawanna, and Western.[18]

At the federal removal Treaty at Buffalo Creek concluded with the Six Nations on January 15, 1838, and its amended treaty at Washington on February 3, both pushed by the nefarious agents of the Ogden Land Company, the United States exchanged lands west of Kansas with the Oneidas for lands near Green Bay, recognizing that the majority of this Indian nation and the bulk of their lands were now in Wisconsin.[19] Other Oneidas left New York and resettled at Southwold, Ontario, between 1839 and 1846. In the decade following the treaty, the Oneida world in New York further shrank in their land sales to the state, once again made in clear violation of the federal Trade and Intercourse Acts.

In 1839 the Oneidas owned 4,509.85 acres and were even more divided than they had been at the time of the partition. On March 8, the New York State Legislature approved an act authorizing the Board of Land Commissioners to purchase Oneida lands. In the following two years, the 172 Oneidas at Windfall sold most of their lands, retaining 1,114 acres, while the 98 Oneidas at Orchard sold 293.62 acres, retaining 742.66 acres. In 1843 the New York State Legislature authorized the dividing of the remaining Oneida lands in severalty. Although the law was not forcibly applied, many of the remaining Oneida families, largely because of the temptation of quick money or out of financial necessity, sought fee-simple patents on their lands, which allowed their allotments to be later sold and alienated out of Oneida hands. Another state law passed in 1847 allowed individual Oneidas to deed lands in transactions supervised and witnessed by local justices of the peace.[20]

In 1845 the legislature authorized Henry Rowe Schoolcraft to conduct a census of the Six Nations remaining in the state. Schoolcraft was to hire his nephew Richard U. Shearman to help him collect data. The census that resulted, albeit incomplete, provides a partial window into Oneida existence in Oneida and Madison Counties at that time. Although some Oneidas resisted giving information to Shearman, seeing it as Albany's efforts to extend state control over them and levy taxes on the Indians, the census, nevertheless, does provide some valuable information, especially about economic activity. In 1845 157 Oneidas, 86 women and 71 men, as well as 7 other Indians—2 Mohawks, 4 Stockbridges, and 1 Lenape/Delaware—resided on the two Oneida territories. Six of the thirty-one households were headed by women. Approximately 11.5 percent of the Oneidas were farmers who raised beans, oats, peas, potatoes, a variety of unspecified field squashes, and wheat on 421 acres. The two communities had fifty head of cattle, twenty-eight of which provided milk; forty-six pigs; and seventeen horses.

The Oneida territories had forty-four fruit trees, most probably apple-bearing ones. Besides the farmers, 6 Oneidas were listed as part-time trappers, 3 as Indian interpreters, and 1 as a mechanic. Although the Schoolcraft census showed that some Oneidas, including Christian Beechtree, Thomas Cornelius, Daniel Scanandoa(h) Sr., William Jourdan, and Cornelius Wheelock, were apparently more successful in making a living, the vast majority were just hanging on to a subsistence existence. Sales of agricultural products resulted in $173 per year, hunters and trappers brought in $85 per year, and Oneidas also received $2.91 per acre on 89 leased acres of their territories.[21]

The Schoolcraft census claimed that only 31 of the Oneidas were Christian, with a congregation organized at the Orchard (under Native preacher Thomas Cornelius's ministry), but that the majority of Oneidas were followers of the native Longhouse religion.[22] Yet it is important to note that by the time of Chapman Scanandoah's youth, a Methodist church had been established at Windfall, and many of the former "Pagan" Party Oneidas were members of its congregation.[23] Although Chapman and his family were Methodists, he admitted later that his religious failings could never lead him to become a preacher.[24] Although he and his brother Albert later attended the Methodist church at Onondaga and their funerals were conducted in that very church, they, along with their first cousin William Hanyoust Rockwell, served as Oneida representatives on the Grand Council for decades, were fluent in the Oneida language, and were well versed in Hodinöhsö:ni´ horticultural and medicinal traditions.[25]

By midcentury, no longer able to survive by merely planting their maize, beans, and squash; hunting deer; and taking advantage of the great fishery at Oneida Lake, now heavily despoiled, Oneida men began working as factory workers, as migrant laborers gathering berries, as hired hands or tenants on nearby white-owned farms, as lumberman in the Adirondacks or New England, or as traveling performers in minstrel shows and dance troupes.[26] Indian women were hired as domestics at John Humphrey Noyes's non-Indian millennial experiment, the Oneida Community at Mansion House, and also by the new white gentry in and around Windfall and the Orchard.[27] While their men were away working in distant lumber camps in the Adirondacks or in New England, women would maintain small gardens and can foods for winter storage at their two central New York Oneida communities. The women would also supplement their income by selling berries and by making and selling handicrafts such as baskets and beadwork to beachgoers at Oneida Lake, at Erie Railroad stations, or as far away as at Niagara Falls and Saratoga Springs.[28]

Although the majority of lands in central New York remained rural and agricultural for much of the nineteenth century, the Oneidas were also affected by the coming of the Industrial Revolution to Oneida and Madison Counties. They were to adjust to these changes by finding employment in these new industries. Down the road from the Indian lands, several manufacturing enterprises and mills had taken advantage of the abundant and readily available waterpower offered by their proximity to Oneida Creek. By the Civil War, the Oneida Community, just two miles from Windfall, had the largest plant in the United States for manu-facturing animal traps. Later it produced silk thread, even before it started its flatware production at what became Oneida Silver, Ltd., in the 1880s.[29]

By the early 1880s, Oneida Silver became the best-known enterprise in the area because of its famous production of silverware. It was hardly alone, and there were earlier enterprises in the environs of Windfall and the Orchard territories. The richness of central New York's agriculture led to its becoming a major area of hop growing and with it the founding of breweries. As early as the 1820s, Munnsville Plow Company produced axes, edge tools, and scythes, until its operations were destroyed in a fire. Two tanneries—Berry's Tannery and H. B. Phelps' Tannery—were established by the middle of the nineteenth century. After the Civil War, Holmes Stringer and Company, subsequently renamed several times—Holmes and Van Brocklin and finally Stringer, Dexter, and Coe—man-ufactured a wide variety of agricultural implements, including plows and cultivators as well as hops- and fruit-evaporating stoves until its closing in 1927. In 1879, with the founding of the Powell and Goldstein Company, the area became a manufacturing center for cigars and chew-ing tobacco. From the early 1870s well into the 1920s, the region around Windfall and the Orchard also became a major manufacturing center for different modes of transportation, namely, steam engines, horse-drawn carriages and buggies, and later automobiles. Among the newly estab-lished enterprises were the Oneida Steam Engine and Foundry Company, which later became the Westcott Chuck Company; the Oneida Carriage Works; and the Oneida Manufacturing Company, which became the Schubert Bros. Gear Company, which subsequently acquired the Oneida Chuck Company.[30] Chapman was later to find employment in the city's manufacturing center at Schubert Bros. Gear Company and at Westcott after his graduation from Hampton Institute in the mid-1890s. Chapman's cousin William Hanyoust Rockwell worked for many years at Westcott, while other Oneidas, including Chapman's older brother, Albert, sought employment farther away from the Oneida homeland at Solvay, the mas-sive salt-processing company in Syracuse.[31]

In the decades after New York's allotment legislation in 1843, the Oneida-held territory in central New York shrank even further. Numerous

Oneidas from Windfall and the Orchard began to sell off their allotments. With the declining ability of many Oneidas to make a suitable living off the land in their territory, and enticed by rising land values in eastern Madison County and western Oneida County that increased dramatically with the rapid rise of large-scale non-Indian settlement in the region, Oneidas sold their allotments and went off to reside elsewhere. Even members of Scanandoah's own family at Windfall went to join up with the majority of Oneidas living near Green Bay, Wisconsin. These descendants, part of the tribe known as the "Homeless Oneidas," were not enrolled there because they arrived well *after* the 1838 Buffalo Creek Treaty and thus had no political standing or land rights. They were later accepted as full tribal members in Wisconsin in the years that followed the passage of the Dawes General Allotment Act of 1887.[32]

A significant number of Oneidas, especially from the Civil War onward, went to live at the Onondaga Reservation, the central fire of the Hodinöhsö:ni´ where the Grand Council of the Six Nations held forth. In 1870 there were only 52 Oneidas residing among the Onondagas.[33] Sixteen years later, 174 Oneidas lived in Madison and Oneida Counties, and 66 lived at Onondaga. Thirty years later in 1916, the entire Oneida population was approximately split in half—124 Oneidas were residing at Onondaga, while 131 were still living in the two counties. By that year, the Oneidas made up well over 25 percent of the overall population of the Onondaga Reservation![34] Seeking more opportunity as a mechanic that was available in the growing industrial city of Syracuse, Chapman Scanandoah joined this migration, moving back and forth from Oneida lands until 1916, when he and his family, including his mother, Mary, became residents of Onondaga. Until his death in 1953, Chapman and his wife, Bertha Crouse, an Onondaga, whom he married in 1905, raised their five children on this reservation.[35]

Even when the Oneidas were a dispersed population, Oneida identity was reinforced by their retaining a sense of place, an ever-present remembrance of homeland. These lands, including those territories lost as a result of state treaties, were associated with prime fishing and hunting spots, rituals and traditional medicine gathering, place-names and storytelling, and even smells in the air. As anthropologist Keith Basso, a specialist on the Native Americans in the Southwest, has perceptively observed, one must understand a people's sense of place and how they fit into a landscape as much as their spoken words to understand them and the way they think.[36]

Oneidas periodically returned to places of historical importance to them. They frequented Oquaga (Onoquaga), now Windsor, New York, one of their four major villages, which had been acquired by the state in a questionable treaty after the American Revolution. Artist George Catlin, a resident there, recalled that as a child he was intrigued by the presence of Oneidas who camped on his farm. A family of Oneidas had come to fish and camp, just as they had done so frequently before they were dispossessed. The male head of this family put a new hickory handle on Catlin's iron pipe tomahawk, shafted and feathered the boy's flint arrowheads, fashioned a hickory-lined bonnet plumbed with woodpecker feathers, and told the future artist magical stories about the region and its history. Four decades later in 1848, Susan Fenimore Cooper, the daughter of James Fenimore Cooper and one of the founders of environmental literature in America, wrote about being startled when she encountered three gentle and gracious Oneida women basket makers in the environs of her home at Cooperstown, lands that had been historic Oneida territory until 1785. Unlike her father, who saw Native Americans as a vanishing race, Susan, the author of *Rural Hours,* a work that predated Henry David Thoreau's *Walden,* became an advocate for Native Americans in her later writings.[37]

Tiro has pointed out that for the Oneidas, their surrounding environment was a repository of their beliefs, history, and values and added meaning to their actions. Oneida stories also focused on specific locales that were associated with creation of the world, right action, and history. Hope Emily Allen, the noted historian of the Middle Ages who had been born and raised at the Oneida Community's Mansion House, documented many of these Oneida Indian beliefs, especially stories of the supernatural, in her writings and field notes over a thirty-year period from 1916 onward.[38]

One of the central beliefs of Oneida existence is about a "Standing Stone," an inanimate boulder unlike any other stone. Beliefs in this stone and other Hodinöhsö:ni´ legends were told by the elders in central New

York and were part of every child's upbringing when storytelling was at a premium during the harsh winter months. The children were told that the stone had magical powers. Unaided by human hands, it would suddenly appear every time the Oneidas would move their villages in their homeland. When placed in a tree, it was supposed to bring good luck when Oneidas took the warpath. Finally, when the village at Oneida Castle was founded, the stone remained there. Around this sacred stone, the Oneidas conducted their great councils, where they resolved questions presented to them and worshipped the Creator. Consequently, it is no coincidence that the Oneidas to this day call themselves *Onyota'a:ká*: the "People of the Standing Stone."[39]

In 1860 the *Gazetteer of the State of New-York* described the Oneidas as a "small remnant" of a once powerful nation who still managed to reside in the state. They were now viewed as "ancient curiosities," a "race" that had largely vanished from the face of the earth.[40] Fifteen years later, Luna Hammond, an author of a local history of Madison County, described the Oneidas in a similar vein. She claimed that the Oneidas were mere vestiges of the past, slowly becoming extinct. Hammond described the Oneidas and their landholdings: "Indians own farms all along the Oneida Valley, from Oneida Castle southward to the old tavern called 'Five Chimneys,' though white people own farms among them." She added that the Oneida children's education took place at the two state district schools but that their instruction was "hindered by the Indians' speaking almost exclusively their native language in their families." In her contradictory logic, she maintained that the Oneidas faced "impending doom" brought about by the "evils of civilization." However, she then indicated that their only hope for survival was twofold—accepting the "benefits of civilization" and by intermarriage with whites, since "their color in a few generations would disappear." To Hammond, they, nevertheless, should be acknowledged by their successors, the local whites, who should erect a monument as a testament to their past glory and allow the few remaining Indians to have their own cemetery to honor their great chiefs.[41]

The Oneidas had to deal with these types of gloomy predictions made frequently about their future. They were seen by many outsiders much like a soon-to-be-extinct species. In addition, state and federal officials refused, despite court decisions to the contrary, to acknowledge their continued existence as Native peoples. To challenge these assumptions and stereotypes, Chapman Scanandoah was to make his presence felt by showing up in "unexpected places," receiving extensive press coverage for his achievements throughout his lifetime. With stubborn determination, Chapman challenged these popular assumptions well into the 1950s.

2

Growing Up Oneida

WINDFALL IN THE 1870s AND 1880s

Chapman Scanandoah was the son of Abram Sconondoa and Mary Hanyoust (Scanandoah George). On May 16, 1870, Mary, *Gar-gea-junta-tar,* meaning "Plucking Flowers," gave birth to their second son, Chapman, at the Windfall community in Lenox in Madison County, New York. Chapman was given an Oneida name meaning "He Moves the Fire," suggesting that his extended family saw him as a future leader of his Oneida people at the councils of his nation.[1] He was born into the Wolf Clan, whose traditional tribal role was to encourage and promote tribal consensus and cooperation. In his household, only Iroquoian languages were spoken. Until the age of eight when Chapman first entered the state-run district school at Windfall, he spoke only Oneida and had no knowledge of English.[2]

Importantly, three days after Chapman's birth, his cousin William Hanyoust Rockwell was born at Windfall. The two boys were to be "tied at the hip" for the next eight decades, asserting their nation's treaty rights, fighting to retain their people's remaining lands in New York, and resisting US citizenship and the state's attempts to assert its jurisdiction over the Hodinöhsö:ni'. They frequently appeared together in federal courts and before state and federal hearings well into the 1940s.

Campisi has pointed out that the role of strong-willed women was a major factor that allowed for the continuance of Oneida identity in central New York. He added, "Nineteenth century Oneida society in New York centered around two communities," often at odds with each other, "consisting of three or four families dominated by the women who owned

Map 2. Eastern Iroquoia at the time of Chapman Scanandoah's birth on May 16, 1870. The place-name "Oneida" on the map refers to both Oneida Indian communities at the time: Windfall territory in Madison County and the Oneidas' Orchard (Marble Hill) territory less than three miles away in Oneida County, New York. Map by Joe Stoll. Courtesy of Joe Stoll and the Syracuse University Department of Geography.

the land."[3] Although the Oneida clan structure had significantly declined from the late eighteenth and throughout the nineteenth centuries, women elders, such as Chapman's mother, Mary, still continued to designate headmen or chiefs. The women also shared in the distribution of annuities provided under the provisions of the Treaty with the Six Nations at Canandaigua in 1794 and maintained the list of enrolled members.[4] Anthropologist Anthony Wonderley has best described the power of these women and the overall Oneida social structure in central New York in the late nineteenth and early twentieth centuries: "Structured around a matriarchal core, the family was an extended matrilineage, the traditional Oneida unit of residence for centuries. . . . It seems likely the women were reasserting traditional roles as overseers or supervisors of the land on behalf of all, regardless of who was said to own the land in nonnative terms."[5]

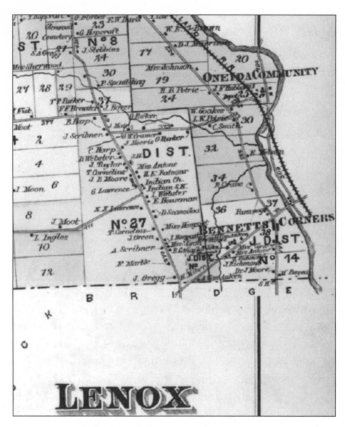

Map 3. Detailed map of the town of Lenox, New York, 1875.
The lower right side of the map (between the letters *I* and *D*)
shows the names of Oneidas at Windfall, including several
Hanyousts. No formal listing of a reservation is noted on
this map or on most federal and state maps of the time, even
though the Oneida lands had been recognized in federal treaties! Also shown is the Oneida Community, the famous communal experiment, founded by John Humphrey Noyes, where
some of the Oneidas worked. *Source*: D. G. Beers, *Atlas of Madison County, New York* (Philadelphia: Pomeroy, Whitman, 1875),
56–57. From the collections of the New York State Library, Manuscripts and Special Collections, Albany, New York.

Chapman's mother, Mary, was one of these powerful women. Indeed, in one interview of Electa Doxtator Johns, this Oneida woman mentioned a conversation with another Oneida, Sophie Dennie (Denny). In it Dennie referred to Mary as *gehsik*, a Seneca word for a woman with supernatural powers similar to a witch. She added that "people ought to be good to her or they don't know what will happen to them."[6]

Whether believed by most Oneidas or not, Mary was, nevertheless, a powerful and most influential individual. At the Hanyoust residence in the southeast corner of Windfall situated on thirty-two acres, along today's West Road, she; her sister, Margaret; her brothers, Isaac and William; and their families were determined to hold on to their land, even when most family members were forced by economic necessity to migrate elsewhere to survive. In his testimony before the Whipple Committee, a New York State Assembly investigation of the so-called Indian problem in 1888, William Dockstader, an Oneida, had testified that Mary Scanandoah along with Polly Antone, Barley and Lucy Dockstader, and several Charles (Mary's mother's family) and Cornelius family matrons held on to their land while the men accepted allotment and squandered their lands away from the 1840s onward. By the turn of the twentieth century, Mary's thirty-two acres at Windfall, first transferred to her brother Isaac and subsequently to her son Chapman, were the only land not allotted. They were later to be at the forefront of the major Oneida court case.[7]

In the 1870s and 1880s, at a time when Scanandoah was reaching maturity, the Oneidas had to contend with inferior educational opportunities offered to them by New York State. Even though Albany officials had established a school in each of the two Oneida communities in the 1850s, the education provided was suspect at best, and both schools were to close by the late 1880s. In 1889 the Whipple Report revealed that there had been thirty-one children of school age in the two schools, but that no more than sixteen showed up on a daily basis. The report never questioned why the truancy rate was more than 50 percent, asked what was being taught in the schools, or inquired about teachers' qualifications.[8]

A year earlier, Andrew Draper, the New York State superintendent of public instruction, in his annual report, reflected on Indian education. He asserted that the state was throwing money at the "Indian problem" and that the policy was "not very promising" and did little to prepare their children for the goal of American citizenship. He then blamed the victim. Draper indicated that the real reason for the "Indian problem" was Indian parents. Incredibly, he even suggested that the children at the Thomas Asylum for Destitute and Orphan Indians on the Cattaraugus Reservation, one that housed children from all the Hodinöhsö:ni´ communities, were better off than pupils in the state district schools because they were more controlled and had little contact with outside corrupting family influences.[9]

Superintendent Draper then went on to advocate the "breaking up of the reservation system" and justified it by referring to the reservations in New York as "nests of uncontrolled vice," where "superstition reigns supreme," where "impure ceremonies are practiced by pagans," where no law operates to protect or punish, where "chronic barbarism" exists, and where too few Indians speak English. Bemoaning this state of affairs, he questioned why it continued to exist "in the heart of our orderly and Christian Nation." Although recognizing state treaty obligations to the Hodinöhsö:ni´ that needed to be fulfilled "in equivalents if not in kind," Draper insisted that "when treaties perpetuate barbarism and protect vice, they should be broken." After all, he maintained, the Hodinöhsö:ni´ "are not to be considered equals; they are unfortunates; they are the children of the State."[10]

Thirty years later in August 1919, Scanandoah reflected on the early schooling he received at Windfall. At a conference dealing with the conditions on Hodinöhsö:ni´ reservations in New York held at the Onondaga Historical Association in downtown Syracuse, he insisted that he had wanted to further his education by attending school "but that the conditions are what drove us away. Sometimes the teacher would sneer at the dirty child because he was poor and had no father or mother." A firm advocate of education, Chapman chided Albany's efforts at helping Hodinöhsö:ni´, insisting that the state had never done anything for his people.[11]

While the Hanyoust family struggled to hang on in the last decades of the nineteenth century, federal Indian agents and judges in central New York and politicians on legislative committees in Albany attempted to define the status of the New York Oneidas. A federal case decided in 1877 had a long-range effect on how the Oneidas were officially viewed. It involved Abram (Abraham) Elm, later one of the founders of the Society of American Indians in 1911–12. Elm, an Oneida from Windfall, was a lumberman who had gone off to New England to find work. When the Civil War broke out in 1861, he enlisted in Company B of the Fifth Vermont Infantry Regiment. After the war, he returned to work his allotment and become a citizen of the United States.[12]

In 1876 Elm decided to vote in the congressional election in his district. The federal judge in the case recounted that the state legislature had enacted a law allotting the Oneida Reservation lands in 1843. He noted that there were about twenty families that constituted the Oneida tribe living in the vicinity of their original reservation, but he inaccurately claimed that they were "no longer set apart by custom, language and color" from their surrounding white neighbors. He maintained that a distinct Oneida community no longer existed in New York because most had migrated out of the state.[13]

The judge then made reference to the recently ratified Fourteenth Amendment to the US Constitution, which had excluded "Indians not taxed" from citizenship and suffrage. However, he insisted that Elm was already a US citizen who now allegedly lacked tribal status, and thus he did not fall into the category of Indians not taxed. Ignoring the Oneidas' acceptance of federal annuities and participation in the annual distribution of treaty cloth under the Treaty with the Six Nations at Canandaigua in 1794, the judge made the argument that the majority of Oneidas had been allotted from 1843 onward and now lived like their white neighbors. Thus, he claimed that the remaining families had no separate tribal status since they "owe no allegiance other than to the government of the United States, and they have been placed by the State upon an equality with its citizens respecting important rights denied to aliens." The court then found that Elm had been illegally arrested and had the constitutional right to vote. Thus, in this serendipitous decision, there was no such thing as dual citizenship. You were either a tribal Indian or a US citizen.[14]

In 1888 the Whipple Committee held hearings in several Hodinöhsö:ni´ communities and issued its report the following year. The report described the Oneidas as US citizens who still received "twelve yards of cotton cloth to each person per year" as part of federal treaty obligations to the Oneidas. Much like the Elm decision in 1877, the committee inaccurately maintained that the Oneidas had "no tribal relations, and are without chiefs or other officers."[15]

In 1890 Thomas Donaldson compiled a special report on the Six Nations in New York for the federal Office of the Census (now the Bureau of the Census). The report, published in 1892, noted that there were 196 Oneidas living in the two communities and "gaining a livelihood by basket making or day's labor, and are less comfortably settled than a majority of reservation Indians." Henry Carrington's account in this same census report then described Windfall and the Orchard: "Two groups of small houses, in each of which are seven families constitute their representative settlements, viz. Orchard in Oneida County, about four miles from the city of Oneida, and Windfall, in Madison County." He indicated that the Oneidas "were honest and well behaved," but his conclusions were hardly flattering, presenting a condescending portrait of the people in the two communities. He informed his readers that the Oneidas were "without sufficient ambition or sympathy to insure much progress." Despite pointing out that these Indians were still receiving their annual share of treaty cloth, Carrington viewed the few remaining residents of these communities as losing their Indian identity. He saw them as a vanishing race and indicated that allotting Oneida lands from the 1840s onward "had only hastened their dissolution, without elevating their industry or their condition." He suggested that in another generation, they would no longer exist as a separate people. Carrington concluded, "Visitors who ride through Windfall, the larger of the 2 villages, should understand that these are no longer Indian villages, and should not confuse any signs of general improvement with ideas of Indian thrift and progress, which do not exist."[16]

Well into the twentieth century, New York State agencies published maps on Iroquoia without listing the Oneida lands as a reservation. Federal agents continued to claim that the Oneidas in New York had no reservation and no treaty annuities and were basically living like their white neighbors.[17] Only in 1905 did a federal court's decision, one rendered in the Kansas Claims case, indicate that those Oneidas in central New York had legal standing under the Buffalo Creek Treaty of 1838, just like most other Hodinöhsö:ni´ communities in New York, and thus had a right to share in monetary compensation. With the Boylan case, federal court decisions in 1919–20, described in chapter 4, Chapman Scanandoah and his extended family and their attorneys were to finally succeed in showing that the Oneidas had not vanished and were entitled to federal treaty guarantees and protection.[18]

Despite the move to Onondaga by many of the remaining New York Oneidas, they retained their distinct identity there largely because of several factors. The Onondaga Reservation was but a short distance, less than forty miles, from the two Oneida communities where some members of Scanandoah's family continued to reside. Its proximity allowed for periodic visits and family gatherings. Campisi has noted, "The persistence of the Oneida community in New York hinged in part, on close family attachments, and in part the feelings of alienation from White and other Iroquois societies." The result was that "the old reservation [the Oneidas' central New York homeland] area continued to be the sentimental capital of the different segments of the [Oneida] Tribe."[19]

Importantly, by the end of the nineteenth and into the twentieth centuries, the Hanyousts' thirty-two acres at Windfall were to become the center of the Oneida world in New York. It was the homeland, the motherland, and the land of one's citizenship, even if an Oneida had migrated to Onondaga. Writing to the Oneidas' attorney in December 1909, Chief Rockwell maintained that the Hanyoust residence there, one in which his entire family had an equal share, was used for the benefit of all band members; it was where they congregated for meetings and ceremonies. To the chief, these points proved that the Oneida Nation not only continued to exist as a distinct tribe in New York, but also had self-government.[20]

By the age of eighteen, Chapman Scanandoah came to the realization that his limited education at the state district school had not prepared him to survive in the rapidly changing industrial order of the late nineteenth century. What was required was more education that would add to his skill set. Consequently, after a visit by a recruiting agent from Hampton Normal and Agricultural Institute to Hodinöhsö:ni´ communities in New York, he sought to further his childhood interest in machines by enrolling in the Virginia school. Although he found himself in a far different environment, his experiences at this African American school were to change the direction of his life.

3

An Oneida in an
African American World

HAMPTON INSTITUTE

nly two years before the massacre of Lakotas at Wounded Knee in
1890, Chapman Scanandoah entered Hampton Normal and Agricultural Institute, a private school established in 1868 to educate the freed-
men.[1] Today, most contemporary Oneidas, as well as Hodinöhsö:ni´ in
general, cannot comprehend why some of their ancestors were sent away
to a private school for blacks and not to a federal Indian boarding school
such as Carlisle. Hampton's Indian program was actually more academic
with more rigorous course work than any federal Indian boarding school
at the time of Scanandoah's attendance from 1888 to 1894. The school's
administrators and teachers attempted to combine what it deemed as cultural uplift with moral and manual training. Hampton Institute's founder,
Samuel Chapman Armstrong, believed in educating the "head, heart and
the hand."[2] Founded a decade before the United States Industrial School
at Carlisle, Pennsylvania, Hampton actually led the way with a combined
academic-vocational curriculum, influencing its adoption nationwide by
the federal Indian boarding-school system.[3]

Armstrong was a former colonel who had commanded black troops
during the Civil War. The son of missionaries who had served the American Board of Commissioners for Foreign Missions in Hawaii, Armstrong
became heavily involved after the war with the efforts of the American Missionary Association and the Freedman's Bureau. In 1868 during
Reconstruction, Armstrong established the school to provide industrial

education and agricultural instruction for former slaves. Although Hampton continued to serve the black community after Reconstruction, he, nevertheless, initiated his Indian program in 1877. Approached by Captain Richard Henry Pratt, subsequently the founder and superintendent at the United States Industrial School at Carlisle, Pennsylvania, Armstrong admitted 62 Indians the next year to his Virginia school.[4]

Between 1878 until the Indian educational program ended in 1923, 1,451 Native American students, 518 girls and 933 boys, representing sixty-five tribes, attended Hampton Institute. One hundred fifty-six of the Native American students were to graduate from the school. The Sioux from nine different reservations and the Oneidas from Wisconsin and New York made up the largest contingent of Native American students at the school. One hundred ninety-three Oneidas, including 109 males and 84 female students, attended the Hampton program. Although the vast majority were Wisconsin Oneidas, at least 12, 8 boys and 4 girls, were from New York, including future chiefs William Hanyoust Rockwell and Chapman Scanandoah. Half of the New York Oneidas in attendance were members of the Scanandoah-Hanyoust family, including Chapman's younger brother, Nicholas.[5]

The Native American experience at Hampton occurred when more blacks were being lynched than at any other time in American history. To both races in the late nineteenth century, Hampton was not merely another boarding school intent on indoctrinating the values of the more powerful white world. Hampton was also looked at as a self-contained institution, a safe haven for Native Americans and African Americans to learn both academic and vocational skills to help themselves and their families earn a living and survive in a hostile world. While Hampton was not completely free of the race hatred found in the larger society, campus life was much more insulated from the virulent prejudices found at the time; however, it should be noted that in the period of time that the school's "Indian program" operated, 1878–1923, all schools that educated Native Americans—Indian orphanages, state district day schools, religiously affiliated schools, and federal or private Indian boarding schools—had an assimilationist focus.[6]

TABLE 1 **New York Oneida Students at Hampton Normal and Agricultural Institute**

Name	Years	Occupation	Other Info
Josephine Bread	1921–22	—	—
Ida Mae Burning	1910–12	Domestic servant	—
Susie Chrisjohn (Spies)	1892–93	Housekeeper; canning factory employee	—
Daniel Honyoust	1894–96	—	Attended Carlisle later
Marshall John	1892–93	Farmer; printer	"Unsatisfactory performance" at school; later chief
Emma Johnson (Skenandore)	1892–96	Domestic servant	Died 1917 or 1918
Stella Johnson (Garlock)	1892–93	Housekeeper	Died 1899
William Hanyoust Rockwell	1892–94	Machinist; toolmaker	Oneida chief; representative on the Iroquois Grand Council for four decades; died 1960
Chapman Scanandoah	1887–94	Machinist; farmer	US Navy veteran; inventor; Oneida chief; died 1953
Joel Scanandoah	1892–96	Railroad watchman; laborer	Married Ellen Crouse, Hampton student; two daughters attended Hampton
Nicholas Scanandoah	1889–95	Machinist; farmer	Chapman's younger brother
William Scanandoah	1903–4	Factory worker; farmer	US Navy veteran

This chart is based on information obtained from the following: Jon L. Brudvig, "Bridging the Cultural Divide: Hampton Institute's Experiment in American Indian Education, 1876–1923" (PhD diss., College of William and Mary, 1996) and Brudvig's website on Hampton's Indians, http://www.twofrog.com/hampton.html. Because of privacy concerns, the chart does not include disciplinary actions such as suspensions or dismissals brought against specific Oneidas.

Although the separation of Indian children from their cultural surroundings and family support systems had both short-term and long-term negative consequences, some parents definitely viewed Hampton admission as both a place of refuge as well as an opportunity for their youngsters because of conditions on reservations at the time. Schooling at Hampton was a viable alternative to the poverty and the unsettled political situation on reservations caused by the constant attempts of outsiders to get at the remaining tribal lands and resources. Sending Indian children away to Hampton would provide them with three meals a day and improved medical care because the Virginia school had a full-time physician (Martha Waldron) and a hospital.[7] Thus, to at least some of the Hodinöhsö:ni´, it was seen as a way for parents to protect their children and, at the same time, have them acquire a trade that then was not provided in state district schools.[8]

Scanandoah's early education at the state district school at Windfall had been quite limited. Some accounts inaccurately suggest that Scanandoah could not read or write English until he was fifteen years of age, but this conclusion appears to be somewhat exaggerated. Nevertheless, his knowledge of written English was well below standards, as evidenced by his early unclear and ungrammatical essays as a twenty-year-old student at Hampton Institute.[9] A highly motivated individual with a desire for self-improvement, Scanandoah dramatically improved his writing abilities at the school. Later, he apparently practiced his writing in his extensive correspondence with both Converse and Keppler. In sharp contrast, Chapman's science and technological abilities were outstanding from the first day he enrolled at Hampton.

Two individuals influenced Chapman's decision to enter Hampton and further his education. His older brother, Albert, born in 1867 and known as Doc, apparently had an enormous influence on his sibling's education as well as his later career path. Albert was an inventor himself and later was an Oneida chief and served as the Oneida representative on the Grand Council of the Iroquois at Onondaga before Chief Rockwell took his place. While the two brothers had limited formal educational opportunities available to them in their childhood at Windfall, they educated themselves in mechanics by tinkering with gadgets and small devices.[10]

A second individual, Chapman's friend Charles Doxon, an Onondaga, had been admitted to Hampton in 1883. For six years, Doxon was a leader of the Hodinöhsö:ni´ students at the Virginia school. He was graduated in 1889 with a certificate in mechanics. The Onondaga spoke glowingly about his residency at Hampton and the opportunities it offered for future employment. After his graduation, Doxon became a successful mechanic in New York City. He later claimed that whatever success he had achieved "was my ability to hold my own along side of many white workmen and my ability to hold my own is largely due to the training I received at Hampton."[11] Chapman followed Doxon's path there, seeking training in mechanics. He was initially admitted as an eighteen-year-old student to the night school program at Hampton Institute, one that was designed to allow students to work during the day to pay for their education and, at the same time, prepare pupils before their entrance into more rigorous course work.

Scanandoah's days at Hampton expanded his horizons. Besides learning from his black classmates about their personal family experiences and the racism they faced in white America, his schooling there brought him into contact with numerous Oneidas from Wisconsin, where his grandfather Daniel Scanandoah Sr. had migrated prior to Chapman's birth. It also stimulated his already existing fascination with machines, provided the necessary training for his future employment as a mechanic, and opened his eyes to a life at sea in the US Navy.

Although some Hodinöhsö:ni´ children had difficulty adjusting to the school's rules and regulations and the separation from their families back home, their experiences, previous to attending Hampton, were far different from pupils from Indian nations in the trans-Mississippi West. The Oneidas were clearly better prepared to deal with change. Unlike the numerous Plains and Southwestern Indians who knew no English, the Oneida children had attended the white man's schools for more than a century and a quarter and had a better understanding of English. Moreover, their relatives had just served the Union in the Civil War, unlike the sons and daughters of Apache, Cheyenne, Comanche, Kiowa, Navajo, and Lakota warriors, who had fought the American Army from the 1860s into the 1880s.[12]

Because of financial necessity, Scanandoah was temporarily forced to drop out of Hampton late in 1889 because, at that time, the federal government was not subsidizing the schooling of Hodinöhsö:ni´. For about a year, he worked in Albany and as a factory worker at Edison Illuminating Company in Schenectady. Later, after the Oneida's return and completion of the mechanic program at Hampton in 1894, Scanandoah went back to work at Edison's plant, then known as General Electric, but at a higher status and pay.

In 1892 Scanandoah attended the Lake Mohonk Conference of Friends of the Indian, where he explained how and why he returned to Hampton after working at Edison Illuminating. Before he had the chance to speak, Clara M. Snow, who taught Bible studies at Hampton, addressed the audience before these reformers that included prominent educators, missionaries, and government officials. In the 1890s, Snow was to make annual visits to the reservations in New York to recruit Hodinöhsö:ni´ for admission to the school. At Lake Mohonk, Snow described one of her visits to Windfall and to the Onondaga Reservation. She had met Chapman's mother, who greeted the Hampton recruiter warmly but "could not talk much English." Another Oneida woman approached Snow, indicating that she wished her children could attend Hampton because the district school had closed. At the end of the visit, Snow thought to herself that she wished she could have taken all of the twenty-four school-age children back to Virginia with her.[13]

Snow then questioned why New York had limited schooling of its Indian population and why the policies of the federal government were so neglectful. In her talk, she had clearly embarrassed T. J. Morgan, the US commissioner of Indian affairs, who was in attendance. She pointed out to her audience that the Office of Indian Affairs in Washington, unlike its policies with respect to western Indians, was not providing moneys to send Native Americans from New York to schools such as Hampton. Because of this neglect, highly motivated students such as Scanandoah had to temporarily drop out of school for several terms, to earn money to pay Hampton's tuition. Then Snow lauded Doxon and Scanandoah for working hard to make money that allowed them to pay their way through Hampton without government subsidies. Scanandoah had told her that completing his education was "worth more than two or three dollars a day" that he had made in the outside world. Snow indicated that Chapman previously "had done very credibly" at Hampton's night school and "now had a chance to go to school during the day." She noted that Scanandoah had even encouraged his younger brother, Nicholas, to attend Hampton.[14]

Then it was Scanandoah's turn to address the audience. As a caveat to his presentation, he informed the gathering of reformers of Indian policy that he had never spoken before such a large congregation. Although some of his family members were now residing at Onondaga, he proudly told his audience that his "home is in this state [New York] on the Oneida reservation." He then elaborated on why he chose to go to Hampton: "When I was young I was inclined to go to school, and I went to one on the reservation; the white neighbors petitioned to have the school closed; they said it was of no use. I would like to say a word for that little school. It was there I got my first knowledge of English." Continuing his speech, the twenty-two-year-old Oneida told his audience that one of his friends (Charles Doxon) had been attending Hampton for several years and spoke glowingly of his days at the school, but warned him that he would have to work hard to stay at the school. Despite some trepidation, Scanandoah recounted that he decided to go to the Virginia school and even pay his way by working ten hours a day in the machine shop to pay his tuition; after supper, he would then attend Hampton's innovative night school until nine o'clock, when he had to report to the male Indian dormitory known as the "Wigwam." However, after completing two years at the school, he told the reformers that he was forced to leave Hampton because he had no money to continue his studies there. He then joined his older brother, Doc, working as a mechanic at Thomas Edison's Electric Light Company (later renamed General Electric) in Schenectady and in a machine shop in Albany. Despite earning $2.50 a day, he decided to return to Hampton to finish his schooling, which he viewed as essential for his future.[15] Significantly, a year after the Lake Mohonk Conference ended, the federal government started to pay for Hodinöhsö:ni´ students' tuition at Hampton. Thus, it appears that Snow's appeal and Scanandoah's talk at the conference had a direct impact on modifying federal Indian educational policies.

In 1886 Samuel Chapman Armstrong had introduced his "Technical Round" at the school, which introduced the Indians to general training in various trades and provided the opportunity for specialized training in the field of their own choosing, which also allowed them to pay for their education at the school. During a six-month rotation, the Indian students were instructed in carpentry, blacksmithing, and wheelwrighting. Enrollment at Hampton's evening school, where Scanandoah first attended for two years, allowed male students to work all day in the trade shops or school farm during the day. He and other students also advanced their skills and earned money for tuition at the same time by laboring on the school's working farm in Massachusetts or on "Outings," but whose ultimate aim was also to advance the acculturation of the Indians into the dominant white capitalist world of the late nineteenth century.[16]

Native Americans were enrolled in several separate divisions of Hampton and taught in very different ways because they entered with different levels of education and English-language abilities. Some, mostly western Indians with little or no knowledge of English, were admitted to a basic course of literacy and introduced to "obedience, courtesy and other qualities." A second level, preparatory to admission to the normal school, included study of arithmetic, drawing, economics, geography, history, physiology, singing, reading English texts, public speaking, and learning to write grammatically. The normal school, or third level, actually equivalent to high school, included course work in "practical" knowledge in arithmetic and science that could be applied to various occupations and trades. There was also an emphasis on civics and economics to prepare the Indians for US citizenship in the future. The more successful students, both men and women, at the senior level were also trained in the basics of teaching methods and entered a special program at the Whittier (elementary) School, formerly the Butler School, at Hampton.[17]

Although the girls took the same academic subjects as the boys, their education at Hampton had a quite different focus. As historian David Wallace Adams has observed, "Victorian America was hardly a prescription for female equality."[18] Principal H. B. Frissell's report for 1894 indicated that the Indian girls were instructed in "domestic science and etiquette."

They were taught housework, seamstress skills, including dressmaking and mending clothes, as well as cooking and baking.[19]

At Hampton Scanandoah was inculcated with the educational philosophy of the school's principal and founder. Armstrong believed in the potential of both African Americans and Native Americans to learn. However, his ethnocentric views were heavily laden with paternalism, and his writings and speeches were filled with the racially charged language of his day.[20] As historian Eric Foner has written about the reformers of the Reconstruction era, we must look beyond their patronizing language. While the Hampton founder believed that racial minorities should accept mainstream American values, Armstrong's motivation was "not simply to promote a form of social control."[21] He stressed the need to inculcate his charges, whether black or Indian, with the gospel of work and the dignity of labor, combined with Christian teachings. Through discipline and hard work, he and his successor and protégé, Hollis Burke Frissell, would instill the Protestant work ethic and produce self-reliant individuals—farmers, mechanics, tradesmen, domestics, nurses, teachers, and school matrons—because the past enslavement of blacks and the "savagery" of the Indian had to be overcome. They had to be led to "civilization" through a Hampton-style education, one that combined "cultural uplift" with moral and manual training.[22]

Armstrong and Frissell set out to train the Indians for American citizenship and suffrage and to value private ownership of property, the goal espoused by the majority of reformers of Indian policy in the post–Civil War era. Both male and female students, black and Indian, were included in the school's celebration of Columbus Day and the "discovery" of America and at Thanksgiving, where they were told of how "noble" Indians such as Squanto, Samoset, and Massasoit had helped the Pilgrim "fathers" found America. Hampton Indian students, both girls and boys, were featured performers in commemorating the four hundredth anniversary of the discovery of America at Chicago's Columbian Exposition. They were also required participants in the Columbia Roll Call pageant on "Indian Citizenship Day," February 8, which celebrated the congressional passage of the Dawes General Allotment Act of 1887, legislation that contributed to the significant alienation of tribal lands in the trans-Mississippi West, but provided Native Americans a route to US citizenship![23]

Although Hampton was not church affiliated, it did receive funding from missionary societies, and its program had more of a religious underpinning than Carlisle, as Pratt had a disdain for missionaries. Historian Jon Brudvig has observed that unlike Pratt's uncompromising belief in the need to rapidly transform the Indian, Armstrong believed in gradualism. Consequently, at Hampton students took course work on the Bible, were encouraged to say their prayers before dining and before bedtime, and were required to attend chapel as well as Sunday services. Christianity permeated student life, and the school promoted proselytizing. Importantly, Hampton's students were encouraged to recognize their responsibility to serve the group and to society as a whole, not to just to further individual pursuits. These same ideas were quite compatible with old Indian values.[24]

Because of the large number of Hodinöhsö:ni´ enrolled at Hampton, especially Oneidas from Wisconsin, Scanandoah was less isolated than most. While Chapman was in attendance, eight other New York Oneidas were also in attendance, which made his transition to this Virginia boarding school somewhat easier. Six Oneida women from Wisconsin, including Lavinia Cornelius, the first Oneida to attend nursing school, arrived in 1888, the same year Chapman entered Hampton.[25] His friend Charles Doxon had started a Hodinöhsö:ni´ club that would meet and discuss issues affecting Hodinöhsö:ni´ as well as Native people in general.[26] As a fluent Native speaker, Scanandoah could converse in his Oneida language when school disciplinarians were not around, since speaking "Indian" was strictly forbidden at Hampton and other boarding schools at the time. His classmates would later fondly recall that he kept a battery in his room in the Wigwam, the all-Indian residence hall, and that he was always willing "to explain the principles to us."[27]

Native American students were a racial minority at the school, and not all black students and alumni welcomed them. Their admission appeared to be a divergence from the school's original mission, established during Reconstruction.[28] In Armstrong's and later Frissell's thinking, black students at Hampton would help lead the Indians to "civilization." To further these efforts, Armstrong felt that the more accomplished black students at Hampton would help educate the Indians. They would serve as models of behavior, tutor English, teach certain skills, emphasize neatness, and enforce discipline. Advanced-level blacks would lead workshops and classes and even command the required military drills for the separate Indian companies at the school. Nevertheless, while Native Americans and African Americans attended both academic and vocational classes together and jointly participated in athletics and musical performances, males of each race sat separately in chapel and at different tables in the dining room. Native American males also had their own residence halls; in most cases, but not all, Native American girls were housed separately from black students.[29]

Although fights did break out between black and Native students, historian Donal Lindsey has claimed that, despite racial tensions, there was an apparent lack of conflict for the most part on the campus between the two groups: "Whenever the Hampton system pushed a black or Indian further than he could accommodate himself, some official of the institute could usually heal the fissure by pointing to the miseries of the other race."[30] Yet there is some evidence that not all Hodinöhsö:ni´ felt comfortable attending Hampton, with its primary educational commitment to African Americans.[31]

During his Virginia schooling, Scanandoah clearly had empathy for his black classmates and was well aware of the scandalous treatment they faced in America. In 1894, at a time when the lynching of blacks was at its height in America, he and his fellow Indian and black classmates, accompanied by Robert Moton, later appointed Hampton's principal, traveled to Lake Placid. They hiked in the Adirondacks and made a pilgrimage to John Brown's farm. When they reached Brown's grave site, the Hampton contingent honored the controversial radical abolitionist by taking their hats off and singing: "John Brown's body lies a smoldering in the clay. His soul is marching on."[32] Scanandoah's views were to change for the worse after he served in the US Navy. Much like a significant number of whites of the time, he was not averse to using derogatory language to describe African Americans. He objected to blacks whom he suspected of "passing" as Native Americans, and his private correspondence reflects those views.[33]

After receiving his mechanic's certificate in 1894, Scanandoah was frequently praised by administrators and by his teachers and held up as a role model for students attending the school. Hampton publications tracked his career as an inventor, as an ardent defender of his people's lands, as a patriotic sailor in the US Navy, as a mechanic working for major companies, and as a chief. He was portrayed as an example of what great accomplishments could be achieved by hard work and an education at Hampton.[34]

In the late summer of 1894, Scanandoah returned to Schenectady. By this time, Edison's company had merged with Thompson-Houston of Lynn, Massachusetts, to form General Electric. In its first fifteen years before its giant leap in other directions, this corporation, with its a board of directors and managerial executives who reported to stockholders, centered on electric lighting, producing incandescent bulbs and lamps of all kinds and turbines for power plants. GE was a highly stratified white male–dominated order. At the top of the company were brilliant design engineers in charge of research, such as Charles Proteus Steinmetz, followed by production engineers, mechanics, and thousands of factory workers. At the bottom of the scale were numerous teenage workers as young as fourteen.[35]

The Oneida machinist started work on September 4, joining an expanded workforce of six thousand employees. He was assigned to the "New Machine Shop," Building #9, a massive single-story concrete structure, 117 by 273 feet long, that contained large motor generators throughout. Instead of depending on rollers and ropes to haul heavy equipment such as turbines, the company installed an internal railroad to haul materials and improve efficiency and speed at the GE complex along the Mohawk River. Yet factory conditions were primitive, and the building did not even have toilet facilities.[36]

For some unknown reason, the Oneida suddenly quit his position at GE on April 29, 1895. Perhaps it was caused by poor working conditions, but more likely by his wanderlust that characterized his whole life. His leaving was not based on his lack of performance at GE. His skill as a mechanic was never an issue there, since two years after he left Schenectady, he was temporarily rehired by GE and assigned to its

Thompson-Houston Electric Works in Lynn, Massachusetts. His decision to leave Schenectady was a major mistake, since he found himself with only temporary employment because the electrical industry was consolidating and fewer and fewer firms were hiring during one of the country's worst depressions.[37]

Scanandoah received even more attention at Hampton when he joined the US Navy in 1897.[38] In one article in Hampton's magazine the *Southern Workman*, the writer took great pride in the Oneida's enlistment. The article contained a photograph of Scanandoah in his navy uniform and pointed out his accomplishments during the Spanish-American War. The reporter indicated that the Oneida was now a machinist first class aboard the cruiser USS *New York*. With little cultural sensitivity and undoubtedly still seeing Native people as impediments to progress and "civilization," the writer of the article insisted that Chapman's success proved that "Indians can be trained to be loyal subjects of our country."[39]

The Oneida's enlistment was no spur-of-the-moment decision. During the years of Chapman's attendance, Hampton students toured the nearby shipyards and were even employed there, learning construction skills and maritime trades. They were inculcated with the importance of military service to the nation and were reminded of the major events in American history that had occurred off the Virginia coast. When Scanandoah's ship the USS *New York*, the flagship of Admiral William T. Sampson during the Spanish-American War, later docked in the spring of 1900 at Newport News, the Hampton students paid a visit to the impressive vessel. Filled with pride, a reporter told his readers in the *Talks and Thoughts*, Hampton's student-authored newsletter, that Scanandoah, one of the school's former students, was assigned to the armored cruiser, spending most of his time "in the engine room working on complicated machinery."[40]

His years at the Virginia school in the vicinity of the shipbuilding center of America, the Atlantic home of the "new navy," was to come into play in his decision to enlist. The proximity of the school to the country's primary naval installations, at Hampton Roads, at Newport News, and at the Norfolk Naval Shipyard, was a major reason that led Scanandoah to enlist in the navy. In the Revolution, the Americans and their French allies achieved their major naval victory at nearby Yorktown in 1781. At the Battle of Hampton Roads on March 8–9, 1862, in the waters nearer to the school, the ironclad USS *Monitor* won its famous victory against the CSA *Virginia* (*Merrimack*), one that significantly changed naval history. Across from Hampton was Fort Monroe, the major Union staging area in the combined land and water operation in the Peninsular Campaign. By the 1890s, Hampton students were assigned work in the shipyards at Newport News, learning shipbuilding trades.

Later, while serving in the navy, Scanandoah would write back to school administrators, teachers, and students, and his letters would be reprinted in the various Hampton publications. They provided valuable geography lessons to the pupils at the school. He described his adventures at sea, including his assignment on the USS *Marietta* accompanying the USS *Oregon* on its famous trip during the Spanish-American War and on the USS *Raleigh* in 1903, when he circumnavigated the globe.[41]

When Scanandoah's ships docked at the nearby naval facilities, he would periodically travel the short distance to Hampton and give encouragement to the students and recount his great adventures in the navy on the high seas. In two visits in November 1910 and January 1911, he spoke to the Indian boys in Hampton's Museum and to the Indian girls at their Winona dormitory.[42] After one of Scanandoah's visits back to the school, Lucinda George, a student from the Onondaga Reservation, reported:

> Chapman Schanadore [Scanandoah] is another New York Indian who left here [a] few years ago. When he was here [at Hampton as a student] he studied some electricity, but devoted most of his time in the machine shop. When he left here he took a position at General Electric in Schenectady, N.Y. Later on he obtained a position in the Government Service [US Navy] as a second class machinist on the Gunboat "Merriatta" [USS *Marietta*]. Last Fall he was promoted to the Battleship "New York", and now he is a first class machinist and has a salary of over $1000. This is what Hampton has done and is doing for the Indians.[43]

Scanandoah's enlistment was also necessitated by the state of the American economy in the mid-1890s. He had received his mechanic's certification at a time when the United States was experiencing one of the country's worst depressions. His enlistment in the navy was largely the result of needing to find a way to pay off a loan/mortgage that threatened his mother's homestead at Windfall. Thus, it was no coincidence that in August 1897, while in Chicago, on his way back from visiting his relatives and former Hampton classmates at Oneida, Wisconsin, he decided to visit the main recruiting station then on Michigan Avenue. There, he indicated that he was now facing financial difficulties and thus he thought it best to sign up.[44]

For the next fifteen years, he served on board ship in war zones and at naval yards, earning money to send home. The presence of an "Indian" in unexpected places was frequently noted in articles in newspapers throughout the United States. While sailing to every part of the world, he received a global education in international relations, power politics, and geography. However, at times, his service was no smooth sailing, largely because of his anxiety and reaction to the troubled waters his Hanyoust family faced back at Windfall.

4

A Global Education

NAVAL SERVICE IN WAR AND PEACE

W hen Chapman Scanandoah entered the Chicago recruiting office on August 6, 1897, naval officers were startled by the presence of an "Indian." A Chicago newspaper found this newsworthy and presented Scanandoah as a novelty, more like a relic of the past that had suddenly made an appearance in America's second city. The naval engineer in charge of recruitment noted that the future sailor was "a member of [the] five nations of early America." He stated that the Oneida was a "civilized" Indian who had taken to engineering and had been educated at a technical school back east, but after finding little opportunity for him in Chicago, he had decided to enlist "and take to the salt water." The engineer then referred to Scanandoah as "a splendid physical specimen of the copper-colored aborigines."[1] The sailor was described in his navy enlistment records as being five feet seven and a half inches tall, weighing 178 pounds, with brown eyes and black hair, and having noticeable scars on his nose and jaw.[2] Several other accounts suggest he was "athletic" in appearance.[3] After passing his physical, Scanandoah was temporarily assigned to a training vessel, the USS *Minnesota*, a wooden steam frigate that dated from the Civil War era.[4]

For the next fifteen turbulent years, Scanandoah served in the US Navy, including in two war zones, and traveled to nearly every region of the world. Despite facing two courts-martial during his naval service, he, nevertheless, was promoted several times—from assistant machinist to machinist first class to chief petty officer—and later received an honorable discharge when he left the navy in 1912.[5]

The US Navy had been undergoing major changes and a significant expansion since the 1880s. These years are often referred to as the "age of the new navy." Starting in 1883, the United States had initiated a shipbuilding program that resulted in the launching of a new class of battleships, including the ill-fated USS *Maine*. By the mid-1880s, the navy added three armored steel-hull cruisers—the USS *Boston* and the USS *Atlanta* as well as the dispatch vessel USS *Dolphin*—to its fleet. In 1890 Congress began an even more ambitious program. Influenced by Alfred Thayer Mahan's *The Influence of Seapower in History, 1660–1783*, Secretary of the Navy Benjamin Tracy pushed plans for further expansion. The same year Congress passed the Navy Act that authorized the building of three more battleships—the USS *Massachusetts*, the USS *Iowa*, and the USS *Oregon*. In the immediate aftermath of the Civil War, the United States had a navy ranked twelfth in the world; however, by the time of the Spanish-American War, the US Navy was ranked fifth.[6]

On April 26, 1898, the United States declared war on Spain and soon began a two-ocean operation in which the American Navy played the decisive role both in the Philippines and in Cuba. Later newspaper articles about Scanandoah claimed he was a hero of the Battle of Manila Bay on May 1, 1898, but his name does not appear in any of the lists of sailors on board the American vessels in Admiral George Dewey's fleet.[7] At the time of the battle, he was aboard the USS *Marietta*. The ship was a schooner-rigged gunboat, only 110 feet long and weighing only one hundred tons. The slow-moving vessel topped out at ten knots. It was commanded by Commander F. W. Symonds of Utica after being been launched a year before the war at the Union Iron Works in San Francisco. With Scanandoah aboard, the *Marietta* departed San Francisco on March 19, 1898. It headed southward for the Peruvian coast to meet up with the USS *Oregon*, the famous predreadnought battleship, which had already set out on its historic sixty-six-day voyage of nearly 14,700 nautical miles from San Francisco to Key West. The USS *Oregon*, which was built in 1890 at the same San Francisco facility as the USS *Marietta*, had been ordered to patrol Caribbean waters because tensions between the United States and Spain had reached a boiling point after the sinking of the USS *Maine* in Havana Harbor in February.[8]

On April 6, Scanandoah's ship rendezvoused with the USS *Oregon* at Valparaiso, Chile. At the time, the Oneida was working in the USS *Marietta*'s coal-fired engine room, where the temperature was excruciating, reaching 110 to 140 degrees! The two ships proceeded through the Strait of Magellan and then up the east coast of South America. The USS *Marietta*, a much slower vessel, had difficulty keeping up with the battleship. By the time it reached the Brazilian coast, the Spanish-American War had started. A Spanish gunboat was sighted off the coast, but quickly left the scene when the American ships made their appearance. After pulling into the River de la Plata at Montevideo and docking at Rio de Janeiro at the beginning of the second week of May, the American crews were informed of Admiral Dewey's victory at Manila Bay and the destruction of much of the Spanish Navy in the Philippines.[9]

After reaching Key West on May 24, 1898, the USS *Oregon* arrived at Jupiter Landing in Florida. The much slower gunboat USS *Marietta* arrived a week later. Both ships were then ordered to Cuba and participated in the blockade of Havana Harbor. On July 3, the American fleet won another crushing naval victory by destroying the Spanish fleet commanded by Admiral Pascual Cervera y Topete at the Battle of Santiago de Cuba.[10] Although the USS *Oregon* was directly involved in the American victory, the USS *Marietta* was in only a supporting role during this major naval battle. Scanandoah later indicated that he regretted not having been directly in hand-to-hand combat during the Spanish-American War.[11] Nevertheless, Scanandoah and some of the crew of the USS *Marietta* subsequently took control of the heavily damaged Spanish gunboat *Sandoval* near Guantánamo after raising it, since it had been partially submerged for forty-two days. They then boarded it, adding it to the American fleet as the USS *Sandoval*, and headed back for major repairs at the Washington Navy Yard.[12] He later wrote about his fascination with Cuba, especially Gibara, what he referred to as a "queer little city" with houses atop the wall that surrounded it. He was not allowed to go ashore to satisfy his curiosity because the city was facing quarantine owing to three separate epidemics.[13]

From 1901 onward to 1912 when he left military service, the Oneida sailor's major assignments were on the armed cruiser-battleship USS *New York* (later renamed the *Saratoga* in 1911); the gunboat USS *Dubuque*; the cruisers USS *Atlanta*, USS *New Orleans*, USS *Raleigh*, and USS *San Francisco*; the monitor-class small warship and training vessel USS *Florida* (USS *Tallahassee*); and several antiquated supply ships and receiving vessels: the USS *Constellation*, the USS *Independence*, the USS *Sherman*, and the USS *Vermont*. He also briefly served on the USS *Franklin*, USS *Hancock*, and USS *Wabash*. After his brief tenure on the captured Spanish gunboat *Sandoval*, renamed the USS *Sandoval*, he was promoted to machinist first class and assigned to the USS *New York*. At the conclusion of the war with Spain, he was later assigned to another war zone, this time in the Philippines. He was on board several different ships from 1899 to 1906—the USS *Raleigh*, USS *New Orleans*, and USS *Sherman*—that supplied American forces fighting Emilio Aguinaldo and his war for Filipino independence and a subsequent insurrection.[14]

Scanandoah received an inordinate amount of attention in newspapers from New York to California during his fifteen years in the navy. When he returned home in December 1898, from service off the coast of Cuba aboard the captured gunboat *Sandoval*, one newspaper described him as "a fine looking man and very intelligent man and a thorough American" who had served as assistant machinist. He was "said to be the only full-blooded Indian in the United States Navy."[15] Indeed, the navy repeated this falsehood with reporters, apparently using it to gain publicity for recruitment purposes. After Scanandoah reenlisted in the navy for a four-year stint in 1900, the *Utica Globe* referred to the sailor "as a fine stalwart fellow of whom his tribesmen have good cause to be proud."[16]

The Oneida sailor's letters to Joseph Keppler Jr. and Harriet Maxwell Converse while in naval service reveal that he had a remarkable sense of humor. In 1899, at the end of the Spanish-American War, Scanandoah was promoted, assigned to Admiral Sampson's flagship, the cruiser USS *New York*, which patrolled the eastern coastline of the United States. In the summer of 1899, while his ship was docked at the US Naval Station in Middleport, adjacent to Newport, Rhode Island, he wrote to Keppler, telling him that he had no complaints except that he was eating too much. He added that he hoped to return to New York before Admiral Dewey made his appearance at the New York City parade in his honor. That August he wrote to Keppler from Bar Harbor, Maine, complaining about the heavy fog, which he blamed on the Eskimos, who he suggested were expectorating their lungs in the open air. In a letter to Converse aboard the USS *New York* on Christmas Eve in 1899, he informed her that his five-star accommodations had ended because the ship was overcrowded and, as a result, the commanding officer had forced him, describing himself as simply a poor Indian, out of his comfortable bed and quarters. After his ship, the USS *Atlanta*, visited Brazil in March 1901, he told Keppler a tall tale. He jokingly reported to the political cartoonist that he had finally reached a region where folks feed their chickens cracked rice to prevent them from laying hard-boiled eggs.[17]

The Oneida sailor's humor helped him pass the time when he faced assignments that were less pleasant. Scanandoah faced boredom, especially when serving on slow-moving vessels such as his temporary assignment on board the USS *Sherman*, an army transport headed for the Philippines in 1906. The excruciatingly long voyage at sea between San Francisco and Manila took one month.[18] When in the tropics, he frequently had to deal with mosquitoes that hovered overhead and took bites out of his body.[19] Another concern was his frequent complaints about postal service, because many of his letters mailed overseas even from South America had to be sent to London and then transshipped to the United States.[20] In 1909, writing from New Orleans, he complained to Keppler that shipboard food had made him fat and that his weight had swelled to 225 pounds.[21]

At other times, he had more serious things on his mind. In November 1900, he worried about the crew's safety after two fires had broken out on board the ordnance-laden gunboat USS *Atlanta*. Most vexing to him was hearing about his family's troubles at home. Although he sent a part of his wages home, he frequently expressed fear that it would not be enough to save his mother's homestead at Windfall and that the land would be lost in foreclosure proceedings while he was at sea. As early as the summer of 1900, he arranged for the hiring of an attorney to undertake a title search and told Keppler he still planned to pay off the loan/mortgage on the property taken out by his uncle Isaac.[22]

After being given liberty after the USS *New York* docked at St. Thomas in the Virgin Islands in late December 1899, Scanandoah was arrested for public intoxication, for having an empty bottle in his possession, and for being out of uniform after overstaying his shore leave by twelve hours. He reported to Converse that he had come back to his ship senseless, having lost every penny he had taken with him. Subsequently, the Oneida faced a court-martial. Fearing twenty days in the brig and a loss of two months' pay, he asked Converse, who had political connections in Washington, to write a letter on his behalf to the ship's captain. He informed his benefactor that he had been disturbed by bad news from home, but that he did not want to use it as an excuse with his highly respected captain, a fair-minded individual but a stickler for regulations. Scanandoah was to receive ten days in the brig and was docked fifteen days' pay, amounting to $27.50. Although Scanandoah expressed the view that he considered not reenlisting after this conviction, he was to stay in service for twelve more years.[23]

His absence from home, nevertheless, continued to weigh heavily on the Oneida sailor. He was torn with thoughts of desertion, to get back as soon as possible to protect his family from being evicted from their home, but he was also quite aware that his family needed his earnings from his naval service to save their property from foreclosure. In the summer of 1902, Scanandoah was to make a decision that nearly led to his ruin. With more bad news emanating from central New York, Scanandoah went "over the hill" for nearly five months. He had become desperate for shore leave to return home to central New York since he had been informed that there were new attempts to dispossess his mother and remove her and his other family members from their lands at Windfall. At the time, Scanandoah had been reassigned to duty on board the USS *Atlanta* that was scheduled to patrol South Atlantic waters.

On August 13, 1902, while on board the USS *Atlanta*, then in Bahia, Brazil, he wrote to Converse, asking her to use her political influence to secure a leave for him. He told her that he was thinking of deserting because he needed to help out back home.[24] Despite pleas to his commanding officer that he needed to return to New York because of exigent circumstances, his requests, nonetheless, were turned down.[25]

When the USS *Atlanta* pulled into port at Buenos Aires for repairs, the Oneida decided that he had had enough of naval life. He left his ship in

Argentina without permission and secured passage on a liner. He then traveled eight thousand miles back to New York where he visited his mother at Windfall. Scanandoah then made his way to Converse's home in New York City. Once again, she came to his defense, explaining the exigent circumstances of why Scanandoah abandoned his ship, emphasizing that the Oneida had served loyally in the war with Spain and in his other naval service. Captain Pendleton of the USS *Atlanta* replied to Converse's lobbying, maintaining that he regarded Scanandoah "as a man of very good disposition and attentive to his duties. He was 'touchy' as regards matters duty, but otherwise a very good man. He was granted a great many privileges and I know of no reason for his leaving the ship."[26] Using her sizable influence in Washington political and New York society circles, Converse's intervention ultimately proved successful.[27]

Scanandoah surrendered to naval officials in Washington, DC, and was placed on trial for desertion. The navy's court-martial convened on December 12, 1902. Perhaps because of the influence of Keppler, well known as the publisher of a leading magazine, the trial received widespread coverage in newspapers. Articles pointed out that his enlistment in 1897 and subsequent reenlistment had been motivated to help out his poor mother, who was struggling to hold on to her land. Reporters emphasized that he was a good son and that his only motivation to jump ship was to provide for his mother's welfare. They mentioned that he had previously sent $330 from his navy wages back home to pay off the mortgage on his family homestead. The articles also described Converse's help and emphasized that the Oneida Indian was patriotic to the American flag and that he was a descendant of Skenando, the great orator and chief who had helped the Americans win their independence in the Revolutionary War.[28]

A navy tribunal convicted the Oneida sailor of a lesser charge, namely, being absent without leave, or AWOL, and sentenced him to confinement for three months; he was to forfeit pay, totaling $80.08, and was to be dishonorably discharged from the navy at the completion of his punishment. However, testimony from friends and supporters about Scanandoah's good character, his distinguished service in the Spanish-American War, and sympathetic newspaper coverage about his care for his mother led the

Department of the Navy to reconsider the decision. It also appears that Keppler, a personal friend of Theodore Roosevelt and a leading Progressive reformer, had direct contact with the president.[29] Subsequently, the assistant secretary of the navy decided that if Scanandoah's commanding officer in his monthly reports deemed the sailor's conduct satisfactory, his court-martial conviction would be expunged after ninety days. The Oneida was also to lose all his pay for his time while AWOL and add five more months of naval service to his enlistment. In January 1903, the Department of the Navy officially suspended the Oneida's sentence of three months of confinement, removed the dishonorable discharge from his record, and conditionally restored him to active duty.[30]

Although he never got into "hot water" again, his concerns for his family's welfare back home continued to eat at him. His life in the navy did not take away his feelings of guilt about being separated from things back home and not being able to be with his family in times of crisis. In Scanandoah's letters to Keppler, it appears that the editor of *Puck* served as his personal psychologist, comforting him when Converse died and bringing him news of what was happening stateside. Scanandoah, always in need of money, would on several occasions borrow some from the editor of *Puck*. The Oneida would inquire from him about "Kansas money," namely, funds from the US Treasury that were later awarded to the Hodinöhsö:ni´ in 1906 by the US Court of Claims, for federal violations of provisions of the Treaty at Buffalo Creek of 1838. Moreover, the editor would serve as his trusted conduit, bringing information from Scanandoah to the attention of Oneida attorneys seeking to save the tribal lands.[31]

As a diversion from his troubles, the Oneida wrote extensively of his travels in naval service. These letters, addressed largely to Keppler and to students, teachers, and administrators at Hampton, are eye-opening. They are clear examples of his keen intellectual curiosity, which was later reflected in his successful patents and in his agricultural achievements. Because of his limited education in writing English before his years at Hampton, these letters also reflect his determined efforts at self-improvement, a goal inculcated by Principal Frissell at the Virginia school. In 1890 his writing had been atrocious both in spelling and in grammar, but four years later it had substantially improved as a result of his Hampton training. By 1903 his letter-writing skills clearly show a mastery of the English language.[32]

In January 1903, Scanandoah was assigned to the cruiser USS *Raleigh*, a ship that was built at the Norfolk Naval Shipyard in 1889, near Hampton Institute, when Scanandoah was studying there. The 305-foot cruiser was launched in 1892. The vessel had a crew of 312 men and was initially assigned to the North American Squadron. The ship and its crew played a major role in the Spanish-American War. In May 1898, the USS *Raleigh* had joined Admiral Dewey's squadron and had participated in the Battle of Manila Bay. Its involvement in the battle led to the capture of the Spanish gunboat *Callao* and to the shelling and surrender of Grande Island.[33]

In March 1903, the cruiser set sail for Honduras and began a six-month voyage that ended in the Pacific. He later wrote that on the voyage, he had seen the most extraordinary things he had ever seen.[34] This expedition was truly another phase of his education. The Oneida's writings while on this global voyage reveal that he had acquired a real understanding of international relations as practiced by the world powers of the time. Especially noteworthy were his comments about the British. He noted that there were numerous British forts from the Indian Ocean to China that flew the Union Jack. When the USS *Raleigh* docked at the British-held "treaty port" of Chefoo (now renamed Yantai) that the English had forced China to cede in an "unequal treaty" in 1862, Scanandoah commented that there was an international crisis brewing in the region of northern China and Korea. He commented that Russia was ferociously holding on to Port Arthur. To Scanandoah, it appeared that war was about to break out, predicting what was to happen the next year with the start of the Russo-Japanese War.[35]

After leaving New York Harbor on this six-month expedition, the USS *Raleigh* first headed to Caribbean waters. From Honduras, the ship sailed to Gilbraltar. After docking in Marseilles, Scanandoah was given leave and traveled all over France, comparing its cities with cities in the United States. He bemoaned that he could have paid less for items he purchased if he could have known the language, because the French, it appeared, were taking advantage of American visitors. The USS *Raleigh* then sailed through the Mediterranean Sea to Egypt.[36]

Scanandoah's impressions of the Arab world reveal much about him, his interests, and his faith. At Port Said, along the banks of the Suez Canal, he saw camels for the first time.[37] With increasing talk of the United States' plans to develop a way to traverse the isthmus of Central America, he was especially interested in seeing the Suez Canal. Going through the canal and having a keen interest in technology, he postulated that this marvel of engineering would have impressed him more if Uncle Sam would build an isthmian canal through Central America.[38] When the USS *Raleigh* reached the Red Sea, he jokingly reported back to Hampton students that the water was not red at all, as he had expected it to be. He reflected on being in the places described in the scriptures as being where the pharaohs ruled and even where Christ had walked on water. After the USS *Raleigh* docked in Aden in the Persian Gulf for repairs, he noted that it was one of the ancient cities mentioned in the Bible. In this same parched-desert sheikdom, now Yemen, he noted that only one person he met there spoke English. He intentionally pointed out to Hampton's students that the people there were black and dressed in the manner of ancient times.[39]

The USS *Raleigh* then sailed into the storm-ridden Indian Ocean to Ceylon (Sri Lanka), where Scanandoah reported that cheap pearls of every description could be purchased.[40] After traversing this great expanse of water into the South China Sea, the ship made a stop for supplies at Subic Bay in the Philippines and then headed to the coast of China. After he reached the Royal British Colony of Hong Kong, Scanandoah's descriptions there and later at Chefoo were not flattering to the residents and even racist in tone. To him, the Chinese all looked alike and traveled on the ocean in similar-looking junks. He warned that one had to be careful in business dealings with them, as he questioned the Chinese merchants' honesty. The USS *Raleigh* then sailed to Japan, docking at Yokohama. Unlike his Chinese experiences, he complimented the Japanese and considered the stop one of the highlights of his voyage.[41]

The ship then headed to Pearl Harbor. Scanandoah was clearly disturbed by what he saw in the Hawaiian Islands, now part of the American empire after being annexed by the United States in 1898. He had great empathy for the Native Hawaiians. In his mind, he equated what had happened to Hawaiians with his own Oneida people's struggles. He indicated that the Americans were taking the best jobs there and that there was significant discontent among Native Hawaiians because they were losing out politically, as outsiders were beginning to outnumber them. Much like his Hodinöhsö:ni´ people, the Native Hawaiians were forced "to take a backseat" when confronted with Western civilization.[42]

Scanandoah's global education was to continue later in his naval service. From 1908 through 1910, he was to serve a stint aboard the USS *Dubuque*, a thirty-five-foot gunboat that had been launched in 1904.[43] He reflected on what he witnessed in Central America. In the "age of dollar diplomacy," the vessel's mission was to protect American lives and property in the Caribbean and environs. Much of the time, his ship was in the waters between Honduras and Nicaragua. In Honduras he described Puerto Cortez as "the banana port," exporting twenty-four thousand bunches of bananas annually from the port, and said that the price was so much cheaper there for the product than back in the United States.[44] He questioned why the United Fruit Company had a controlling interest throughout the region. The company had its own security force and even purchased and refitted Scanandoah's old ship the *Marietta*, now decommissioned by the navy, for its own use.[45]

Scanandoah was also quite disturbed by what he witnessed in Nicaragua, then the site of a major rebellion against the government in power. After initially favoring the Nicaraguan rebels, who were seen by the United States as being more honest, the Oneida was to soon change his mind. Subsequently, he claimed that both the rebels and the government forces were greedy and simply fighting for control of gold mines in the interior. He labeled both sides as being equally detestable. Nevertheless, sailors from the USS *Dubuque* were called on to intervene in the port of Bluefields, which he apparently opposed because he saw since American political and economic interests there as being infinitesimal. Moreover, he thought it foolish for Americans to get further involved in a war in the unfavorable jungle climate of Nicaragua. To him, it did not matter which members of the two sides were killed, although he expressed concern for the Miskito Indians caught in the middle between opposing forces.[46]

While on shore leave during his naval career, Scanandoah searched for Native Americans and their communities to visit and with whom to socialize. In 1899 he proudly wrote the students at Hampton when he brought the captured Spanish gunboat *Sandoval* back for refitting at the Washington Navy Yard. He indicated that he was surprised to find so many Indians in Washington while he was stationed there. Scanandoah served as their tour guide when they showed up at the navy yard. With typical humor, he recounted the story of a visit by one elder. After Scanandoah showed him the massive naval gun factory, the elder turned to him and remarked that the big guns he was shown there were useless because they were no good for his hunting requirements in the woods![47]

At Tampa in 1910, he was happy to see more Native peoples. At an event in the city celebrating the building of the Panama Canal, one that would greatly benefit this major Gulf port in the future, the Oneida reported that he was to see numerous Indians, presumably Seminoles, at the celebration.[48] Earlier while on shore leave in 1900, the Oneida came face-to-face with a "fortune teller" who portrayed himself as a sagacious Indian with special powers. Scanandoah exposed the man as a "fake Indian."[49] His anger in this regard apparently made him forget his favorable experiences that he had received at Hampton. The racist language employed by sailors in the US Navy seemed to replace his earlier education and sensitivity training at the Virginia school. In 1911, after reading an article and seeing an illustration in a newspaper showing what he interpreted as blacks in American Indian regalia, he reacted angrily by employing the racial slur "nigger" in his descriptions in a letter to Keppler.[50]

On several occasions, Scanandoah received official leaves to venture back to New York. In 1905 he married Bertha Crouse, an Onondaga, while on shore leave in Manhattan.[51] Although he received official leaves when his cousin Nicholas Hanyoust was charged with manslaughter in 1907 and when his newborn son, Bennie, became seriously ill in 1909, he was stuck in Nicaragua on the USS *Dubuque* when his brother Albert nearly died.[52] While on leave, he was able to testify in court in 1907 in an attempt to stop foreclosure proceedings on his family's homestead at Windfall; however, he was aboard ship in 1909 when the New York Supreme Court foreclosed on the same property.[53] Once out of service, he later helped his family lead the fight to regain this thirty-two-acre parcel of land.[54]

Scanandoah spent his last two years in naval service at Norfolk and at the Washington Navy Yard. In his spare time, he tinkered around, trying to perfect a new type of megaphone, one that could receive as well as transmit messages. He also spent time listening to congressional debates about appropriations affecting naval pensions for Spanish-American War veterans.[55] By August 1912, after completing the requirements of his third reenlistment and five years before he could officially retire and receive his full twenty-year pension, Scanandoah had had enough and left the navy, although he later came to regret his decision and attempted unsuccessfully to reenlist. In 1920 he secured a pension for his service during the Spanish-American War and Philippine insurrections; seventeen years later, he was awarded the Spanish-American War Campaign Medal.[56]

His departure from the navy in 1912 was largely because of two factors: his determination to challenge the loss of his family's homestead in court and his hope for success as an inventor after receiving a job offer to return to work at GE. Schenectady was now the "Electric City," and the company was the world leader in manufacturing electrical equipment of all kinds. It dominated every aspect of the industry, from the lightbulb all the way to the giant turbines that produced electricity. By 1900 it had become heavily involved in marine electrical apparatuses, including the manufacture of boat cranes, fan motors, hoisting machinery (including those designed for raising ammunition in storage), launch motors, marine wiring supplies, search lights, and signaling systems. By the time Scanandoah left naval service, GE had major US Navy contracts to supply turbines for its ships.[57]

While his days at sea were largely empty of direct involvement in combat, his civilian days that followed brought him and his Oneida people into a herculean struggle whose ramifications extended right down to the first decade of the twenty-first century.

Fig. 2. Samuel Chapman Armstrong, founder and principal of Hampton Institute. Chapman Scanandoah attended Hampton during the years 1888–94. *Source*: Edith Armstrong Talbot, *Samuel Chapman Armstrong: A Biographical Study* (New York: Doubleday, 1904).

Fig. 3. The Wigwam, Native American boys' dormitory, Hampton Institute. Native American male students had their own separate residence hall at Hampton Institute. Courtesy of Wisconsin Historical Society, Image #76477.

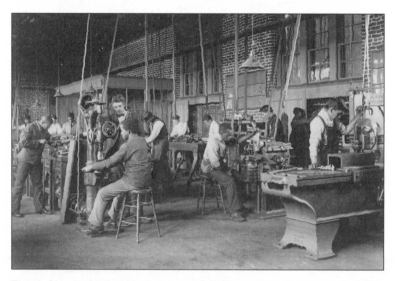

Fig. 4. Young Native American and African American men training in the use of machinery at Hampton Institute. Chapman Scanandoah was trained as a mechanic at Hampton Institute. Photograph by Francis Benjamin Johnston, ca. 1899–1900. Courtesy of the Library of Congress, Image #76477.

Fig. 5. Hampton Institute campus from offshore Hampton Inlet, leading from the Chesapeake Bay to the James River. The surrounding historical region with its major naval installations influenced Chapman Scanandoah's decision to enlist. Photograph by Frances Benjamin Johnston, ca. 1899–1900. Courtesy of the Library of Congress. Image LC-DIG-ppm sca-17491.

Fig. 6. Young Thomas Edison with an early model of his phonograph, 1878. Courtesy of the Library of Congress, LC-USZ62-98128.

Fig. 7. General Electric factory complex, December 1895. Originally founded as Edison Illuminating when it opened in Schenectady in 1889, the massive complex became General Electric in 1892. Chapman Scanandoah worked at GE at three different times of his life. *Source*: Horace L. Arnold, "Modern Machine Shop Economics," *Engineering Magazine* 11 (1896).

Fig. 8. Interior of GE Building #9 at GE factory complex in Schenectady, where Chapman Scanandoah worked in 1894 and 1895. Courtesy of the Museum of Innovation and Science, Schenectady. Image G.E.7052.

Fig. 9. Chapman Scanandoah in his US Navy uniform, 1898. Chapman served for fifteen tumultuous years in the US Navy. *Source*: "Chapman Schanandoah," *Talks and Thoughts* 14 (November 1898): 1.

Fig. 10. USS *New York*. The USS *New York* was an armored cruiser commissioned in 1896. Chapman Scanandoah served on this ship immediately after the Spanish-American War. Hampton students would visit and tour this ship when it docked at the Norfolk Naval Shipyard. Courtesy of the Naval History and Heritage Command, Image NH63559.

Fig. 11. USS *Marietta*. The USS *Marietta* was a schooner-rigged gunboat commissioned into service in 1897. Chapman Scanandoah served on this ship during the Spanish-American War. Courtesy of the Naval History and Heritage Command, Image NH411.

Fig. 12. USS *Oregon*. The USS *Oregon* was a predreadnought battleship commissioned into service in 1896. It made a famous voyage of 14,700 nautical miles from San Francisco around South America to Florida and to Cuba during the Spanish-American War, thereby showing the need for an isthmian canal. For part of its historic voyage, the USS *Marietta* accompanied it as its supply ship. Courtesy of the Naval History and Heritage Command, Image NH43148.

Fig. 13. USS *Sandoval*. On July 3, 1898, the Spanish gunboat *Sandoval* was heavily damaged in the Battle of Santiago de Cuba during the Spanish-American War. The crew of the USS *Marietta*, including Chapman Scanandoah, worked to salvage the vessel and transported it back to the Washington Navy Yard. The ship was subsequently placed into the US naval service and commissioned as the USS *Sandoval*. Courtesy of Naval History and Heritage Command, Image NH44246.

Fig. 14. USS *Atlanta*. The USS *Atlanta*, commissioned into service in 1884, was a protected cruiser and one of the first steel warships in the US Navy. In 1902, desperate to help his family save their homestead at Windfall, Chapman Scanandoah deserted this ship when it docked in Argentina. He made his way back to New York and was later convicted at a court-martial. Because of favorable publicity generated by his influential supporters, Scanandoah's conviction was later officially modified by the Department of the Navy, and the Oneida was to serve out the rest of his naval service and receive an honorable discharge in 1912. Courtesy of the Naval History and Heritage Command, Image NH63595.

Fig. 15. USS *Raleigh*. The USS *Raleigh* was a protected cruiser commissioned into service in 1894. In 1903 Chapman Scanandoah circumnavigated the globe while serving on this ship. His writings reveal keen insights about the world at that time. Courtesy of the Naval History and Heritage Command, Image NH67898.

Fig. 16. Harriet Maxwell Converse, poet and writer on the Iroquois, 1894. She was also an advocate for the Hodinöhsö:ni´ and was adopted by the Snipe Clan of the Senecas and condoled as a chief by the Iroquois Confederacy. Converse befriended Chapman Scanandoah and his family and served as their benefactor until her death in 1903. From the William M. Beauchamp Collection, New York State Library, Manuscripts and Special Collections, Albany, New York.

Fig. 17. Interior of gun shop, Washington Navy Yard, 1903. Scanandoah was assigned on different occasions to this naval yard and wrote about showing visiting Indians these big guns. Photograph by Frances Benjamin Johnston. Courtesy of the Library of Congress, LC-USZ62-924O4.

5

Saving the Thirty-Two Acres in the White Man's Courts

In a brief autobiographical sketch of his life, Chapman Scanandoah's cousin Chief William Hanyoust Rockwell claimed that he, above all others in his family, had been totally committed to fight the battle to save the Hanyoust homestead and the thirty-two acres of unallotted land at Windfall. Unlike other Oneidas, he frequently stated that he gave up everything—a residence in Rochester and a good job at Gleason Die Casting in that city—to return to live at Windfall and work as a mechanic at Westlake Manufacturing Company in nearby Canastota, New York, and later at Franklin Auto Service in Syracuse. The chief insisted that his cousin Chapman had taken the position that the effort to reclaim the thirty-two acres of Windfall was hopeless and that the remaining Oneidas in New York should all move onto the Onondaga Reservation.[1] To the public at large, the peripatetic and photogenic Rockwell, wearing his Plains headdress at numerous forums, was the epitome of the struggling Indian attempting to fight back against civilization. Largely unknown in this story of Oneida courage and fortitude was the role Rockwell's cousin Chapman played in the fight to save the thirty-two acres.

Rockwell's statement about his role in this litigation seems implausible based on his cousin Chapman's actions. Although in the traditional Iroquoian way, Scanandoah went to live with his wife's family at Onondaga once he returned from the navy, Chapman's commitment to the cause was just as firm as Rockwell's. As we have already seen, Chapman was even willing to risk imprisonment for desertion because of his concern for the future of the Hanyoust lands. As early as the summer of 1900, he arranged for the hiring of an attorney to undertake a title search of the Hanyoust family property at Windfall and told Keppler he planned to pay off any indebtedness on the property taken out by his uncle Isaac.[2] During his naval service, he had sent his salary home and had developed key relationships with influential non-Indians such as Converse and Keppler that he used to gather funds and information for his people.[3] In both 1907 and again in 1916, he testified in two cases involving Oneida efforts to save the thirty-two acres.[4] Scanandoah was partly responsible for getting the brilliant attorney George Decker, then serving as the deputy attorney general of New York, to volunteer his legal services to the Hanyousts.

Even before his family was evicted from the thirty-two acres, Scanandoah wrote to Keppler, indicating that he wished that he was home and out of naval service so that he could help in the legal fight to stop the eviction. On December 8, 1909, after the eviction of the Hanyousts had occurred from Windfall, Scanandoah wrote Keppler that he was pleased that such a prominent attorney as Decker was helping the Oneidas and was not going to charge anything for his work. Scanandoah asked Keppler to write Decker to find out the status of the case.[5] After expressing disappointment that he was far away and thereby could not be home to help, the Oneida indicated that he hoped that his family's efforts could lead to a victory in the case. Scanandoah also expressed concerns about Rockwell's leadership and what he saw as his cousin's inaction in pursuing the case. Rockwell had left the area for employment and was somewhere in Texas and had not forwarded his address to his cousin. Scanandoah described his cousin as flighty as a wild goose.[6]

The peripatetic Rockwell was born at Windfall on May 19, 1870, just three days after his cousin Chapman's birth. Despite their growing up together much like brothers and having a common interest in machines and how they worked, it appears that there was sibling rivalry between the two. Unlike Chapman, Rockwell had left Hampton after less than two years there. He had later taken course work in bookkeeping in Schenectady. Rockwell, known as Willie, was the illegitimate son of Chapman's aunt Margaret Hanyoust and Winthrop Jay Rockwell, a white man. Because of the circumstances of his birth, William Hanyoust Rockwell was set apart by some members of his family and referred to as "Willie the Bastard."[7] However, he was quick to point out that his mother, Margaret, Chapman's aunt, had not been shunned for her indiscretion with a white man. She had a special role at Windfall, taking care of tribal members when they were sick and feeding them when they were hungry.[8]

In 1906 Katherine Burney, the daughter of a deceased Oneida chief, had designated Rockwell as a chief of the Oneidas. Unlike Chapman, Rockwell sought out publicity as the Oneidas' head chief, becoming the "poster boy" for all tribal members living in central New York. Consequently, for the next half century, Rockwell was recognized as the Oneida spokesman in and around the thirty-two acres and frequently made appearances at public events and commemorations talking about Oneida culture and history.[9]

Scanandoah's hope that his family's lands could be saved were raised as a result of congressional legislation and federal court decisions involving the Hodinöhsö:ni´'s Kansas Claims case. He believed that a financial payout in the case would allow him to pay off his family's debt and avoid foreclosure on the property at Windfall.[10] Under the provisions of the Buffalo Creek Treaty of 1838, the US government had ceded to the Hodinöhsö:ni´ 1,824,000 acres "directly west of the State of Missouri" in order to entice them to leave New York. Article 3 of this treaty required that "such of the tribes of the New York Indians as do not accept and agree to remove to the country set apart for their new homes within five years, or such other time as the President may, from time to time appoint, shall forfeit all interest in the lands so set apart, to the United States."[11] Approximately two hundred Hodinöhsö:ni´ emigrated to Kansas; some died of disease, and most returned to New York by 1847.

By 1857 the lands assigned as the "New York Indian Reservation," which ran from the Missouri border into central Kansas, were overrun by trespassers in the aftermath of the Kansas-Nebraska Act of 1854. In the sectional conflict that led to "Bleeding Kansas," the Indians were the real losers, with squatters, using excuses of promoting slavery or free soil, laying claim to these lands.[12] By the late 1850s, there were nearly five thousand white settlers occupying lands assigned to the "New York Indians." In the fall of 1857, James W. Denver, the commissioner of Indian affairs, reported on the lands assigned to the "New York Indians" in Kansas and

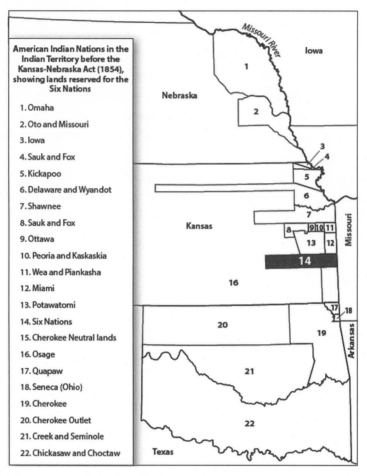

American Indian Nations in the Indian Territory before the Kansas-Nebraska Act (1854), showing lands reserved for the Six Nations

1. Omaha
2. Oto and Missouri
3. Iowa
4. Sauk and Fox
5. Kickapoo
6. Delaware and Wyandot
7. Shawnee
8. Sauk and Fox
9. Ottawa
10. Peoria and Kaskaskia
11. Wea and Piankasha
12. Miami
13. Potawatomi
14. Six Nations
15. Cherokee Neutral lands
16. Osage
17. Quapaw
18. Seneca (Ohio)
19. Cherokee
20. Cherokee Outlet
21. Creek and Seminole
22. Chickasaw and Choctaw

Map 4. American Indian nations in the Indian Territory before the Kansas-Nebraska Act (1854), showing lands reserved for the Six Nations. Lands in Kansas, the so-called New York Indian Reservation (designated as Six Nations on this map), were assigned to all the Hodinöhsö:ni´ from New York, including the Oneidas from New York under the Buffalo Creek Treaty (1838). These lands were overrun by trespassers after the Kansas-Nebraska Act of 1854. They were eventually sold off by the US Land Office. Hodinöhsö:ni´ claims against the US government continued until the first decade of the twentieth century, when there was a US Court of Claims financial settlement. Please note that the area on the map marked "Seneca" was land assigned to separate Iroquoian communities removed from Ohio in 1831 and 1832. Map by Joe Stoll. Courtesy of Joe Stoll and the Syracuse University Department of Geography.

proposed a "solution." He recommended the allotment of these lands to the few Six Nations people living there and the selling off of the rest, presumably to satisfy those non-Indians rushing into the territory as well as the lobbying by railroad interests.[13] President James Buchanan issued an executive order making these lands part of the national domain and allowing them to be surveyed. By the Civil War, federal Indian agent E. L. Terry complained to the commissioner of Indian affairs that no one was coming to the aid of the destitute "New York Indians" in Kansas who were "now outcasts," victims of "lawless violence" and facing "extinction."[14]

Subsequently, over the next decade and a half, the commissioners of Indian affairs ordered the allotment and sale of nearly two million acres of the "New York Indian Reservation." The federal government also granted some of the lands that had been reserved for the "New York Indians" to railroad interests. Thus, millions of acres of prime farmland were eventually sold off, and the United States made a significant profit, doing a "land office business" at the expense of the Hodinöhsö:ni´. Subsequent petitions filed by the Oneidas later claimed that they had not been protected and given supplies that they had been promised and that the federal government had failed to carry out its obligations as set forth in the treaty of 1838.[15]

For the next two decades, the settlement of the Kansas Claims was delayed primarily by the Civil War, by divisions within the Hodinöhsö:ni´, by congressional resistance, and by the US government's formally ending treaty making with the Indians in 1871.[16] On March 3, 1883, Congress passed the Bowman Act, authorizing the US Court of Claims to determine the facts surrounding the Hodinöhsö:ni´ claims.[17] In 1895 the Court of Claims decided that the "New York Indians" had abandoned their claim and thereby dismissed the case.[18] The attorneys for the Six Nations then appealed the decision. On appeal the decision was overturned and remanded back to the Court of Claims.[19] On November 14, 1898, the Court of Claims reversed its earlier decision and awarded $1,967,056 to the Hodinöhsö:ni´.[20] The US government then appealed the decision. On March 20, 1899, the US Supreme Court affirmed the Court of Claims' decision of 1898. The Court held that "the title acquired by the Indians had legal title to clearly defined lands, totalling 1,824,000 acres in Kansas."

The decision added that "the Indians had neither forfeited nor abandoned [except for the Wisconsin Oneidas and the Tonawanda Senecas who had exchanged their claims to Kansas lands for lands in Wisconsin and New York in 1838 and 1857, respectively] their interest in the Kansas lands, and that they were entitled to judgment."[21] On February 9, 1900, Congress appropriated $1,998,744.46 to pay the judgment and accrued interest on the claim for damages arising out of the sale of Indian lands in Kansas ceded to the Indians by the Treaty of Buffalo Creek of January 15, 1838.[22]

From 1903 to 1905, the Office of Indian Affairs assigned Guion Miller as a special agent to do research, scrutinize names, and prepare eligibility lists of individuals entitled to "Kansas money." Upon orders from Washington, the federal Indian agent was strictly authorized to distribute these moneys regardless of "sex, age, or family relations, and that minors' warrants could be delivered only to duly qualified guardians." He was also to prepare lists of those individuals who were not eligible. All those Indians who sought moneys had to provide documentation that they were tribal members or "descendants of such persons or that they were affiliated or associated with one of said tribes" on January 15, 1838, and "further establish that since said date of 1838 they have not affiliated with any tribe of Indians other than one of the tribe of New York Indians parties to said treaty."[23]

Applicants were denied based upon a number of factors: no evidence of Hodinöhsö:ni´ bloodlines back to 1838, honorary adoptees into the Hodinöhsö:ni´ members or members of other tribes, or descendants of fathers or grandfathers who had taken a white bride. Unlike their central New York and Southwold, Ontario, kinsmen, the Wisconsin Oneidas were not eligible to receive "Kansas money," as it was called, since they had negotiated an amendment to the Buffalo Creek Treaty on February 3, 1838, exchanging their interest in Kansas lands for 65,400 acres of lands in Wisconsin; the Tonawanda Senecas also were not eligible because, in a federal treaty in 1857, they had used money for the sale of Kansas lands to repurchase 7,500 acres of their New York homeland from the Ogden Land Company, whose agents had defrauded them in treaties in 1826 and in 1838. Most Hodinöhsö:ni´ living on the Six Nations Reserve in Canada were also denied these moneys because many had left New York well before the treaty of 1838. In the largest category of denials, Guion and the Indian Office followed the ruling of the secretary of the interior that the children of white mothers and Hodinöhsö:ni´ fathers were not entitled to share in the fund.[24]

Until the awards of the Indian Claims Commission (ICC) in the late 1960s and 1970s, the allocation of Kansas money in 1906 was the only compensation that the Hodinöhsö:ni´ ever received for the "surrender" of much of New York State. Of the 5,585 who received payments, the Oneidas, 1,220 of them, were the second largest in number of Hodinöhsö:ni´ to be awarded money.[25] The payout was smaller than most Hodinöhsö:ni´ had anticipated—approximately $170 per individual. Moreover, the settlement resulted in intratribal fights over eligibility.[26] Chief Rockwell noted that James B. Jenkins, the Six Nations white lawyer from Oneida, New York, received $70,000 as payment for his services, while a slew of less scrupulous but well-placed Washington, DC, attorneys also shared in the pot. Rockwell and others also complained that some who received payment from the federal government "had little or no Indian blood."[27]

The final settlement of the Kansas Claims had a major impact on the Oneidas in New York, even more than other Indian nations. For years, both the federal and the state governments had claimed that Oneida tribal reservation lands in New York no longer existed and that these Indians had assimilated and were living much like their white neighbors. Despite the state and federal governments' continued denial that the thirty-two acres constituted an official reservation right through the post–World War II era, the federal courts had set an important precedent with the Kansas Claims decision.[28] The existence of a continued Oneida tribal presence in New York could not be totally dismissed anymore.[29]

The Kansas Claims case also had a long-range impact within other Oneida communities. For several years prior to the award, Wilson K. Cornelius, an Oneida from Southwold, Ontario, had begun writing to the Office of Indian Affairs in Washington about the claim. He first came to Onondaga in 1895 and soon became involved in the pursuit of the Kansas Claims.[30] Inspired by the favorable outcome in the case, Cornelius shifted his focus to writing to Washington about Oneida claims to other lands in their homeland of central New York. He was to be persistent in his argument, namely, that US officials had forsaken their treaty obligations to the Oneidas and had stood idly by while New Yorkers stole the massive tribal estate. He and later his daughter Mary Winder raised issues that had been brought up before by earlier generations of Oneidas about the frauds perpetrated, especially in state treaties in 1785, 1788, and 1795, that cost the Oneidas millions of acres of their homeland. Cornelius and his family moved back and forth from the Oneida and Muncy Reserves in Canada to Onondaga, promoting their call for justice. Eventually, most of his family settled at Onondaga and were adopted into the New York Oneida tribal membership.[31]

The Hanyousts fought their battles in courts in the Boylan case, actually a series of cases, involving the thirty-two acres of their property at Windfall. These lands had been recognized as Oneida territory in two federal treaties in 1794, and, despite the state allotment act of 1843, the Hanyoust plot had never been divided in severalty.[32] Margaret Charles Hanyoust (Chapman's grandmother), Margaret Hanyoust (Chapman's aunt), and Mary Hanyoust (Chapman's mother) had resisted accepting fee-simple title and the selling off of the family's lands. The two sisters' families and their brother Isaac viewed this tract as their home, as did Chapman and Albert Scanandoah and their cousin William Hanyoust Rockwell.[33] All the members of the family had an equal interest in the tract and viewed their homestead at Windfall as a central meeting place for the benefit of their entire band of Oneidas. To them, as Rockwell later wrote to attorney Decker, the acreage was the symbol of Oneida self-government and independence.[34]

Long before Mary Hanyoust Scanandoah left for Onondaga, she had transferred the administration of the property, a lease, to her brother Isaac. In 1887 Isaac Hanyoust had secured a $1,250 mortgage from Philander Spaulding, a white man, who later signed the debt over to Patrick Boylan, another non-Indian, whose widow, Julia, was to later initiate foreclosure proceedings on the property. Because the thirty-two acres were part of Oneida lands recognized in federal treaties, the mortgage was an illegal transaction. In 1897 Isaac Hanyoust transferred the lease back to his sister Mary. A year later, Chapman Scanandoah assumed responsibility on the

$1,250 debt, hoping to save the property. In 1905, after continued threats of foreclosure, Joseph Beal, a local attorney and executor for the estate of Patrick Boylan, publicly announced his client's intention to recover a debt on the property, $1,250 plus $400 in interest that he claimed was owed by the Hanyoust family.[35]

The next year Beal filed an action to have these thirty-two acres foreclosed and partitioned into lots. In order to counter this action and slow down the snowballing efforts at foreclosure, W. J. McCluskey, the Oneidas' attorney, agreed that an arbitrator be appointed by the state court judge who would determine if the parcel could be partitioned. On leave from the navy in 1907, Chapman testified at this arbitration hearing. Much to the regret of the Hanyousts, Charles Coville, the arbitrator, was to conclude that the Oneidas were no longer tribal Indians and had no tribal government. Colville then ordered the auctioning of the property to the highest bidder. Julia Boylan was to purchase it for $725.[36]

In an attempt to stop Boylan, twenty-four members of the Hanyoust family petitioned Governor Charles Evans Hughes. Rockwell and two other Oneidas were to meet with Hughes in Albany.[37] The governor then ordered William Schuyler Jackson, the New York State attorney general, to provide a legal analysis of the issues in the case. Fortunately for the Indians, Jackson appointed George Decker, his brilliant deputy attorney general, to do the research and writing of this report. Decker's analysis concluded that the arbitrator and the New York Supreme Court were wrong in their conclusions and that the Oneidas, despite state law allotting Oneida lands in 1843, continued to have a unique legal status as an Indian tribe. He argued that if this Oneida band was dispossessed, it would constitute a violation of federal Indian treaty rights. Decker's official report concluded unequivocally that the disputed thirty-two acres were part of the original Oneida Indian reservation and that some of their lands in the town of Lenox, Madison County, were held jointly and had never been allotted. He pointed out that the federal government still recognized the New York Oneidas, as evidenced by the dispensing annuity of goods provided to their chiefs under the 1794 Canandaigua Treaty with the Six Nations. Decker also found that New York continued to recognize the existence of the Oneidas' tribal government in its laws and in the actions of Albany's commissioners of the land office. He maintained that these Oneidas had never agreed to the state legislature's law of 1843 law and that the thirty-two-acre parcel, in the southeast corner of Windfall, had never passed out of Indian hands, making the mortgage on the property and Boylan's claim of ownership invalid.[38]

Decker's findings were transmitted to Hughes by Attorney General Jackson, who recommended presenting the facts outlined in Decker's report to the New York Supreme Court, which was then hearing the Boylan case. Governor Hughes wrote back, concurring with the recommendation that "if the band is dispossessed under a sale in the pending suit . . . that act would constitute a violation of Indian rights."[39] The next year, the New York Supreme Court ruled against Boylan. Important to note, Decker continued to pursue justice even after he left his post as deputy attorney general to become the counsel for the New York State Conservation Commission in 1912. In 1914 he returned to his home in Rochester and worked for the next two decades as the lead attorney for the Oneidas as well as the Cayugas and Senecas in both the United States and Canada.[40]

Despite Decker's report, the foreclosure auction on the thirty-two-acre tract had already taken place. Attorneys for Boylan then appealed the ruling of the New York Supreme Court. The New York State Appellate Division overturned the previous New York Supreme Court decision of 1907 and ordered the deed be given to Boylan.[41] Rockwell then sent a letter of protest to Hughes on behalf of fourteen members of his family, including Chapman and his two brothers, Albert and Nicholas, and their mother, Mary. The governor then passed off the petition to his new state attorney general, Edward O'Malley. Unlike Decker, O'Malley was hardly sympathetic toward the Oneidas. As his authoritative source, he drew on conclusions made in the Whipple Report of 1889, one that demeaned the Hodinöhsö:ni´ beliefs, customs, and leadership and advocated the breakup of all tribally held lands. O'Malley concluded that there was no obligation for the state to enter the case. He rejected the idea that the thirty-two acres were communal property, mistakenly insisting that all Oneida lands in New York were held in severalty since the 1843 state allotment law. He even went beyond ruling on the thirty-two acres, stating that it was his opinion that the Oneida tribe had ceded all their rights, titles, and interests to several parcels "along the north shore of Oneida Lake to the people of the State of New York in 1795."[42]

On June 24, 1909, the Appellate Division of the New York Supreme Court in *Boylan v. George, et al.* held for the plaintiff, allowing her to maintain a partition action on the thirty-two acres, which would allow her to sell off the property. Before the court, William J. McCluskey, the attorney for the Oneidas, argued that the land in question was part of the original reservation guaranteed by the United States in treaties and thus could not be partitioned or sold. However, McCluskey's argument was rejected by the court. Judge J. Cochrane ruled that the plaintiff, Boylan, was entitled to the earlier interlocutory decree because those Oneidas who remained behind while their kin left for Wisconsin had "mingled with the whites, dealt with the whites, and lived among them. That said parties have no relation with the said Oneida tribe, nor have they for the last forty years maintained or supported any tribal government."[43] Thus, to Cochrane, the Oneida Nation was seen as being extinct!

On November 29, 1909, Undersheriff Michael Mooney of Morrisville, Officer Ross Beckweth of Oneida, and several other officers threw the Hanyousts off the thirty-two acres. Several family members, including Chapman's mother, were carried out of the house by force, and their personal effects and furniture were placed in the street, despite their insistence that the thirty-two acres were federal treaty lands and thus could not be transferred to Boylan by foreclosure. Rockwell described the incident, an account that was confirmed in an article in the *Oneida Dispatch*:

In 1909, my poor old helpless aunt Mary Schenandoah—on the day following after Thanksgiving she was carried out and dropped in the highway which is now Route 46. Mary Schenandoah was carried to the road five times because she managed to return to the house each time. She was picked up bodily and dropped so heavily into the roadway, she was not able to walk back to the house again that was her home. My uncle William Honyoust was treated in the same way. He kept returning to the house that was his home too. Seven burly sheriffs kept putting these two defenseless Indians out in the road until they were completely exhausted so that they could not return to their home. The horse William Honyoust owned was turned out of the barn. Our furniture was thrown out to the road. Finally it was carted away into a lot by the woods by a white person.[44]

Chapman Scanandoah and his family were devastated by the foreclosure. Chapman's uncle Isaac, perhaps blaming himself for taking out the mortgage, fell into a deep depression and died soon after. In December 1909, lamenting the situation, Chapman wrote Keppler after the foreclosure that his family's beloved home was now in white men's hands. Four days later, he asked Keppler to help him make contact with George Decker.[45] In May 1910, attorney Decker petitioned Governor Hughes and the New York State Legislature on the Oneidas' behalf, but his effort was quickly dismissed. Decker then wrote the governor on June 14, insisting that the Oneida Indians were politically independent and beyond the jurisdiction of the state and its agencies; however, by this time, Hughes had been appointed to the US Supreme Court.[46]

While serving as chief attorney and counsel for the New York State Department of Forest, Fish, and Game Commission from 1911 to 1914, Decker continued to volunteer his legal services to the Oneidas.[47] He undertook historical research on their history and treaties, gathered affidavits from Oneidas concerning their customs, and appealed to federal and state officials to intervene on their behalf.[48] Stonewalled by Albany officials and by the Office of Indian Affairs in Washington, the attorney was relentless in his advocacy. After Decker sent his supporting documents and briefs to various federal officials and even secured the support of influential senators such as Elihu Root, former secretary of state, the US Department of Justice Department agreed to take action in 1913 because Decker had convinced their attorneys that there was a constitutional issue involved in the case, namely, violations of federal Indian treaty-right guarantees to the Oneidas.[49] When the US Department of Justice delayed court action even though he had given their attorneys all of the necessary research to pursue litigation, Decker criticized the department for being inadequately staffed, allowing for the stealing of Indian lands.[50]

Decker's tireless efforts coincided with Scanandoah's leaving naval service. In 1911, while still in the navy, he won attention for one of his inventions, receiving a patent on it. Consequently, the next year he felt confident enough to leave naval service for a position in the private sector at General Electric in Schenectady. No longer fighting Spaniards in Cuban waters, supplying American forces to put down insurrections in the Philippines, or commenting on civil wars in Nicaragua, his attention was largely directed at another conflict, winning back his mother's homestead and the thirty-two acres at Windfall.

Finally, in 1916 US attorney Frank J. Cregg entered federal court on behalf of the Oneidas in an attempt to regain the thirty-two-acre territory by suing Boylan and Anna Siver Moyer, who had purchased a part of the Hanyoust property from Julia Boylan. Scanandoah, by now an elected chief, was heavily involved in the case as it progressed through the maze of the American judicial system. Importantly, Chapman, his brother Albert, their mother, Mary, as well as Chief William Hanyoust Rockwell were to testify at the federal district court. They appealed for justice and recounted the Oneidas' long alliance with the federal government, as symbolized by the Polly Cooper shawl given to them by Martha Washington. Joseph Beal, the attorney for Boylan and Moyer, claimed that the Oneidas were now scattered all over the country, had abandoned their lands as well as their allegiance to tribal control, and had become US citizens. Assistant US attorney Cregg responded that the Oneidas were not citizens and that it would take a special act of Congress to bestow citizenship upon them. Importantly, he went on further to say that New York had no jurisdiction over the seven Oneidas who testified. To win the sympathy of the court, Chapman Scanandoah and the other Oneidas who testified employed familiar themes used by their tribesmen in the past: they insisted that their ancestors had helped the United States win its independence during the Revolution and that the Oneidas were always a peaceful, thrifty tribe.[51]

America's entry into World War I delayed the decision in the case. After deliberating for two and a half years, Judge George Ray declared Boylan's title invalid and decided that the Oneidas retained aboriginal title and had not abandoned their tribal relations.[52] Ray's decision was appealed by the Boylan attorneys. In 1920 at the Federal Court of Appeals in *United States v. Boylan*, Judge Martin T. Marion accepted Decker's argument and found for the Oneidas, indicating that the Boylan mortgage, which had been executed by a member of the Oneida tribe, was invalid "in the absence of federal legislation authorizing it." He added that the Oneidas "constitute a distinct tribe or nation, and exclusive jurisdiction over them is vested in the federal government which may maintain actions in the behalf."[53] Thus, in effect, this historic decision held that the Oneidas remaining in New York, despite their small numbers and minuscule land base, were a bona fide federally recognized tribe with treaty rights that prevented the alienation of their lands. The court ordered the return of the thirty-two acres to them.[54]

The Boylan decision was met with open hostility and threats by non-Indians in central New York, causing Oneidas, who desired to return to their small reservation, to remain at Onondaga; others moved to Rochester, where Decker found them employment.[55] Scanandoah, nevertheless, remained at Onondaga with his wife, Bertha, and their four sons, Benjamin, Chapman Jr., Donald, and Earl; his mother, Mary; and his brother Albert and his family.[56] Moreover, while the Boylan decision had recognized the thirty-two acres as federal treaty lands that could not be foreclosed by a failure to pay off a mortgage, Bureau of Indian Affairs (BIA) officials both in New York and in Washington, DC, continued to ignore the implications of the ruling. They viewed the New York Oneidas as having no reservation lands and merely recognized these Native Americans' right to pursue further land suits only as a segment of the Oneida Nation of Indians of Wisconsin, where the majority of their tribesmen resided.[57]

Although the federal government had been minimally involved in administering Indian policies and services in New York and had left it to Albany officials for three-quarters of a century, the Boylan decision maintained that the federal government had exclusive jurisdiction over the Hodinöhsö:ni´. Consequently, the New York State Legislature, at the behest of the state attorney general, established an assembly commission to deal with what he considered the ambiguous line between federal and state jurisdiction over the Hodinöhsö:ni´ nations. The commission was headed by Assemblyman Edward A. Everett of Potsdam and included Charles Newton, the state's attorney general; three members of the state senate; five members of the assembly; one representative each from the state departments of education and board of charities; and one official Indian representative, Chief David R. Hill. Arthur C. Parker, the noted anthropologist at the New York State Museum of Seneca ancestry, was also on the commission. Members were instructed by the legislature to examine "the history, the affairs, and transactions had by the people of the state and to report to the legislature the status of the American Indian residing . . . in New York." They were to make on-site visits and hold hearings on the reservations in the state.[58]

On August 16, 1920, the commission held a hearing on the Onondaga Reservation. In attendance were Everett and five other members of the commission. Chief Andrew Gibson gave the invocation in the Onondaga language. He was followed by Chief George Thomas, who presented a resolution that had been adopted by the Onondaga chiefs. The memorial clearly stated that Albany had no jurisdiction over the Hodinöhsö:ni´; that the chiefs preferred the federal government, not New York State, as their "guardian"; and that Albany officials needed to live up to their agreements made in the past.[59]

After the discussion that followed, one New York Oneida, Joseph Johnson, interjected. He asserted that despite being "quartered off in a little bit of land called a reservation," the Indians "are a separate country from the United States as long as we have treaties and yet we are called aliens." He then blamed the missionaries, especially Samuel Kirkland, and agents of the Ogden Land Company for what had befallen his Native people. He insisted that the recent federal court decision in the Boylan case had settled the jurisdictional question. Johnson continued sarcastically: "If they [New York State officials] appropriate a few dollars for the benefit of my health, is that protecting me or not?" He added that most Indians didn't care who took care of them, only that they be "treated right by state authorities."[60]

When it was brought to the chairman's attention that Johnson was an Oneida and not an Onondaga and that the present hearing was specifically set to take Onondaga testimony, the meeting turned somewhat contentious. Chapman Scanandoah then tried to pose a question to the commissioners. Everett asked that the Oneidas wait until the next day's hearing to voice their opinions. Angrily, Scanandoah then reacted to Everett's comments by claiming that the state commission was purposely "trying to separate the tribes." He added, "We [Hodinöhsö:ni´] are a league of nations, like you are today with Uncle Sam as boss and when the South tried to get away [and secede] we had a civil war." Everett quickly responded by insisting there was no need to have a civil war, as the Oneidas would be given a full forum the next day.[61]

On August 17, the commission met with the Oneidas. Joseph Johnson resumed his testimony from the previous day. Two other Oneidas who resided at Onondaga—Chiefs Marshall John and Chapman Scanandoah—testified at this hearing. Chief John, a Hanyoust from Windfall who had been directly involved in the legal fight over the thirty-two acres, stated that his people had the "greatest grievance of any nation of the Iroquois League." He then explained that the Oneidas had made numerous treaties with the state, that his people had existing land claims, that Albany had failed to pay its treaty annuities, and that the state had failed to protect the Oneida land base when local farmers began moving their fences and furrowed inch by inch onto tribal lands.[62]

Scanandoah then followed. He presented a brief historical overview on Indian-white relations from earliest colonial times. He then brought up that the Oneidas had always been loyal to the United States from the era of his ancestor Chief Skenando in the American Revolution through World War I. Scanandoah stated that he had traveled the globe in his younger days and saw too many awful things, and thus he was content to shy away from documenting the crimes and injustices of the white men toward the Indians. Yet Scanandoah did just that in his testimony. He insisted that the Indians were the first to establish independence, because "it is natural born in him," as it is for the rest of nature, be it a turkey, fox, raccoon, or coyote. He insisted that despite efforts by colonial powers and the white man's propensity for violence, no efforts were successful in completely controlling and changing the Indians, and none would succeed in the future. "A great amount of money has been spent to establish other nations as Cuba and the Philippines, for self government. We [Hodinöhsö:ni´] don't want it until we get fair treatment." He rejected the idea of awarding US citizenship to the Hodinöhsö:ni´, which he insisted was no surefire panacea for the Oneidas. Scanandoah concluded by emphasizing that his people "in their hearts" favored federal jurisdiction and strongly opposed the idea of transferring criminal jurisdiction to New York State. Later that day, acting as the secretary for the Oneida delegation at the hearing, Scanandoah requested that the commission accept written testimony and attached historical documents before the commission finalized its report to the New York State Legislature.[63]

Despite Everett's urgings, the New York State Legislature refused to pay for second on-site visits to reservations or to pay for official Indian delegates to come to Albany to testify. The commission's final report was to reflect only the opinions of the chairman and the commission's researcher and stenographer, Lulu G. Stillman. The report concluded that the Hodinöhsö:ni´ were legally entitled to six million acres of New York State, having been illegally dispossessed of their title after the Fort Stanwix Treaty of 1784. It stated, in part:

> The Indians of the State of New York are entitled to all the territory ceded to them by the treaty made with the Colonial government prior to the Revolutionary War, relative to the territory that should be ceded to the Indians for their loyalty to said colonies and by the treaty of 1784 [at Fort Stanwix] by which said promise by the colonists was consummated by the new Republic known as the United States of America and in a speech by General Washington to the Conference of Indians comprising the Six Nations and recognizing the Indians as a Nation.[64]

When the final report, completed on March 17, 1922, was filed with the assembly in early April, neither the New York State Assembly nor the New York State Senate even bothered to print it. Despite being buried by state officials, the report and the commission's statewide hearings combined with the earlier Kansas Claims settlement and the favorable Boylan decision fed into an already existing Hodinöhsö:ni´ land-claims movement.

That summer the federal courts formally ordered that the thirty-two acres revert to the Hanyousts. Although this ruling involved only the family's homestead and parcel, the decision had a tremendous impact on the Hodinöhsö:ni´ psyche. These Windfall lands were to become a great symbol of Oneida fortitude in facing what appeared to be insurmountable odds. The successful litigation over the thirty-two acres also raised hopes among other Hodinöhsö:ni´ nations, now determined to pursue legal options in their quest for a return of their lands taken from them by state and federal treaties.

On August 18, 1922, the Hanyousts held a celebration at Windfall to mark their victory in the Boylan case. Oneidas from Wisconsin and Canada and from Onondaga were joined in the festivities by prominent Mohawks, Onondagas, and Tonawanda Senecas as well as a representative from the BIA. Chief Rockwell, the master of ceremonies at the event, praised Judge Ray for his courageous decision on the Oneidas' behalf.[65]

Among those individuals in attendance was Laura Minnie Cornelius, a Wisconsin Oneida activist now married to Orrin Kellogg. Minnie Kellogg, as she was better known at home on her Wisconsin Oneida Reservation, was to use the Hanyoust victory in the Boylan case as her springboard for leadership within the Iroquois Confederacy. Although judged as a usurper by the Hanyousts and by many others throughout Iroquoia, she, nevertheless, gained a wide following with her pursuit of the Six Nations' land claim for millions of acres within the Empire State.[66]

By the mid-1920s, Chapman and Bertha Scanandoah were to be thrust into the middle of the political upheaval caused by Minnie Kellogg, her husband, and her followers, by then known as the Kellogg Party. Until then, the Oneida and his brother Doc remained above the fray, committed to their work as inventors. From 1916 onward, Chapman had turned his inquisitive mind to backyard experiments with chemical compounds. Taking up farming, both brothers attempted to revive traditional Iroquoian varieties of maize and other crops. Despite being outsiders on the Onondaga Reservation, the brothers' reputation as inventors insulated them well until political chaos brought on by the Kelloggs forced them to choose sides.

6

A Native American Inventor in the Age of Edison

In his experiments that started during his US Navy career and carried over into civilian life, Chapman Scanandoah achieved recognition for his mechanical abilities and later for his work as a chemist and as an agronomist. His efforts resulted in the US Patent Office awarding him two patents. It also led to his receiving a significant amount of press coverage throughout his long life. Picturing him in these stories as an "Indian" who somehow unexpectedly leaped into "modernity," reporters generally ignored what had shaped him, namely, his Oneida identity as well as the history and culture of the Hodinöhsö:ni´. In this regard, in one of his later accomplishments, he helped revive an ancient variety of Hodinöhsö:ni´ maize and won recognition for it in statewide agricultural circles.

Growing up at Windfall, Chapman and his brother Albert, known affectionately as Doc, took joy in assembling and dissembling small machines. When he went off to Hampton, he continued to be fascinated by what his teachers were instructing in his vocational course of study. While at the Virginia school, Scanandoah became known for experimenting in the Indian dormitory known as the Wigwam. After Scanandoah left Hampton in 1894, a student reporter writing in a Hampton Institute newsletter fondly remembered the Oneida as the student who kept a battery "in his room while here and how willing he was to explain the principles to us." A year and a half later, the same publication noted Scanandoah's accomplishments after leaving Hampton: "Chapman is a machinist who takes no back seat for a machinist of his age [twenty-four]."[1]

His inquisitive brother Doc had had a strong influence on him. In the 1890s, Doc began working at Solvay, the nation's largest producer of soda ash, just outside the northwest boundary of the city of Syracuse. One of the major problems faced by the company, which was later bought out by Honeywell and Company, was its problem of waste disposal that produced a ring of toxic chemicals around the southeast end of Onondaga Lake. Besides polluting the lake and desecrating a major holy site of the Hodinöhsö:ni' associated with the Iroquois Confederacy's founding, the wastes hardened and formed high dikes.[2] Until his death in 1934, Albert, aided by Chapman, worked with Cornell University scientists, hoping to remove and make use of the residue. His plan was to make construction materials five times lighter than bricks out of the residue. Doc's plan was later dubbed impractical and rejected by the US Patent Office.[3] The brothers' collaborative efforts did not stop there. As an Oneida traditional herbalist with a keen interest in scientific endeavors, Doc and Chapman conducted agricultural experiments after World War I on their farms at Onondaga. They also worked with Dr. Albert Gilmore, a staff member of the Museum of the American Indian, in collecting and documenting traditional Indian remedies.[4]

Chapman first received recognition as an inventor on his own while serving in the navy. As early as 1901, the *New York World* reported that the Oneida was a machinist who had previously worked at Thomas Edison's plant in Schenectady while he had temporarily taken a break from his studies at Hampton in the early 1890s to pay for his schooling.[5] In February 1904, Scanandoah wrote to Keppler describing an invention that he was trying to perfect. He enclosed a sketch for Keppler's benefit. At the time, the Oneida was working on improving the accuracy of big-gun sightings while on board the USS *Raleigh*. In the design, Scanandoah fitted a small telescope to the barrel of the large shipboard gun, much like a standard telescopic rifle. The naval gunner was thus able to pinpoint the object made by the bisecting of the two straight lines crossing at right angles upon the lens. When the marksman obtained the position, he was assured of success when firing, providing the object was not moving too fast. If the object moved too rapidly, Scanandoah recommended that the marksman needed to raise the elevation of the gun and adjust the range finder. Realizing that it would take "many moons" (Scanandoah's own words) for his specifications to reach the US Patent Office in Washington, DC, Scanandoah asked Keppler to take up the matter with Munn and Company, the publisher of *Scientific American* and the most successful firm in helping individuals secure patents for their inventions.[6] The US Navy eventually introduced telescopic sighting to its big guns; however, Scanandoah was not credited with the innovation.

Later, on board ship during downtime, the Oneida observed that sailors often could not communicate easily across deck or when ships were side by side. The noises produced by high winds and waves were frequently too intense and interfered with communication. In order to deal with this real problem, Chapman began to fiddle around with a megaphone, attempting to invent an attachment that would allow it to receive messages back. As chief machinist's mate stationed at the Norfolk Naval Shipyard in 1911, he successfully invented a new type of megaphone, one with a receiving device, which was adopted for use on ships at sea. The US Patent Office awarded Scanandoah a patent on it on October 8, 1912. His success in receiving this patent on his invention was well publicized in publications at Hampton and at Indian boarding schools around the country, and he was once again presented as a role model for students to emulate.[7]

In US Patent application #1040775, filed on December 19, 1911, Scanandoah explained what he referred to as a "simple and efficient device," an attachment to the traditional megaphone. He described this attachment as allowing sound waves to be caught so that the device could be "used as an audiophone." One objective of Scanandoah's invention was to provide a device "with certain wiring arrangements to assist in the collection and reproduction of sound waves." In his application, he described how to use the modified megaphone and provided a diagram:

> In using the device the ear pieces are placed upon the ears with the tube 18 extending around beneath the chin and this will bring the mouth opposite the mouth piece 11. The operator may face in the direction of the person with whom he wishes to communicate and by speaking into the mouth piece sound will be conveyed to him in the ordinary manner.

When using the device to speak [into it,] it is preferred to shut off the sound waves by closing the valve so that the only opening that remains is the small opening 27 which is provided for the reception of a wire 32 when said valve is closed. When the other person desires to speak, the valve is opened and sound waves enter the megaphone and strike the wires 15, also passing down through tube 17.[8]

After leaving the navy in 1912, Scanandoah went to work once again at GE's manufacturing and project development center in Schenectady. At that very time, GE had invented and was building the first electrically propelled turbine generators for the navy. Apparently, Scanandoah's past experiences as a mechanic in engine rooms serving on battleships, cruisers, and naval tenders were seen by some in GE as needed skills and an important addition to its workforce. Both Chapman and his brother worked as mechanics there for nearly two years. However, in the corporate culture of GE, company managers favored and mentored young aspiring engineers from major universities, a fact that limited the Oneida chief's upward mobility at the Schenectady plant. Eventually, these college graduates soon were to replace all shop engineers.[9]

After the sinking of the *Lusitania* in May 1915, Chapman left Schenectady for employment at the famous New York Navy Yard at Brooklyn. At this major naval installation at the Wallabout Basin, a semicircular bend of the East River across from Manhattan, the Oneida worked there for about a year. This two-hundred-acre shipyard, established between 1801 and 1806, had a remarkable history. In 1862, the USS *Monitor*, the first ironclad in the US Navy, was assembled at this navy yard, and in the mid-1890s, the USS *Maine* was built there.

With new war clouds on the horizon, Scanandoah, perhaps nostalgic for life at sea and regretting that he had never served in combat, attempted to reenlist in the navy. He wrote the secretary of the navy and other prominent officials, even indicating that he would be willing to be assigned to submarine service. Because he was now forty-six years of age, had been separated from active navy duty for four years, and wore corrective glasses, his attempts to reenlist were rejected. When this effort failed, he returned to Onondaga to work with Chief Rockwell and attorney Decker in their determined attempts to reclaim his family's property at Windfall. In much demand because of his growing reputation as a mechanic, he began working off and on for the next decade at two enormous plants: Crouse-Hinds, the major high-grade electrical and instrumental products company that invented the traffic light based in Syracuse, and later at New Process Gear, first established in Syracuse and then in DeWitt, which later made automotive gears and transmissions.[10]

Upon his return to Onondaga in 1916, Scanandoah began experimenting with explosives. His longtime naval service and news of war coming from Europe pushed him in this direction. The chemical science of weaponry intrigued him as well because this field had grown exponentially since the Civil War. In 1863 Julius Wilbrand, a German scientist, safely poured trinitrotoluene, better known as TNT, into a shell casing for the first time. In the mid- and late 1860s, Alfred Nobel, a Swedish engineer, invented both blasting caps and dynamite, a special formatting of nitroglycerin. By the first decade of the twentieth century, at the time of Scanandoah's service, the US Navy started using TNT in mines, bombs, depth charges, and torpedo warheads. By the time he left the navy, Scanandoah had become familiar with other ordnance, including the explosive amatol, TNT mixed with ammonium nitrate, and widely used pitric acid and phenol, all of which proved unstable, volatile, and sensitive to vibrations.[11]

Scanandoah's experiments came at a time when chemistry was coming to the fore in military thinking. Indeed, World War I has been labeled "the chemist's war." Germany, France, England, and later the United States produced chlorine, monochloride for mustard gas, bromine for tear gas, and phosgene, also known as "white star," a colorless, odorless compound that was sometimes mixed with chlorine. German companies first developed these chemical weapons, but the Allies soon followed suit. American companies—Dow and DuPont—produced a significant array of these chemicals when the United State entered the war in April 1917. Although outlawed at The Hague Declaration Concerning Asphyxiating Gases in 1899 and The Hague Conference of 1907, both the Allied and the Central Powers placed these chemicals into canisters and hurled them by artillery indiscriminately outward toward the enemy. Perhaps as many as 1.3 million people were affected by poison gas, and 90,000 people were killed in chemical warfare from 1914 to 1918.[12] DuPont alone grossed a billion dollars in World War I, two hundred million of which came from explosives such as TNT and so-called smokeless powder.[13]

Scanandoah's interest in explosives dated back to his service on the USS *Dubuque* off the coast of Central America from 1908 to 1910. At that time, he noted the effect of temperature upon chemicals in shell canisters. He later recalled that once in the tropics, he watched an entire magazine of explosives "dumped because it had been ruined by the climate." Scanandoah's aim was to produce an explosive more powerful than dynamite that could be safely handled and sent through the mails. The Oneida inventor was to eventually succeed with what he labeled "shanandite" (also at times spelled "schanadite" or "schenedite"), by mixing two powders together, each one alone incapable of producing an explosion. Much to the curiosity of his Indian and non-Indian neighbors, he began mixing compounds in his backyard shed on the reservation. Subsequently, he made contact with officials of manufacturing plants in the environs of Syracuse to explore the possibilities of producing a new stable gunpowder—"shanandite"—that could be safely handled and transported. It would take him another decade to perfect this explosive that he intended to use for commercial nonmilitary uses.[14]

While experimenting in his backyard shed and working at Crouse-Hinds in Syracuse, Chapman also took up farming. As an Oneida living at Onondaga, he was eligible only to acquire a life lease on the property from the Onondaga Council of Chiefs. Because he was not an Onondaga tribal member, the "sale" entitled him to farm there, but the land could not be passed down to other family members after his death. As a farmer in 1917, he successfully produced 400 bushels of corn; 225 pounds of potatoes; 200 head of cabbage, turnips, onions, and beans; as well as 50 tons of hay.[15] By the fall, the Scanandoah brothers were winning prizes for their agricultural produce of apples, beets, carrots, corn, potatoes, and squash at Onondaga. In a one-thousand-dollar contest sponsored by the *Syracuse Herald*, Albert won the best all-around prize and Chapman secured third place. Unfortunately, Chapman's early effort at farming was short-lived when a fire destroyed the barn, and with it, one thousand dollars' worth of hay; insurance money covered only about half of his loss.[16]

Now in need of more money to rebuild and with the Boylan federal decision not forthcoming, Scanandoah decided to once again leave Onondaga. After the US entry into World War I in April 1917, and now beyond the age for reenlistment, Scanandoah joined up with several other Hodinöhsö:ni´ and began work as a civilian employee to aid the war effort. His decision was apparently also based on his experiments with shanandite.[17]

Early in 1918, he began working at the Frankford Arsenal in the Bridesburg neighborhood in the northeastern section of Philadelphia. Founded immediately after the War of 1812, the arsenal was an extensive complex, with its own medical, fire, and police departments. Ordnance and machines to produce ordnance were manufactured at the site. After the Civil War, it manufactured, among other things, percussion caps and fuses for detonating explosives. By the 1890s, the twenty-acre site had become the nation's center for powder chemistry, which was tested in a special facility, the Proof House, with its 109-foot shooting gallery. Before the US entry into World War I, the arsenal, which employed thousands of civilian workers, was primarily involved in manufacturing small-arms ammunition at a new factory at the site. In one of his letters to Keppler, Chapman reported that employees' jobs there were to manufacture all different types of explosives. The Oneida, however, indicated to Keppler that his employment was temporary because he had plans to return to Onondaga to once again take up farming.[18]

After returning to Onondaga later that year, he was to formulate and refine his plan for his explosive. For the next five years, he continued to test it. In the wake of the horrors of World War I, Scanandoah envisioned that his explosive would be used for peaceful purposes. In September 1923, he wrote to Keppler that his time was largely taken up trying to perfect the explosive in his backyard shop and to convince companies of its practical use in industry.[19]

Early in 1925, the local *Oneida Democratic Union* praised the Oneida inventor for creating shanandite. Unlike much of the ordnance used in World War I, the reporter pointed out, shanandite was the safest explosive in existence, one that "a baby could play with without blowing its hands off." The reporter added that the explosive, a compound of elements, could be safely sent through the mails. After mentioning Scanandoah's excellent naval record, the reporter was flabbergasted that an Oneida could make such an explosive compound with his own tools and in his backyard shop. In one of his first demonstrations of the power of shanandite, Scanandoah drew hundreds of people, both experts on explosives and local Indians, to the Jones Quarry on the reservation to witness his experiment. The first try to set off the explosive proved faulty when wires to the switch box had not been connected right. A local newspaper reported on the success of his second attempt: "The charge of eight large wads and two small ones placed in a rock hill on the southwest side of the quarry, was touched off by voltage wires and 500 yards of solid rock of nearly the same depths, rolled in the gully below."[20]

This explosive, which Scanandoah claimed was twice the powder of dynamite, was directly related to his second patent, a method of condensing metals by explosive force, a scientific way of subjecting iron, steel, or other metals to the concentrated force of a rifle volley to give it strength and hardness. In effect, Scanandoah viewed his discovery of this powerful explosive as a way to produce metals of even quality that were needed in precision instruments and not for war. In his experiments, he placed two guns, end to end, with heavy rams in the place of bullets, with a frame in which the metal was gripped, and then detonated the guns simultaneously. The rams filled with shanandite struck and condensed the metal with tremendous pressure, producing metals of even quality. By using his method, he maintained that the molecules of a body of metal would be suitably condensed by a single application of opposing compressive forces. He suggested that his proposed method of compressing metals would produce the necessary uniformity and lower production costs because it would eliminate steps.[21]

In his application filed April 1, 1925, Scanandoah, now spelling his name "Schanandoah," set out two objectives: to "compress and condense metal so that it could withstand greater resistance and have greater endurance than previously achieved" and to "produce a condensing of a body of metal by means of rams or projectiles of suitable size, weight and material, that may be impelled suddenly and with great force toward the body simultaneously as by explosives that may be detonated in unison, whereby the rams or projectiles may strike with equal force against the opposite sides of the body of metal." He added that he preferred to use explosives in effecting the compression, although a powerful hydraulic force could be substituted but with less uniformity and greater costs. The Oneida then described the method:

> The invention relates to the treatment of steel, iron, and other metals, by means of which the molecules of the metal may be brought into closer relation with each other, for condensing, hardening and increasing the resistance of the metal, for certain purposes. The object of the method is to compress and condense a body of metal by subjecting said body to great pressure, said pressure preferably being greater than that usually effected by casting rolling or forging, as commonly practiced, and the said pressure preferably being applied to the metal from opposite directions and in the same plane simultaneously, thereby subjecting the body of metal to two like forces that preferably move towards the body at the same speed and exert substantially equal pressure against the opposite sides of the metal.

On February 2, 1926, Scanandoah was awarded his patent, "Method of Condensing Metals," by the US Patent Office.[22]

Despite his patent, the corporate megaliths—Dow and DuPont—had no place for an aging backyard inventor. In the antiwar climate that followed World War I, these companies were diversifying, using their immense profits gained in producing armaments. They followed GE's earlier model, establishing specialized departments with university-trained scientists. Chemical departments of Dow and DuPont focused on other projects besides explosives. In the 1920s and 1930s, DuPont became a chemical empire, producing among many other items cellophane, Freon, nylon, rayon, Teflon, and an antiknock additive for gasoline. After World War I, Dow scientists focused much of their attention on light-metals research, especially experimenting with magnesium for use in automobile pistons; furniture and luggage frames; sports equipment, such as baseball bats, canoes, and skis; airplane propellers and boats; as well as home items that included lawnmowers and cooking grills. Thus, the world of the inventor-tinkerer, so prevalent in the late nineteenth and first decades of the twentieth centuries, soon gave way to academically trained scientists from major universities.[23]

With little success pitching his patent, he turned his attention once more to working his farm at Onondaga. By this time, Chapman was now a father of five children born nearly twenty years apart—his fifth child, Louella, was born in 1925. He turned his attention once more to farming at Onondaga.[24] Yet his inventiveness had not come to an end. His energies were now focused on experimenting in his fields, reviving older varieties of Iroquoian crops, and promoting horticulture among the Hodinöhsö:ni´. By 1935 Chapman Scanandoah was so successful in reviving an Iroquoian variety of maize that he won the first prize at the New York State Fair in Syracuse.[25]

In the 1920s, Chapman had become active in the Six Nations Agricultural Society, which had been founded in 1917. He again followed the lead of his older brother. Encouraged by Erl [sic] Bates of Cornell University's Agricultural Extension Service, Doc had become part of Cornell's Indian Board and the New York Indian Welfare Society and spoke on Indian agricultural methods at their meetings, demonstrations, and picnics throughout New York State. Chapman joined his brother in these endeavors. As a leading mechanic, Chapman headed the society's tractor committee. Both brothers, working with the Six Nations Agricultural Society, led initially by Seneca Nation president William C. Hoag and Grant Mt. Pleasant of Tuscarora, encouraged Hodinöhsö:ni´ youngsters to take up farming and hoped that some would be admitted to the New York State Agricultural College at Cornell University.[26]

In 1928, because of the lobbying by Bates and Cornell University's Agricultural Extension Service, the New York State Legislature allocated two thousand dollars to establish the "Indian Village" at the New York State Fair.[27] For the next quarter century, Scanandoah was instrumental in the administration and planning of the annual events held there in the two weeks leading into Labor Day weekend. His carving of a giant ear of corn became the symbol of the Indian Village.[28]

The Indian Village at the New York State Fair has evolved over the years away from the stereotypical portrayal of Hodinöhsö:ni´ wearing Plains headdresses. Oneidas, including Albert and Chapman Scanandoah,

William Hanyoust Rockwell, Ray Elm, and Maisie Shenandoah and her extended family, played vital roles in highlighting Hodinöhsö:ni´ culture, namely, arts and crafts, music, dance, and horticulture.[29] It soon became an annual event where Hodinöhsö:ni´ gathered with their extended families and friends to socialize, renew old ties, and talk about their concerns about US and Canadian policies that threatened their existence. When the Indian Village was rebuilt in 1950, Chapman Scanandoah was the honored Hodinöhsö:ni´ chief who presided over the ceremony.[30] Today the Indian Village teaches visitors about the living traditions of Native peoples in New York and engenders pride among the Hodinöhsö:ni´, especially on the annual Six Nations Day at the fair. It is a vital part of contemporary Indian existence in New York State, one that the Scanandoah brothers, two inventors, helped bring about.

While the Scanandoah brothers were busy throughout the 1920s experimenting as chemists and agronomists and working to promote agriculture in Six Nations' communities, the Hodinöhsö:ni´ faced new challenges. By the end of the decade, all Hodinöhsö:ni´ had to deal with what they perceived as a looming threat, namely, the push to transfer criminal and civil jurisdictional from the federal government to New York State. Internally, the Hodinöhsö:ni´ debated the merits of trying to bring their land claims for millions of acres into the federal courts, legal actions that had been denied them for nearly a century. Despite its nationalist appeal, this land-claims movement created major fissures in every reservation community. Consequently, as outsiders at Onondaga, the brothers Scanandoah and their families had to walk a fine line to survive in the turbulent Six Nations politics of the day.

7

An Outsider at Onondaga

By the 1920s, Scanandoah, now in his fifties, had become a highly respected Oneida elder. Hence, it is not surprising that the Oneidas elected him their chief, representing them at Onondaga. At the time, his reputation as an inventor was widespread, and his experiments drew large crowds. Most important, Scanandoah and his family's successful struggle in the federal courts to regain the thirty-two acres had brought them accolades and contributed to igniting land-claims movements in all of the Six Nations' communities. Fluent in several Iroquoian languages and well versed in Hodinöhsö:ni´ customs, he participated in solemn Iroquoian rituals, including Condolence Councils at Onondaga, in which new chiefs were raised.[1]

Although whites were ordered to be removed from the thirty-two acres in 1922, Scanandoah and almost all of the Oneidas in New York were not to return to Windfall. Only Rockwell and his family continued to occupy these lands as permanent residents. One hundred seventeen remained at Onondaga, and others were to move to the environs of Rochester. There were several reasons for not returning to Windfall. The return to the minuscule homeland, merely the Hanyoust parcel, did not seem economically realistic to hundreds of Oneidas. Many were well settled and earned a living elsewhere. Although 138 Oneidas still lived in Madison and Oneida Counties, strong anti-Indian sentiment by local non-Indian residents existed around Windfall, including by those individuals who had been ejected. Some of these non-Indians saw the decision in the Boylan case as a dangerous precedent, especially after the Hodinöhsö:ni´, emboldened by the Everett Commission report, began talking of filing larger Indian land-claims suits.[2]

Scanandoah was one of the Oneidas who remained at Onondaga. Married to an Onondaga, he, in the traditional matrilocal Hodinöhsö:ni´ manner, maintained his residence there. Because of Hodinöhsö:ni´ rules of matrilineal descent, his four boys and later his daughter, Louella, born in 1925, were all enrolled as Onondagas. He and the rest of the Hanyousts on this reservation attempted to fit into their conservative surroundings. As outsiders, Scanandoah and other Oneidas there had to be careful not to offend and tried to follow the lead of the Grand Council whenever possible.

Oneida-Onondaga relations were affected by historical realities. Onondagas had long memories about the Oneidas that lingered from the time of the American Revolution when the two Indian nations found themselves on opposite sides of the conflict. Onondagas recalled their ancestors' accounts about the Revolutionary War and how their villages were destroyed by American general Goosen Van Shaick, and most became refugees at the Senecas' Buffalo Creek Territory, on the Niagara frontier.

In contrast, most Oneidas served in General Washington's army in the War for Independence. With the massive influx of Windfall and Orchard migrants to Onondaga beginning in the last decades of the nineteenth century, the Oneidas faced a precarious situation there. Oneidas had no right to own land outright on the reservation and thus could not pass land titles on to their children at the time of a parent's death. They were also subject to the resolutions as well as the political whims of the Onondaga Council of Chiefs, who on occasion turned against these resettled Indians. To complicate matters for Scanandoah and his family, a significant number of Canadian Oneidas had resettled on the reservation, and the influx was not always welcomed by their Onondaga hosts or by the federal Indian agent.[3]

Although Chapman had similar views as the ones expressed by followers of the Hodinöhsö:ni´'s Longhouse religion, he and his extended family attended the Methodist church on the reservation. This practice was not unusual, because at that time Christian chiefs, including Chapman's brother Doc and later his cousin William Hanyoust Rockwell, served as Oneida representatives on the Grand Council. Like most Hodinöhsö:ni´, he insisted the United States had treaty obligations to protect his people from Albany policies and that state laws were not applicable. The Oneida was a determined foe of US citizenship and jurisdictional transfer in criminal and civil matters from the federal government to New York State. The Oneida was also an ardent defender of Hodinöhsö:ni´ rights to fish and hunt without state licenses required by Albany. During a contentious time in the 1920s in which the Iroquois Grand Council became fractionated, Chapman supported a clan mother's traditional right to nominate chiefs.[4]

This belief was reflected during World War I. In 1917–18, the United States attempted to draft Indians into military service. Several Oneidas were drafted and sent overseas. Although the Oneidas were willing to voluntarily enlist, they and other Hodinöhsö:ni´, as in the past, saw themselves as allies and not subject to being conscripted. Consequently, Scanandoah and others on the reservation protested the federal policy. Denying the federal government's right to draft Indians led to a backlash against them and charges that they were unpatriotic. In order to calm the flames of resentment, the Oneidas, in step with the Grand Council of the Six Nations at Onondaga, declared war against the Central Powers and pledged their allegiance to the American cause.[5]

In 1921 and 1922, the Oneidas at Onondaga were also to assert their sovereignty in ways apart from the directives of the Grand Council. One incident directly affected the Scanandoah brothers and reveals a rising sense of their family's sovereignty-minded activism. While the Everett Commission was conducting its business, Doc Scanandoah, on September 1, 1921, decided to travel to meet some of his friends on the Seneca reservations in western New York. As Doc drove on a public highway about ten miles outside of the village of Canandaigua, he stopped at a service station to repair his vehicle and obtain gas. When he removed the cushions from the seat of his automobile, a blanket fell. Wrapped in the blanket was a loaded pistol that discharged when the blanket hit the ground. The bullet tore through the car's windshield, while startled bystanders looked on. Doc had no local or state permit to carry a gun. Although no bystander was injured, Deputy Sheriff George E. Colhecy arrested the Oneida and took him to the police station in Canandaigua. He was brought before Judge Leon W. Van Deusen and convicted of a misdemeanor for violating

Section 1897 of the penal law, namely, carrying a firearm without a license. The judge imposed a fine of fifty dollars, at which time Doc protested; in order to secure his freedom and with a fear of imprisonment, he was forced to pay out ten dollars on the spot and agreed to pay the difference to the judge by September 6.[6]

The Oneidas immediately protested, turning once again for help to attorney Decker. On February 6, 1922, the Oneidas sent a formal protest to New York State governor Nathan L. Miller, who forwarded it to both the Attorney General's Office and to the Conservation Commission. The signatories on the petition included the names of five Oneida chiefs—Chapman Scanandoah as well as Alexander Burning, Andrew Elm, Marshall John, and William Hanyoust Rockwell. The chiefs insisted that New York State had no jurisdiction since Scanandoah "was traveling upon a lawful occasion, in an orderly manner," and that federal treaties guaranteed him and his brethren the right "to carry on such travels with ordinary equipment, baggage, and effects as may suit their convenience and purposes of their journey." Emboldened by the favorable Boylan decision and testimony at the Everett Commission hearings, they insisted that "no further invasion" of their treaty rights be undertaken by state and local officials and threatened to pursue the matter further by appealing to federal authorities.[7]

To support the Oneidas' efforts, Decker prepared a detailed argument and sent it to Governor Miller. To the Rochester attorney, the sheriff who apprehended Scanandoah and the magistrate who fined him "acted in the name of the State of New York, and the State cannot deny responsibility to those who are not its subjects or within its sovereignty, for wrongs committed by such officials." He also insisted that when the state agreed to the federal Constitution in 1788, "it subjected itself in Indian affairs to the action of the federal government." He stated that in the 1794 federal Treaty at Canandaigua, New York gave members of the Six Nations the right to travel and visit unimpeded between Hodinöhsö:ni´ territories and that New York State had no right to assert its own sovereignty in the matter. He pointed out that Article 1 of this treaty aimed to promote peace and friendship *in perpetuity*. To Decker, just because the Iroquois became more separated from each other over the years did not end federal treaty obligations, including the right of unrestricted passage over the state highways. He also cited Article 7 of the treaty, pointing out that the Six Nations had the right if needed to bring their complaints to the attention of federal authorities. Besides the US Constitution and the Treaty of 1794, Decker cited Article 3 of the Jay Treaty, arguing that it provided the Indians the right to "freely carry on trade and commerce with each other."[8]

Decker concluded that Doc Scanandoah had not lost treaty rights by traveling on state highways and that there was "no acknowledged law which denies to a separate people any natural right on the score only of color." Indeed, his travels were actually equivalent to "a diplomatic official of one European country passing through the country of another at peace to reach a third to which he is accredited." The state Attorney General's Office and the New York State Conservation Commission quickly dismissed these arguments. They insisted that all the laws of New York State were applicable both to Doc Scanandoah as well as to all the Indians in the Empire State.[9]

In April 1922, the Everett Report was formally submitted to the New York Legislature, supporting Hodinöhsö:ni´ land claims to millions of acres of New York State. A renewed hope that justice would prevail for the Oneidas and other Hodinöhsö:ni´ arose. Favorable outcomes in the Kansas Claims settlement and the Boylan decision and testimony and the final report of the Everett Commission had stirred the kettle, an Iroquoian metaphor for community, identity, and territory, bringing up old grievances against the "white man." In the fall of 1922, Scanandoah wrote Keppler, alluding to the rising tide of Hodinöhsö:ni´ activism around him.[10]

The Hodinöhsö:ni´ in New York were also affected by their kin across the international boundary in Canada. A new activism promoting Hodinöhsö:ni´ sovereignty was already under way at this very moment and added fuel to the push for recognition of Indian grievances in the United States. In Canada Chief Levi General, Deskaheh, with the help of attorney Decker, attempted to bring Native complaints against the government in Ottawa before the League of Nations in an attempt to get to the World Court in The Hague. Deskaheh insisted that the Canadian government was interfering in Hodinöhsö:ni´ political affairs and violating Indian border-crossing rights guaranteed in the Jay Treaty. Decker also represented the Cayugas at Grand River, successfully getting a settlement of claims of one hundred thousand dollars from a joint British-American commission in 1926.[11] A year earlier, Paul Diabo, a Mohawk ironworker from Kahnawake, was arrested for violating the Immigration Act of 1924 by failing to get a permit to work in Philadelphia. Diabo eventually won his case against deportation, arguing that the Jay Treaty of 1794 recognized his right to freely cross the border.[12]

For well over a hundred years, Oneidas in Canada as well as in New York and Wisconsin had complained about state treaties, especially ones negotiated in 1785, 1788, and 1795, that had dispossessed them of more than five million acres of their homeland.[13] They frequently petitioned the New York State Legislature about these lost lands, especially around Oneida Lake. Since the first decade of the twentieth century, Wilson K. Cornelius, a member of the Oneida Band of the Thames, had written extensively to the Indian Office in Washington in an effort to challenge the legitimacy of New York State–Oneida treaties and secure compensation for his people, not just in his Southwold, Ontario, community, but for all Oneidas, including in New York and Wisconsin.[14] By 1906 Cornelius had made his presence felt among the New York Oneidas, and he and his two daughters, Mary and Delia (Dolly), were counted by the federal census taker as Oneidas living on the reservation.[15] Wilson Cornelius went from community to community in both the United States and Canada, urging Oneidas to pursue their claims to millions of acres of lands illegally taken in the decade after the American Revolution. After World War I right through midcentury, his remarkable daughters, Mary (later Mary Cornelius Winder) and her sister, Delia (later Dolly Waterman), were instrumental in keeping the land-claims movement alive. Mary would repeatedly write to the US Interior and Justice Departments for the next three decades, seeking relief.[16]

By the mid-1920s, the Hodinöhsö:ni´ in New York, in the wake of the Everett Commission hearing and report, initiated a suit for millions of acres of their lands that they maintained had been forced out of their hands from 1784 onward. At the forefront of this claim was Laura Minnie Cornelius Kellogg, a controversial but brilliant Wisconsin Oneida activist. Twenty years earlier, in the same year as the Kansas Claims payout,

Laura Minnie Cornelius, then using her maiden name, had first made her appearance in the Oneida homeland. In the first days of summer in 1906, the *Oneida Dispatch* praised her as a bright young women intent on learning by traveling through the country. The reporter informed readers that she was intent on helping all Native Americans "devise practical methods for encouraging industry sobriety and organization."[17] The highly controversial Minnie, as she was known to her people, was fluent in all six of the Hodinöhsö:ni´ languages. By the 1920s, she was to promote the idea of resurrecting the ancient greatness of the Iroquois League, seeking the return through litigation of millions of acres taken from the Hodinöhsö:ni´ people, not just the Oneidas, from 1784 to 1842.[18]

Minnie Kellogg clearly had exceptional abilities—a distinguished Oneida lineage that could be traced back to prominent chiefs Daniel Bread and Elijah Skenandore. She had a brilliant mind, educated at major universities and not at the inferior Indian boarding schools of the day; employed a magnetic oratorical style of speaking in both English and the Iroquoian languages; and had charisma and exquisite beauty. Kellogg was to gain wide influence from her home in the West at Oneida, Wisconsin, to the Mohawk Territory. As a feminist, advocate for Native American treaty and civil rights, and reformer of urban and factory conditions during the Progressive Era, she received national attention in the press when she appeared at forums throughout the United States and Canada. The peripatetic Oneida even toured Europe as a performance artist and as a spellbinding speaker. In 1911 she was one of the founders of the Society of American Indians, the first major national Native American–run organization. However, members saw her as contentious and labeled her a provocateur, and consequently by 1915 she was dismissed from the organization.[19]

The Hanyousts were to have a negative opinion of Minnie Kellogg and her husband, Orrin, who claimed to have Seneca ancestry, and her many followers. Despite their hard-won victory in the historic Boylan case, the Hanyousts were now being pushed aside by this dynamo coming out of Wisconsin. To them, she was a flimflam women making false promises and preaching pie-in-the-sky solutions to desperate and downtrodden

Indians. Both Chapman Scanandoah and his cousin Chief Rockwell spoke out against her and suffered the consequences for doing so.

Kellogg's ideas spread throughout Iroquoia and on both sides of the international boundary line. The activist spoke in proud terms of the Six Nations' past; of her detailed reconstruction idea, the "Lolomi Plan," for the economic, political, and spiritual revival of the Six Nations; of her unyielding hatred for the Office of Indian Affairs in Washington, DC, for failing to properly educate Indian children and provide them with the necessary skills needed to survive in the modern world; and of her intention to file litigation to reclaim millions of acres.[20] In 1925 at Oneida, Wisconsin, she went so far as to revive chiefly titles associated with matrilineal lineages and brought Longhouse preachers from Onondaga to Wisconsin to conduct rituals for the purpose of overseeing the installation of nine sachems. Although she was never convicted of a felony, authorities in both the United States and Canada arrested her on several occasions for impersonating a law enforcement officer and for allegedly using the mails to illicitly raise money.[21] Her many defenders suggest that her arrests were the result of her "rattling the cage" of both Canadian and American officials with her criticisms of both governments' Indian policies.[22] On the other hand, Kellogg's detractors saw her and her husband, Orrin, as "scam artists."[23]

The Kelloggs promoted the idea of a test case, a class-action suit on behalf of *all* of the Six Nations, not just individual nations. Orrin, who was an attorney, and Kellogg's brother Chester collected money wherever Hodinöhsö:ni´ had communities—New York, Oklahoma, Wisconsin, Ontario, and Quebec—with the stated intention of using it for a great Hodinöhsö:ni´ claim to lands in New York and Pennsylvania. They collected a considerable sum from economically hard-pressed Indians, and they apparently never used the money raised for the intended purpose. In an outright lie, the Kelloggs told the Hodinöhsö:ni´ that if they did not contribute, they would not be eligible for the claims once the courts made their determination. They gave tax receipts or due bills, which indicated that the contributor was entitled to 10 percent interest and a 40 percent bonus after the case was settled. The Kelloggs also formed claims clubs on every reservation and reserve and charged dues for membership. They levied a tax of approximately a dollar and a quarter per month on each member. The Kelloggs were later accused by some of their own people of swindling them of hundreds of thousands of dollars in their abortive efforts to bring their land claims to fruition.[24]

Unfortunately, Minnie Kellogg's life has a sense of tragedy to it since her goal initially was to use her extraordinary abilities to help her people; however, in the end, she was accused by many of them of becoming a common outlaw. As historian Douglas Kiel of Williams College, a Wisconsin Oneida, has recently written, "Kellogg's sensible recommendations for economic development were offset by her participation in suspect business schemes."[25]

Kellogg was hardly the first to champion the Six Nations' claim. The Everett Report, largely the work of Lulu Stillman (the commission's stenographer and Everett's chief researcher), and Oneida grievances expressed in petitions to Albany and Washington expressed over a century and a half shaped her thinking.[26] Wilson K. Cornelius had lobbied over the previous two decades and had filed complaints with federal officials about the Oneida-state treaties of 1785, 1788, and 1795. Thus, it was not surprising that by the mid-1920s, Cornelius became associated with the Kellogg Party and served as its treasurer.[27]

In November 1922, the Grand Council hired Assemblyman Everett as its attorney and contracted with Carl Whitney, the assemblyman's nephew and a partner in the New York City law firm of Wise, Whitney, and Parker, in a determined effort to pursue the Six Nations' claim. However, as early as 1923 and 1924, Kellogg and her supporters had created deep splits within Iroquoia. Some objected to her speaking for all Hodinöhsö:ni´ because Kellogg's Oneida community had formally separated from the confederacy structure when they left New York for Wisconsin and then Michigan Territory. Others were intrigued by her ideas of hope and were less concerned about whether she had a right to speak for all Hodinöhsö:ni´. Kellogg's ideas gained influence in some quarters of the reservation, leading certain Onondaga chiefs to invite her to speak about her ideas within the walls of the longhouse. Ironically, while presenting herself as an advocate of traditional Iroquoian culture and values, she and her supporters were also offending some, including the Hanyousts, by her and her followers' nontraditional methods. In 1924 her allies on the reservation appointed George Thomas (not to be confused with his son, George A. Thomas, who served as *Tadodahoh* in the 1950s through early 1970s) as *Tadodahoh*, the principal chief and spokesman for the Iroquois Confederacy Council of Chiefs, bypassing the traditional role played historically by clan mothers.[28] The result was a bitter split on the reservation that continued right through the decade.

By the mid-1920s onward to 1930, the Grand Council itself was divided, leading to claims by two Onondaga sachems—Joshua Jones and George Thomas—that they were the rightful *Tadodahoh*. The Kellogg Party supported Thomas, while the Hanyousts favored Jones. The schism made it quite uncomfortable for Oneidas living there. Scanandoah and a sizable number of Hodinöhsö:ni´ objected to this break with tradition. Among the most outspoken critics were Chapman Scanandoah and his Onondaga wife, Bertha, who pointed out not only that this decision was a violation of the Great Law of the Hodinöhsö:ni´, but that Wisconsin Oneidas such as Kellogg had no standing within the Grand Council and thus should not be listened to. When the women's efforts failed, Joshua Jones was raised by the women as their *Tadodahoh* in opposition to Thomas. Nevertheless, from 1924 through 1930, both Thomas and Jones claimed to be "head chief."[29] Eventually, Chief Jones was to win out.[30]

The Kellogg Party chiefs retaliated against their enemies on the reservation when they gained political control. They attempted to take *all* the profits from a sand and gravel mining lease held by Minnie and Bertha Scanandoah and their family members, outspoken opponents of Kellogg's choice of *Tadodahoh*. In countering the Kellogg Party, Chapman's wife, Bertha, played a major role. Bertha was a well-respected, powerful Onondaga. Her prominence on the reservation led to her appointment as custodian and gatekeeper of the Onondaga tribal rolls and receiver and distributor of the federal treaty cloth, the annual symbolic renewal of the government-to-government relationship between the Hodinöhsö:ni´ and the United States. She was to battle the Kelloggs head-on. She helped bring the mining-lease case to court, questioning the legitimacy of Thomas as *Tadodahoh* and the actions of the Kellogg-allied chiefs. The Kellogg Party's effort eventually failed when the court limited the Kellogg-dominated Chiefs' Council to only one-third of the lease moneys.[31]

In 1927 the Six Nations' land-claims case *Deere, et al. v. State of New York et al.* finally reached federal district court. The litigation involved a one-mile parcel of land, in traditional Mohawk Territory, taken in a state treaty with the Mohawks in 1824. The plaintiff was James Deere, an Akwesasne Mohawk who brought suit on behalf of his own Mohawk Nation and the other five nations of the Iroquois Confederacy. He contended that the 1824 accord was in clear violation of the federal guarantees given to the Six Nations at the Treaty at Fort Stanwix in 1784. The attorneys for the Iroquois Confederacy argued that the sale of the land was null and void because no single tribe of the Six Nations could make such an agreement and because only the Confederacy Council and the federal government could conclude such a land transfer. At the time of the litigation, the one-mile parcel of land was in the hands of the St. Lawrence River Power Company, a subsidiary of Alcoa, and seventeen other occupants. The case was dismissed by the federal district court in 1927 for what it claimed was a lack of jurisdiction.[32] After attempts to appeal the decision failed, the Kelloggs slowly began to lose influence. Some of those individuals who had originally supported her efforts blamed them for the loss, and others began to question what had happened to the substantial moneys that had been raised in pursuing the suit.[33]

The Kellogg Party, nevertheless, received a new life in 1928 when a scathing report critical of federal Indian policies was published. Lewis Meriam and nine assistants at the Institute for Government Research (later known as the Brookings Institution) documented the failures that in some ways echoed ones that had been expressed by Minnie Kellogg for several decades previous. As a consequence of the Meriam Report, the US Senate passed Resolution 79, calling for its Committee on Indian Affairs to undertake a survey of the conditions on reservations throughout the United States. This massive undertaking was to stretch over fifteen years. These hearings allowed the Kelloggs to have one last forum to express their grievances and present themselves as the sole voice of the Hodinöhsö:ni´.[34]

In March 1929, at a hearing in Washington, DC, before the US Senate Subcommittee on Indian Affairs, the Kelloggs once again made their appeal about the Six Nations' land claim. Minnie and Orrin Kellogg opened the hearing with their formal testimony, even though in Iroquoian protocol chiefs were required to speak first. Although their testimony exposed the inefficiency, outright incompetence, and cultural insensitivity of BIA bureaucrats, the hearing backfired for the Kelloggs when some of their questionable tactics and fund-raising activities were exposed. The Kelloggs presented themselves as agents hired by the Hodinöhsö:ni´, revealing that they had a contract that would pay a 2 percent commission on a half-billion-dollar financial settlement in the claim. Minnie Kellogg cited the importance of the Boylan decision, mentioned the battle over control of Grand Council and Onondaga finances, brought up the issue of Hodinöhsö:ni´ border-crossing rights set forth in the Jay Treaty, and opposed the transfer of criminal jurisdiction from the federal government to New York State. After their extensive testimony, they then deferred to allow other members of their party, including several allied Cayuga, Mohawk, and Onondaga chiefs, to express their displeasure with the decision in the Deere case.[35]

Not surprisingly, the Kellogg Party testimony and the New York Oneida tribal testimony occurred at different times. When the subcommittee reconvened its hearings that November in Syracuse, Chiefs Rockwell and Scanandoah testified and attempted to separate themselves from the controversial Kelloggs. Rockwell started off by telling the subcommittee that he was a toolmaker by trade who for a brief time had attended Hampton Institute and later took a business course in Schenectady. Rockwell then described his people's loss of much of their land base in the sixty years after the American Revolution. He emphasized his Indian nation's federal status and its annual treaty renewal by its acceptance of cloth distribution. The Oneida chief expressed his concerns about Albany's and Washington's failures to provide for the health and educational needs of his people. He also stated his personal objection to the Indian Citizenship Act of 1924, claiming that he would never vote in the white man's elections.[36]

Chapman Scanandoah was to follow Rockwell's testimony at the November 1930 hearing. Questioned by Senator Burton K. Wheeler, he described that he could not own land at Onondaga because he was an Oneida and thus could obtain only a life lease on property. He insisted that the matter was a real concern because he had used part of his earnings from naval service to purchase his farm there, but his children had no right of inheritance from him there because the Indian law was far different from the written laws of the United States. He made a veiled reference to the turmoil caused by the Kelloggs: "Now as an individual I am going through this life the same as any other man. I have enemies among my own people, and let me tell you something—the Indian has stumbling blocks to overcome in making progress by lazy white men and lazy Indians holding him back."[37]

In March and April 1930, the House Committee on Indian Affairs held hearings in Washington and Syracuse on a bill proposed by Congressman Bertram Snell of New York that called for the transfer of criminal jurisdiction over Indian affairs from the federal government to New York State.[38] When Congressman Snell first put forth his bill, Chief Rockwell, with his cousin Chapman Scanandoah at his side, testified against its passage. Rockwell insisted that New York State had done little to improve Indian existence in the Empire State, that it had arbitrarily enforced their laws regarding hunting and fishing over the Indians, that New York State had paid a pittance for millions of acres of Oneida land, and that Albany politicians had done nothing to help him or his family when they had been evicted from the thirty-two acres. He told the congressmen at the hearing that he did not vote in town, county, state, or federal elections because their votes would not count anyway: "If you put all the New York State Indian votes together, they would not carry the first ward of Syracuse." Rockwell then went after the Kelloggs, labeling their leadership the "hot dog chiefs" who were surreptitiously conspiring against Hodinöhsö:ni´ interests. He accused Minnie Kellogg of secretly selecting "her own officers, secretaries, treasurers, and field agents." He claimed that they operated in secret off the reservation at the Onondaga Hotel in downtown Syracuse, which served as the headquarters for their questionable fund-raising efforts.[39] The Snell bill of 1930, opposed by Scanandoah and most Hodinöhsö:ni´, failed to pass, although it was periodically revived and finally secured enough votes to become law in 1948.

With worsening economic conditions and fewer employment opportunities because of the deepening of the Great Depression, Kellogg's ideas were less attractive and were now seen as quixotic. The Hodinöhsö:ni´ were more concerned with the immediate needs of family survival than with what they saw more and more as unrealistic pipe dreams. The Kellogg movement slowly dissipated, and Minnie Kellogg faded into history.

For the last two decades of his life, Chapman Scanandoah turned more of his attention to farming and pontificating on Oneida and Hodinöhsö:ni´ subjects to visiting newspapermen wanting to write about "real Indians." Although still wary of Albany's intentions, he kept abreast of doings in Albany and in the nation's capital, but his major attention was devoted to the work of the Six Nations Agricultural Society and the Indian Village at the New York State Fair.

8

The Wise Tribal Elder
Tends His Garden

The Oneidas, including the Scanandoah brothers and some of their Hanyoust family members, were given shelter in symbolic and real terms under the "Great Tree of the ancient League of the Iroquois at Onondaga." Despite living in these foreign waters, Scanandoah's residence at Onondaga allowed him and his wife, Bertha, to raise four sons and a daughter there. Residence there gave him access to participate in Iroquoian rituals on the reservation, at events at the nearby Indian Village at the New York State Fair, and at meetings and commemorations at the local chapter of the Veterans of Foreign Wars. Although most Oneidas at Onondaga were now allied, politically or otherwise, to the Grand Council, most never felt the reservation was their real home, even though, as in Scanandoah's case, more than a few had married Onondagas. They were a distinct minority group set apart on the reservation, a major reason for their continued ability to maintain their separate identity as Oneidas.

Scanandoah was also set apart from others on the Onondaga Reservation by the plethora of experiences in his extraordinary life. Chapman was no ordinary individual living at Onondaga. Undoubtedly, Chapman's marriage to Bertha Crouse, a prominent and well-respected Onondaga, insulated him from what most other Oneidas faced on the reservation. His Hanyoust family had held on to their land despite the temptation of allotment and the quick money gained from selling off the thirty-two acres. They had helped win a great legal decision in the Boylan case, the first major Hodinöhsö:ni´ victory in federal courts since 1857.[1] For fifteen years in naval service, Chapman had participated in war, been court-martialed twice, circumnavigated the world, witnessed rival world powers attempting to extend their imperial schemes, and empathized with Native peoples from Nicaragua to Hawaii. He had worked for the great Thomas Edison and had achieved recognition as an inventor. Chapman and his brother Doc had also consulted with leading academics, attempting to preserve Oneida languages, medicinal plants, and indigenous horticulture. Through his experiments and inventions, Scanandoah had achieved national acclaim and was frequently interviewed by the local media, most of the time identified as *the* Oneida chief at Onondaga.[2]

From the 1930s into the 1950s, Scanandoah, now among the most accomplished and respected elders in Iroquoia, served his people in a variety of capacities. He was one of two chiefs representing the Oneidas at Onondaga in the elected Oneida Chiefs' Council of five (three resided in Madison and Oneida Counties and two on the Onondaga Reservation). Besides being the custodian of the Polly Cooper shawl, Scanandoah also had the honor of receiving the annual treaty cloth, symbolic of the accord made by the federal government with the Six Nations at Canandaigua in 1794. Importantly, as an unofficial tribal historian and philosopher, he kept the memory of past events alive and was sought out by both Hodinöhsö:ni´ and outsiders for his knowledge.[3]

The Oneida elder was frequently interviewed by reporters who visited Onondaga looking for a good story about "real Indians." In these news stories, Scanandoah challenged stereotypes and racial epithets directed at American Indians. As a proud Hodinöhsö:ni´, he pointed out to them that, in his opinion, the first United Nations was not the one in operation in New York City but the ancient League of the Iroquois. He would recount the exploits of his ancestor Chief Skenando and other Oneidas who served the Americans in the Revolutionary War. In his interviews, he noted that present-day major highways followed the same routes as the trails used by the Hodinöhsö:ni´ in the past and informed these newsmen that Thanksgiving was a feast copied by the Pilgrims from the New England Indians. At other times, Scanandoah received attention by challenging scholars and their writings, insisting that the Indians had not migrated across the Bering Strait and that the US government was modeled on the Hodinöhsö:ni´.[4]

Despite the respect and favorable publicity he received, Scanandoah, nevertheless, faced major challenges in the last two decades of his life. Right through the late 1930s, Chapman had to contend with one personal crisis after another. In 1931, while driving on a road to Syracuse, he tried to avoid a man on construction equipment coming at him. He slammed on his brakes, skidded, and went off the road. Although Chapman was not seriously injured, the man on the machine was thrown off and killed, as was a boy riding his bicycle. He was not charged with a crime.[5]

For the next six years during the Great Depression, the Scanandoah family faced financial hardships. Although Chapman still putted around in his backyard workshop, he stopped commuting to work as a machinist in Syracuse. In the spring of 1931, agricultural production on his farm plummeted because of a continuing frost that delayed planting. He noted that the only thing going for him that year was work in his backyard workshop. To make things even worse, the next year the US Bureau of Pensions slashed his naval pension by 70 percent.[6] In the summer of 1934, Doc Scanandoah died after a long illness, a heavy blow, since Chapman so often followed his brother's lead.[7] Things improved for the family financially in 1935, when Congress passed the Social Security Act. After four years of appeals to Washington, his pension was finally restored in 1937. From then on, he received sixty dollars per month.[8]

By the 1930s, Chapman's home life at Onondaga had changed considerably. Two of his sons—Chapman Jr., born in 1907, and Bennie, born in 1909—had reached maturity and resided elsewhere; Donald, born in 1914, would soon leave the nest by the mid-1930s. Only their younger brother, Earl, born in 1920, and their sister, Louella, born in 1925, would remain in their parents' home at Ononodaga.[9] All of the Scanandoah boys became mechanics, although none had the interest in schooling that their father craved. In 1927 Chapman Scanandoah Jr. followed in his father's footsteps by enlisting in the US Navy. He served until 1932; however, three days after the Japanese attack on Pearl Harbor, the younger Chapman once again reenlisted for naval service. Later, two of his brothers enlisted.[10] While sovereignty-minded Hodinöhsö:ni´ protested against being drafted into military service during World War II and several brought legal actions against being conscripted into World War II, almost all eligible recruits such as the Scanandoahs *voluntarily* enlisted for duty.[11]

With the United States at war against the Axis powers, Congress slowly began a reexamination of federal Indian policies. Washington policy makers became determined to push for termination, namely, federal withdrawal from Indian affairs and a shift of responsibilities to state governments. At the federal level, termination was both a philosophy and specific legislation applied to the Indians. As a philosophy, the movement encouraged assimilation of Indians as individuals into the mainstream of American society and advocated the end of the federal government's responsibility over Indian affairs. To accomplish these objectives, legislation fell into four general categories: the end of federal treaty relationships and trust responsibilities with certain specified Indian nations by lump-sum cash commutations of annuities or Indian claims; the repeal of federal laws that set Indians apart from other American citizens; the removal of restrictions of federal guardianship and supervision over certain individual Indians; and the transfer of services provided by the BIA to the states and their localities or to other federal agencies, such as the Department of Health, Education, and Welfare.[12]

The termination laws that were to follow in the Truman and Eisenhower administrations ended federally recognized status for approximately one hundred Indian tribes. Other laws established relocation programs to encourage Indian out-migrations from reservations to urban areas. Moreover, in the postwar years, both Democrat and Republican legislators sought to promote parks, dams, and other projects that impinged on Indian tribal rights and landholdings.[13]

During World War II, Albany policy makers had once again raised their intention to push for the transfer of jurisdiction over the Hodinöhsö:ni´. The issue surfaced anew in 1942 in a decision made by the US Court of Appeals. The case, *United States v. Forness*, involved undervalued long-term leasing by non-Indians on the Seneca Nation's Allegany Indian reservation. Finding against the Fornesses, car dealers in the city of Salamanca that sits on the Allegany Reservation, Justice Jerome Frank, writing for the majority, restricted the application of state laws, insisting that the lessees were "customarily lax about paying their rent," that all too frequently in the past they had been in default, and that the Senecas had previously attempted to cancel the delinquent leases in the past.[14] Because the decision concluded that the federal government, not New York State, had sole jurisdiction over all the Hodinöhsö:ni´ and their reservations, Albany politicians reacted by pushing for new legislation.

In 1943 the New York State Legislature created the Joint Legislative Committee on Indian Affairs. The committee, dominated by politicians from southwestern New York, just a few miles from three Seneca reservations, was to hold hearings in Albany and on several of the reservations, including at Onondaga. The major representatives on the committee included its chairman, Assemblyman William McKenzie from Allegany County; its vice chairman, Senator George H. Pierce from Olean; and its attorney, Leighton Wade, also of Olean. Wade became the driving force pushing for jurisdictional transfer. Indeed, attorney Wade was to become the most important state official dealing with the Hodinöhsö:ni´ for the next two decades and drafted the outlines of the bill to transfer jurisdiction to New York State that Congress eventually passed by 1948.[15]

On the morning of September 30, 1943, at a meeting held at the Onondaga School on the reservation, the New York State Joint Legislative Committee on Indian Affairs took testimony from Oneidas and Onondagas. Suspicious from the beginning of the committee's intentions, Scanandoah, accompanied by his wife, Bertha, and his cousin Chief Rockwell, came to the hearing with the view that he would seek information about why the committee was taking testimony. Scanandoah was cross-examined by Wade.[16]

Before Scanandoah had a chance to ask questions, Wade attempted to dominate the proceedings. For the first part of the hearing, Scanandoah answered questions about his life at Onondaga. He indicated that he farmed one hundred acres at Onondaga, where he held a lease, informing committee members that as an Oneida, he could not will his farm to his children. He mentioned that his former longtime occupation was as a mechanic and that he had served in the US Navy. He told the committee that he was now farming by himself since his four sons had left the nest. He proudly mentioned that two of his sons were then in military service. After being asked about education available on the reservation, he lamented that his sons, all mechanics, had not been academically motivated, as he was a strong advocate of more schooling.[17]

Annoyed that attorney Wade had not yet allowed him to ask questions of the committee, Scanandoah finally posed a question: "What I want to know is this: Is it trye [true] that this commission is going to report to the Legislature to change the wardship of the New York Indians of the government and the state?" In response, Wade deflected the question, stating that only the full legislature had the power to do so and that his committee was merely collecting information. Dissatisfied with Wade's reply, Scanandoah responded with a follow-up question: "It is just a friendly investigation?" In an outright lie, Wade then answered Scanandoah, replying that the committee was only undertaking "a friendly investigation" to "see if there is something that can be done by the Legislature of the State of New York with the cooperation of the Indians themselves, to make the proper application of such laws as are available in case of disputes or any other questions that arise."[18]

Taking the attorney at his word, Scanandoah then continued his testimony. The chief indicated that he had always wanted an education, but acknowledged that a man without one sometimes "gets along better than a man with an education." In questioning by Wade and Senator Pierce, he indicated that he was an Oneida (although the stenographer recorded it wrong in the transcript) but that his sons were Onondagas, and thus he was concerned about the two Indian nations and their future welfare. He added that he was pleased that the committee members had "an interest in the Indians" and that members were "trying to devote their time" in the various hearings to get information. Scanandoah then concluded his testimony by stating proudly that he was a member of the Iroquois Confederacy, the oldest democracy in the Western Hemisphere.[19] Three months later, the Joint Legislative Committee completed a draft of two jurisdictional transfer bills. Hoping for speedy action in Congress, the committee forwarded the drafts to members of the New York State congressional delegation, hoping that these bills would soon be introduced.[20] In February 1944, the Joint Legislative Committee issued its report, drafted by Wade, calling for the transfer of federal jurisdiction over the Indians to the state.[21]

Ironically, while Washington officials were pushing for an end to federal treaty obligation to American Indian nations and a transfer of jurisdiction to the states, the Hodinöhsö:ni´, the Six Nations, were commemorating the 150th anniversary of the Treaty of Canandaigua. The ceremony honored all veterans, as it coincided with Armistice Day, November 11. The venerable Scanandoah, now seventy-five years of age, was the honored chief at this commemoration.[22]

With the congressional passage of the Indian Claims Commission Act in August 1946, the Oneidas pushed for compensation for past land losses and the failures of the United States to protect them and carry out its full trust responsibilities.[23] Three years before the creation of the ICC, Mary Winder had renewed her lobbying efforts for compensation for tribal lands taken illegally around Oneida Lake. Much like what her father had done in the early decades of the twentieth century, she collected maps and documents about Oneida landholdings and state treaties. Winder dictated letters to her daughter Gloria, who sent them off to the New York office and to the BIA office in Washington, requesting information and asking these offices to investigate Oneida claims.[24]

The 1946 ICC Act had provided for the creation of a commission of three persons, later enlarged to five, with appropriate staff, to adjudicate claims against the United States on behalf of "any Indian tribe, band, or other identifiable group of Indians residing within the territorial limits of the United States or Alaska." Before the work of the Indian Claims Commission ended in 1978, the act allowed tribes to file claims against the United States for Washington officials' failures to properly carry out the government's treaty obligations to protect tribal resources, including land, minerals, timber, and water. Under the act, all claims had to be filed within five years, awards would be monetary, and no land or other property would be returned. Judges could deduct "offsets," namely, money spent by the US government for the benefit of a claimant. Decisions of the ICC could be appealed to the US Court of Claims.[25] To many Native Americans, including Hodinöhsö:ni´ and their supporters, the act was originally seen as their opportunity to be heard, their day in court to seek redress. Yet the act was also an important part of termination policies. It was advanced by numerous members of Congress for a final accounting of Indian grievances, a payout leading to federal withdrawal from Indian affairs.[26]

The next year, Winder boldly announced her intention to push ahead with an Oneida land claim.[27] In the process, Winder's revival of the Indian claims movement helped once again to bring together the New York Oneidas and their kin at Southwold, Ontario, and at Oneida, Wisconsin. By the late 1940s, much of the bitter infighting that occurred during the heyday of the Kelloggs two decades earlier had apparently subsided. Although all was not forgiven regarding the intratribal tensions and controversies of the past, Winder and her sister, Delia (Dolly) Waterman, much like Chapman's mother, were soon to become the most powerful voices within the New York Oneida community. It should also be noted that Winder and her daughter Maisie (Shenandoah) soon joined Chief Chapman Scanandoah in the planning of the annual events at the Indian Village at the New York State Fair.[28]

Chief Scanandoah was chosen as the Oneida delegate to a general conference of the three communities held in early 1948. Its agenda was to consider bringing a case before the ICC.[29] The movement of the New York Oneidas to coordinate strategy with the other two communities was in part motivated by the Interior Department's denial of their legal standing to bring suit. Despite the Boylan case that recognized the thirty-two acres of the New York Oneidas as federal treaty lands, BIA officials refused to recognize them as "an identifiable group within the meaning of the ICC." The BIA officials insisted that if a claim was filed, it had to be prosecuted through the Wisconsin Oneidas.[30]

Under congressional pressure, William A. Brophy Jr., the acting commissioner of Indian Affairs in September 1946, had indicated that his agency, the BIA, should set a time limit within which it would cease to exist.[31] The following year, William Zimmerman Jr., acting commissioner of Indian affairs, testified before the Senate Civil Service Committee. The senators on the committee had demanded that he provide a list of Indian nations ready for "release" from federal supervision. In his first category—those nations he labeled as "predominantly acculturated population[s]"—Zimmerman included ten groups, including the Hodinöhsö:ni´ in New York, whom he claimed could be immediately removed from federal supervision.[32] Prompted by the New York State Joint Legislative Committee on Indian Affairs and the lobbying by Congressman Daniel Reed of Dunkirk, New York, Senator Hugh Butler of Nebraska proposed legislation, starting in 1947, to accomplish this objective.[33]

Chief Scanandoah and the vast majority of the Hodinöhsö:ni´ opposed the bills and spoke out against their passage.[34] Despite the condemnation of the Butler bills by diverse constituencies within the Six Nations, Congress passed the legislation, transferring criminal jurisdiction over all the Hodinöhsö:ni´ communities to New York State in 1948.[35] The next year, the Special Presidential Commission on the Organization of the Executive Branch of the Government, better known as the Hoover Commission, filed a task-force report on Indian affairs that, among other suggestions, advocated the transfer of federal programs to the states, urged policies that would encourage and assist Indians to leave the reservation and enter the mainstream of American life, and called for the "ending of tax exemption and of privileged status for Indian owned land and the payment of the taxes at the same rates as for other property in the area."[36] It is little wonder that in the same year, the BIA closed its New York office. In 1950 Congress transferred civil jurisdiction over the Indians to New York State.[37]

Right up to his death in the winter of 1953, Scanandoah worked with the Grand Council in trying to overturn the jurisdictional transfer acts of 1948 and 1950 and Washington officials' further efforts to buy out federal treaty obligations to the Hodinöhsö:ni´. Scanandoah worked with Lulu Stillman, writing to Senator Zales Ecton of Montana, who was on the Indian Affairs Committee, in an effort to stymie the proposed move. They insisted that New York State actions flew in the face of federal-Hodinöhsö:ni´ relations.[38] When Governor Thomas Dewey suggested that there was no Indian problem in New York because the Indians were assimilated into the white population, Stillman reacted angrily, noting, "Her [New York's] history from Colonial date has been to secure control and elimination of these Indians and often she acted contrary to the Federal Constitution."[39]

In the late evening of February 21, 1953, Chief Scanandoah suffered a heart attack and was rushed to St. Joseph's Hospital in Syracuse, where he died the next morning. In the obituary appearing in the local *Oneida Democratic Union*, the reporter praised the well-respected Scanandoah as an American legend, noting that he had suffered a heart attack on George Washington's birthday. The newspaperman saw special significance of the date of the Oneida's death because the chief's ancestors had helped the first president win the American Revolution. Like Doc, his funeral was conducted by a Methodist minister but included a color guard with full military honors. His pallbearers included prominent Oneidas such as Ray Elm, who had succeeded the chief as the keeper of the "old Oneida Indian ways" at Onondaga. His tombstone recognized his military service and included the words "CMM [Chief Mechanics Mate] U.S. NAVY SP AM WAR [Spanish American War]." Even in death, Scanandoah found himself in foreign waters, buried not on the thirty-two acres or in historic Oneida territory, but at the Onondaga Valley Cemetery, just off the Onondaga Reservation, in Nedrow, New York.[40]

Six months after Chief Scanandoah's death, the Eighty-Third Congress passed House Resolution 108, declaring that Washington's policy was to abolish federal supervision over tribes as quickly as possible and subject the Indians to the same laws, privileges, and responsibilities as other citizens of the United States. The resolution specifically mentioned New York State, declaring that it was "the sense of Congress that at the earliest time, all of the tribes and the individual members located within the following states of California, Florida, New York, and Texas should be freed from federal control and from all disabilities and limitations specially applicable to Indians."[41]

After Chief Rockwell's death in 1960 and Mary Winder's passing, Delia (Dolly) Waterman, Mary Winder's sister, attempted to fill the political vacuum within the Oneida polity. She, as Mary before her, increasingly questioned the legality of numerous New York State treaties with the Oneidas made in the six decades after the end of the American Revolution. Waterman was to designate Jacob (Jake) Thompson, a Mohawk ironworker married to her daughter Geralda, to pursue land-claims litigation.[42] Thompson was to soon petition New York State officials, congressmen, and even President Lyndon Johnson in an effort to win support for the resolution of Oneida land claims. In 1965 Thompson approached

George Shattuck, a prominent attorney in Syracuse, about the case. Shattuck was hired to pursue the claim. In 1974, as a result of Shattuck's able arguments, the US Supreme Court voted eight to zero, overturning the landmark case *Cherokee Nation v. Georgia*. The historic decision allowed federally recognized tribes in the original thirteen states the right to bring land-claims suits for the first time in federal courts. Although the Oneidas were not able to win their lands back in court and actually had to buy thousands of acres back with moneys gained from gaming revenues, this 1974 US Supreme Court decision, nevertheless, affected the return of hundreds of thousands of acres to other American Indian nations Indian lands from Maine to South Carolina because it led to land-claims settlements confirmed by congressional legislation.[43]

Fig. 18. Chief William Hanyoust Rockwell (1870–1960), Chapman Scanandoah's first cousin, principal spokesman for the Oneidas, and Oneida representative at the deliberations of the Iroquois Grand Council. From the Collection of the Madison County Historical Society, Oneida, New York.

Fig. 19. Mrs. Marion John Miles holds a baby while Chief William Hanyoust Rockwell demonstrates how stripes on squash determine the celebration of the gathering of the harvest, Oneida Lake, 1949. Library of Congress, Prints & Photographs Division, *World Telegram and Sun*/Acme Collection, LC-USZ62-118443. Courtesy of Corbis.

Fig. 20. Albert "Doc" Scanandoah. Noted chief, farmer, and herbalist, he had great influence on his younger brother Chapman. He was one of the first to question Solvay's dumping of wastes into Onondaga Lake, and he attempted to alleviate the problem of contamination. *Source*: "Medicine Man Seeks Forgotten Herbs," July 1, 1928, *Syracuse Post-Standard*. Courtesy of the *Syracuse Post-Standard*.

Fig. 21. Diagram of Chapman Scanandoah's megaphone with audiophone attachment. From megaphone, application #1040775, filed on December 19, 1911, US Patent Office, patent #1040775, October 8, 1912, US Patent Office, *Index of Patents for the Year 1912* (Washington, DC: USGPO, 1913), 475; US Patent Office, *Official Gazette* (1913), 183.

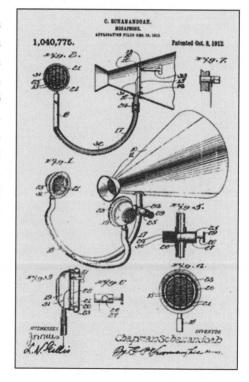

Fig. 22. Dry Dock #4, New York Navy Yard at Brooklyn, 1910–20. Scanandoah worked here from 1915 to the first half of 1916. Courtesy of the Library of Congress, LC-D4-73024.

Fig. 23. Hodinöhsö:ni´ at the New York State Fair, ca. 1950. The group photograph includes Chapman Scanandoah (*third row, fourth from the left*) and Mary Winder (*third row, third from the left*). Courtesy of the Great New York State Fair and the New York State Department of Agriculture and Markets.

Fig. 24. Six Nations Agricultural Society Building, New York State Fair, 2015. The Indian Village at the New York State Fair has promoted agriculture since its founding. Chapman and Albert Scanandoah, both agronomists, were involved from the first in this endeavor. Photograph by Laurence M. Hauptman.

Fig. 25. Longhouse at the Indian Village at the New York State Fair. Courtesy of the Great New York State Fair and the New York State Department of Agriculture and Markets.

Fig. 26. Hodinöhsö:ni´ flag (the Hiawatha Wampum Belt). On Friday, September 4, 2015, Six Nations Day at the New York State Fair, the Hodinöhsö:ni´ flag was raised and flown at the fairgrounds for the first time in the event's 175-year history. *Source*: "Revitalized Six Nations Day Will Bring Iroquois Story to Wider Audience at 2015 Great New York State Fair." Courtesy of the Great New York State Fair and New York State Department of Agriculture and Markets.

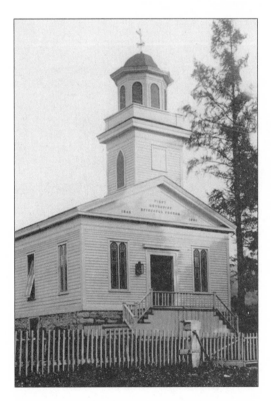

Fig. 27. The Methodist church on the Onondaga Reservation, 1915. Chapman Scanandoah and his family attended this church. The ministers of the church included Louis Bruce Sr. and Chief Livingston Crouse. Photograph by Fred Wolcott. Courtesy of the Onondaga Historical Association.

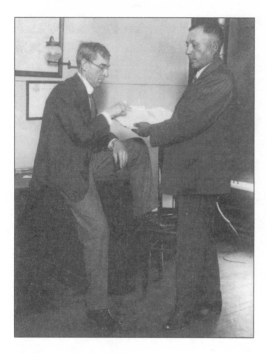

Fig. 28. Attorney George Decker and Chief Levi General (Deskaheh), ca. early 1920s. Deskaheh, from the Six Nations Reserve, brought Hodinöhsö:ni´ concerns to the attention of the world at the League of Nations before his death in 1925. Working with George Decker, the attorney for the Oneidas, he championed Iroquois sovereignty and nationhood. Courtesy of Special Collections, Lavery Library, St. John Fisher College, Rochester, New York.

Fig. 29. Laura Minnie Cornelius Kellogg, 1911. Laura Minnie Cornelius Kellogg was a brilliant but highly controversial Wisconsin Oneida activist. Her ideas and methods split Hodinöhsö:ni´ communities into pro-Kellogg and anti-Kellogg parties. Chapman Scanandoah and his entire family opposed her efforts, which they deemed on occasion as "pie in the sky" solutions. At other times, they saw her as being simply corrupt. *Source: Report of the Executive Council of the Proceedings of the First Annual Conference of the Society of American Indians* (1912).

Fig. 30. Chapman Scanandoah, ca. 1950. Courtesy of the Joseph Keppler Jr.—Iroquois Papers, #9184, Division of Rare and Manuscript Collections, Cornell University Library.

Fig. 31. Chapman Scanandoah's grave site in Onondaga Valley Cemetery, Nedrow, New York, 2015. The grave site reflects Chapman Scanandoah's naval service in the Spanish-American War. Note that by 1953, the Oneida chief's name is spelled differently from how it was spelled at his birth. Photograph by Caleb Abrams. Courtesy of Caleb Abrams.

9

Conclusion

Chapman Scanandoah's life clearly illustrates the balancing act of trying to maintain and preserve one's identity in "foreign waters." He was adrift, away from his homeland for most of his extraordinary life—be it in the US Navy or on land at school at Hampton; at military installations in Brooklyn and Philadelphia; in manufacturing plants in Buffalo, Detroit, Schenectady, and Syracuse; or on the Onondaga Indian reservation. He successfully navigated his way through trouble at every stage of his life: finding employment to pay for his education, facing two courts-martial during his naval service, fighting against the foreclosure of his family's homestead at Windfall, and living as an outsider at Onondaga. In many ways, he faced more danger during these crises than while serving in war zones in the navy or undertaking his many experiments with explosive compounds in his backyard workshop.

Four years before Chapman Scanandoah's death, readers of the highbrow *New Yorker* "discovered" the modern Iroquois. Joseph Mitchell's classic article "The Mohawks in High Steel" introduced the magazine's readers to Hodinöhsö:ni´ ironworkers from the Kahnawake reserve near Montreal who had come to reside in the North Gowanus section of Brooklyn. He described these mobile bands of Mohawks both at their reserve in Canada as well as in their Brooklyn residence. The readers of the article were no doubt surprised to learn about skilled "Indians" working high above the city on massive construction projects. Their risky work in high steel had transformed the landscape of Gotham. Among the many projects Mitchell credited them with included the construction of the George Washington Bridge, the Triborough Bridge, the Bronx-Whitestone Bridge, the Empire State Building, the West Side Highway, and the Waldorf Astoria Hotel.[1]

Mitchell was a well-known author of books and articles for the *New Yorker*. Much of his writings largely focused on describing eccentrics and offbeat individuals on the very fringes of society who inhabited distinct communities in New York City. Hence, the author appears to have been drawn to the subject by what he perceived as an oddity, namely, finding Native peoples in "unexpected places."[2] In his sympathetic and quite accurate treatment, published in the *New Yorker*'s weekly featured column "A Reporter at Large," Mitchell described how these Kahnawake Mohawks were holding on to their culture, bringing their mores and religious practices from their reserve to, of all places, Brooklyn.[3]

Undoubtedly, the article must have astonished some readers of this famous literary magazine. After all, most Americans still held stereotypes of "Indians" as warriors from the distant past. Even to the sophisticated readers of the *New Yorker* in 1949, Mitchell's portrait of Mohawk Indians building the new postwar city did not fit. Just thirteen years earlier, Little, Brown, and Company had published Walter D. Edmonds's best-selling novel *Drums along the Mohawk*, portraying most Hodinöhsö:ni´ as hostiles, threatening American settlements in the Revolutionary War.[4] This image was reinforced in 1939 when the novel was turned into a major motion picture, directed by John Ford and starring Henry Fonda and Claudette Colbert. In an early scene in the film, Edmonds introduces Blue Back, the "good Christian Indian," an Oneida allied to the Americans. Blue Back, played by John Bigtree, a Seneca Indian actor, is presented as being a hopeless drunk.[5] Hence, the American public viewing the film leaves with two distinct pictures of the Hodinöhsö:ni´: as "primitives," "savages" with an outmoded way of life, who challenge the march of civilization, or as downtrodden but friendly Indians with one step in two worlds, incapable of fully adjusting to civilization.

In the late 1950s, the rediscovery of the Hodinöhsö:ni´ continued in the pages of the *New Yorker*. In 1959, influenced by Mitchell, Edmund Wilson wrote a series of elegant articles for the *New Yorker* that later was published as *Apologies to the Iroquois*. Wilson presented a fuller portrait of the *modern* Hodinöhsö:ni´ as a whole, not just of the Kahnawake Mohawks, but one he saw as quickly being consumed by the insurmountable forces of civilization. He focused on how these Hodinöhsö:ni´ were maintaining their traditions while at the same time resisting efforts to take their lands for the building of massive projects—the St. Lawrence Seaway, the Niagara Power Project, and the Kinzua Dam. Now in his brilliant way, the eminent Wilson, a leading light of the nation's intelligentsia, described the reservation life of the Six Nations, informing his readers that an extraordinary indigenous people were living across the breadth of the Empire State into southern Ontario and Quebec, Canada. In sympathetic fashion, he portrayed them as courageously struggling to maintain their lands and way of life.[6]

Wilson, as well as anthropologists and historians writing about the Six Nations, noted the Hodinöhsö:ni´'s remarkable ability to adapt, balancing change with their commitment to maintain their separate nationhood and traditions.[7] These Native Americans had long made adjustments to the changing landscape in both the United States and Canada and had bounced back from devastating policies. In the colonial era, the Hodinöhsö:ni´ were masters of forest diplomacy and filled their depleted ranks by adopting war captives. They bounced back from disaster after their villages were destroyed in the Sullivan-Clinton Campaign during the American Revolution. In the difficult period after the same war, the Hodinöhsö:ni´ resurrected the Iroquois Confederacy along the Grand River in Ontario and at Buffalo Creek in New York, the latter transferred back to Onondaga Territory in the 1840s. Moreover, they underwent a religious revival that led to the establishment of the Longhouse religion, while other Hodinöhsö:ni´ adjusted to the teachings of missionaries and converted to the Anglican/Episcopal, Baptist, Catholic, Methodist, Mormon, and Presbyterian faiths. While being dispossessed from most of their lands in New York in the period from 1784 to 1842 and told to move west of the Mississippi, many, including the Hanyousts, remained on or in the vicinity of their central New York homeland.

Long before Chapman Scanandoah, individual Hodinöhsö:ni´ had competed in the marketplace brought on by the Industrial Revolution. As early as the late 1840s, Ely S. Parker had learned the basics of engineering while working as an ax man on the Genesee Valley Canal. Parker later secured an engineering position, constructing a customs house and marine hospital in Galena, Illinois, just prior to the Civil War.[8] From the second half of the nineteenth century onward, Hodinöhsö:ni´ worked on railroads and served in a variety of capacities on board ships on the Great Lakes. During Scanandoah's lifetime, Oneidas and other Hodinöhsö:ni´ quickly followed the Kahnawake Mohawk example by entering the building trades.

Chapman Scanandoah's full life illustrates the Hodinöhsö:ni´'s ability to adapt to change, a major reason all of the Six Nations in New York still maintain today a government-to-government relationship with the United States. With fierce determination, they hold on to their diminished territories or seek to reacquire parts of their original homeland by court action or by repurchase. In the case of the Oneidas, they have added more than thirty-five thousand acres to their landholdings in central New York in the past twenty years! In August 2014, the Bureau of Indian Affairs converted eleven thousand acres of these Oneida lands in central New York into trust, making them exempt from local and state taxation.[9]

Much like the surprises Mitchell and Wilson found in writing about Iroquoian peoples, reporters doing stories on Scanandoah, an extraordinarily accomplished "Indian," were taken back because he broke the popular stereotypical mold. He had grown up in the rapidly changing world of the late nineteenth century and was quite successful in adapting to changes all around him. While maintaining his Hodinöhsö:ni´ traditions, the Oneida sought to become a mechanic and developed his skills by attending Hampton Institute. Although beset with financial problems, Scanandoah worked his way through school. When he faced the depression of the 1890s and needed money to send home to help his family hold on to their land, he joined the navy. Cultivating a close friendship with powerful white benefactors, he escaped punishment in two courts-martial. Aboard ships or stationed in naval shipyards, he worked to improve his skills as a mechanic and as an inventor that led to opportunities with General Electric and other companies. While he was pursuing these paths, he collaborated with his cousin Chief Rockwell and their attorney George Decker in fighting to resecure the Hanyousts' thirty-two-acre parcel at Windfall. When the clouds of war began to arise, he started working at the Frankford Arsenal in Philadelphia. Returning to central New York, he furthered his inventive streak, receiving his second patent and reviving an ancient strain of Iroquoian maize.

With his abilities recognized by both the Hodinöhsö:ni´ as well as non-Indians, he subsequently helped establish and maintain the Indian Village at the New York State Fair, a special place of importance every late summer for Six Nations people. Scanandoah was also an active participant in the annual commemoration of the Treaty of Canandaigua each November 11, one that recognized the friendship, alliance, and reciprocal obligations between the United States and the Six Nations. Moreover, as a respected chief and elder, he, time and time again, championed Hodinöhsö:ni´ sovereignty, resisting state efforts to obtain jurisdiction over the Indians in civil and criminal matters.

The present Oneidas in New York owe much to Chapman Scanandoah and his family. The courageous Hanyousts, aided immensely by attorney Decker, fought against all odds to win back their Windfall lands. Although the Oneidas had long been in a diaspora, the thirty-two acres, saved by the Hanyousts, became the touchstone of Oneida existence. It was this sense of place—the homeland—that reinforced a common interest and resulted in the Oneida pursuit of a joint land claim. Although the Hanyousts were not successful in repopulating the homeland with Oneidas or in pursuing larger land claims, those Oneidas who followed them could not have succeeded without the foundation that Chapman and his family built.

Abbreviations

⌒

Notes

⌒

Bibliography

⌒

Index

Abbreviations

AD	(New York State) Assembly Document
APS	American Philosophical Society
ARCIA	*Annual Reports* of the US commissioner of Indian affairs
BIA	Bureau of Indian Affairs
CCF	Central Classified Files
CU	Cornell University
DANFS	*Dictionary of American Naval Fighting Ships*
DHI	Francis Jennings et al., eds., *Iroquois Indians: A Documentary History of the Six Nations and Their League*
EB	Erl Bates
FRC	Federal Records Center (New York City)
GE	General Electric
GPD	George P. Decker
HEA	Hope E. Allen
ICC	Indian Claims Commission
JBI	Joseph Keppler Jr.—Iroquois MSS
KCNYIR	Kansas Claims New York Indian Records
KL	Carl A. Kroch Library's Rare and Manuscript Division, Cornell University
LBJ	Lyndon Baines Johnson
LS	Lulu Stillman
MCHS	Madison County Historical Society
MiSci	Museum of Innovation and Science, Schenectady, NY
MR	microfilm reel
MSS	manuscript collection
NA	National Archives
NAA	(Smithsonian) National Anthropological Archives
NPRC	National Personnel Records Center, National Archives, St. Louis

NYIAR	New York Indian Agency Records
NYSA	New York State Archives
NYSL	New York State Library
NYT	*New York Times*
OHA	Onondaga Historical Association, Syracuse
OIA	Office of Indian Affairs
RG	Record Group
SD	(New York State) Senate Document
SH	*Syracuse Herald*
SJF	St. John Fisher College
SHJ	*Syracuse Herald-Journal*
SPS	*Syracuse Post-Standard*
Stat	*United States Statutes at Large*
SU	Syracuse University
SW	*Southern Workman*
T&T	*Talks and Thoughts of the Hampton Indian Students*
USGPO	US Government Printing Office
Whipple Report	New York State Legislature, Assembly Document #51, *Report of the Special Committee to Investigate the Indian Problem of the State of New York*
WMB	William M. Beauchamp

Notes

Preface

1. Keith Reitz, interviews by Laurence M. Hauptman, July 21, 1982, Rochester, NY; May 2–4, 1982, New Paltz, NY.

2. Hauptman, interview of Reitz, July 21, 1984; *Boylan v. George, et al.*, 133 AD 514 (June 24, 1909); *United States v. Boylan, et al.*, 256 F. 468 (Mar. 3, 1919); *United States v. Boylan, et al.*, 265 F. 165 (Mar. 3, 1920); "The Oneida Indian Case: *Boylan vs George et al.* Decision," *Oneida (NY) Dispatch*, Dec. 3, 1909; "Oneida Land Must Be Returned, to the Indians," *Oneida (NY) Dispatch*, Mar. 7, 1919; "Court Gives Land Back to the Indians; Judge Ray's Decision Upheld," *Oneida (NY) Dispatch*, Mar. 12, 1920; "Indians Win Long War for Oneida Lands," *SH*, Apr. 19, 1922.

3. Keith Reitz, "George P. Decker and the Oneida Indians"; "G. P. Decker, 74, Lawyer, Friend of the Indian," *Rochester Democrat and Chronicle*, Feb. 25, 1936. See also Laurence M. Hauptman, *Seven Generations of Iroquois Leadership: The Six Nations since 1800*, 117–42.

4. For summaries of Scanandoah's extraordinary life, see his obituaries: "Chief Skenandoah of Oneida Dies at 82 in Syracuse Hospital," *Oneida (NY) Democratic Union*, Feb. 26, 1953; "Chief in Indian Tribe, 82, Dies," *NYT*, Feb. 23, 1953; "Chief Schanandoah Dies: Circled Globe with Navy," *SPS*, Feb. 23, 1953; "Full Military Honors Paid to Chief Schenandoah," *SPS*, Feb. 26, 1953. See also Susan Hébert George, "An Oneida Renaissance Man: Chapman Scanandoah."

5. "Indian Chieftain Granted Patent on Metal Press," Mar. 4, 1926, unidentified newspaper, newsclipping folder, Vertical Files: Indians—Onondaga [Reservation] individuals, Schanandoah, Chapman, OHA. For his patents, see Chapman Scanandoah of Norfolk, Virginia: Megaphone, Application filed, Norfolk, VA, Dec. 19, 1911, Serial #666,739, Patent #1040775, Patented, Oct. 8, 1912, US Patent Office, *Index of Patents for the Year 1912* (Washington, DC: USGPO, 1913), 475; US Patent Office, *Official Gazette* (1913), 183:7; Chapman Schanandoah: Method of Condensing Metals, Application filed, Nedrow, NY, Feb. 2, 1925, Serial #19.902, Patent #US 1571737A, Patented, Feb. 2, 1926, US Patent Office, *Index of Patents for the Year 1926* (Washington, DC: USGPO, 1926), 577.

6. Philip J. Deloria, *Indians in Unexpected Places*, xiv, 234.

7. William Hanyoust Rockwell, autobiographical sketch, Vertical Files: Rockwell, William, MCHS. See chap. 5.

8. Keppler also wrote on Iroquois subjects. See Joseph Keppler Jr., "Comments on Certain Iroquoian Masks," *Contributions from the Museum of the American Indian* (Heye Foundation) 12 (1941): 1–40; Joseph Keppler Jr., ed., "Tawahnyos [Blacksnake], Some Seneca Stories," *Indian Notes* 6 (Oct. 1929): 372–76. Even though Scanandoah's friend and benefactor was born Udo J. Keppler, he took the same first name as his father, also a famous cartoonist and editor of *Puck*, upon his father's death.

9. For early examples of their close relationship, see Chapman Scanandoah to Joseph Keppler Jr., Feb. 3, May 20, 1900, Dec. 18, 1903, Feb. 24, 1904, Aug. 13, 1908, May 12, Dec. 4, 1909, July 10, 1910, Jan. 7, 1921, Oct. 16, 1922, July 5, 1932, and Bertha Scanandoah to Keppler, May 12, 1909, JKI MSS, Box 2, KL, CU. Keppler subsidized the Hanyoust legal efforts and provided him with money to purchase his farm. He supplied Scanandoah with friendly advice in times of troubles, while Scanandoah sent his longtime friend farm produce raised by him at Onondaga as well as Indian corn soup. Both visited with each other on occasion.

10. "Deerfoot's Funeral . . . ," *Iroquoian* 16 (Fall 1989): 30–31 (reprint of an Apr. 2, 1900, news story).

11. Converse's best-known work on the Hodinöhsö:ni´ was published after her death, *Myths and Legends of the New York State Iroquois*.

12. Joy Porter, *To Be Indian: The Life of Iroquois-Seneca Arthur Caswell Parker*, 45. The Harriet Maxwell Converse–Ely S. Parker correspondence can be found in Arthur C. Parker, *The Life of General Ely S. Parker: Last Grand Sachem of the Iroquois and General Grant's Military Secretary*, 162–80.

13. William N. Fenton, "Converse, Harriet Maxwell"; Arthur C. Parker, introduction to *Myths and Legends of the New York State Iroquois*, by Converse, 14–30; Harriet Maxwell Converse, "Induction of Women into Iroquois Tribes," *Journal of American Folklore* 5 (Apr.–June 1892): 147–48; "A Seneca Adoption," *Master Key* 26 (1952): 94–96; "Rites of Adoption by the Seneca Indians on the Cattaraugus Reservation," June 15, 1885 (Geneva, NY, 1885). Converse's name *Ya-ie-wa-noh* was the same name as Cornplanter's wife.

14. See, for example, Chapman Scanandoah to Harriet Maxwell Converse (1836–1903), Jan. 1900, Feb. 11, 1900, Apr. 13, 1901; and Scanandoah to Joseph Keppler Jr., Dec. 15, 1903, JKI MSS, Box 2, KL, CU. See also "Quit His Ship in Far South: Oneida Indian Deserter Stirs Navy Officials," *SPS*, Jan. 3, 1903; and "White Man's Navy Good to Lo': Oneida Indian Scanandoah May Serve Again," *New York Sun*, Jan. 3, 1903.

15. In well over a hundred articles about Chapman Scanandoah, I found that he was almost always identified as an Oneida. There were some exceptions. See, for example, two *SPS* articles: "Onondaga Chief's Explosive Meets Test: Shenendite Moves Tons of Solid Rock in Test," Aug. 24, 1926; "Onondaga Chief's Tribal Land Defense in Text Book," Sept. 12, 1948. One man, Old Crow, took exception to a reporter calling Scanandoah an Onondaga: letter to the editor, "Sentiment Passes for History," *SPS*, Sept. 21, 1948. The Onondaga

Historical Association filed separate news stories about Chapman and his brother Albert "Doc" Scanandoah in newsclipping vertical files marked "Onondaga," because of the brothers' longtime residence there.

16. Chief William Tooshkenig to Laurence M. Hauptman, personal communication, 1991, in Hauptman field notes.

17. Laurence M. Hauptman and L. Gordon McLester III, *Chief Daniel Bread and the Oneida Nation of Indians of Wisconsin*, xi–xv; Hauptman, *Seven Generations of Iroquois Leadership*, xi–xv.

1. The Oneida World in New York in the Century after the American Revolution

1. For Chapman Scanandoah's genealogy, see Anthony Wonderley, *Oneida Iroquois Folklore, Myth, and History: New York Oral Narrative from the Notes of H. E. Allen*, 195–96. According to numerous newspaper accounts, Scanandoah was named after Benjamin Franklin Chapman, an illustrious attorney and later judge of Clockville, Madison County, NY. "Indian Sailor Boy: Descendant of the Great Chief Skenandoah," Jan. 1903, unidentified newspaper, newsclipping folder, Vertical Files: Indians—Onondaga [Reservation] individuals, Schanandoah, Chapman, OHA. For Judge Chapman, see *Biographical Review: The Leading Citizens of Madison County, New York*, 493–95.

2. For the Oneidas in the American Revolution, see Joseph Glatthaar and James Kirby Martin, *Forgotten Allies: The Oneida Indians and the American Revolution*; Karim Tiro, *The People of the Standing Stone: The Oneida Nation from the Revolution through the Era of Removal*, 39–64; Mark E. Lender and James Kirby Martin, eds., *Citizen Soldier: The Revolutionary War Journal of Joseph Bloomfield*, 66–109; and Barbara Graymont, "The Oneidas in the American Revolution," in *The Oneida Indian Experience: Two Perspectives*, edited by Jack Campisi and Laurence M. Hauptman, 31–42.

3. For the Polly Cooper shawl, see Wonderley, *Oneida Iroquois Folklore, Myth, and History*, 210–17. For Chapman Scanandoah and the shawl, see "Shawl Symbolizes Alliance: Indian Heirloom Was Gift from Troops," *Syracuse Herald-American*, May 7, 1972; "Oneidas Helped the American Cause: A Shawl Given by a Grateful Martha Washington to Polly Cooper . . . ," *SPS*, July 4, 1994. For Oneida perspectives, see "The Legacy of a Shawl," *Oneida (NY) Indian Nation News* (June–July 1993): 7.

4. For the Oneidas at the Battle of Big Sandy (Battle of Sandy Creek), see Greg Chester, *The Battle of Big Sandy*. See also Carl Benn, *The Iroquois in the War of 1812*, 155–63; Donald R. Hickey, *The War of 1812: A Forgotten Conflict*, 185; J. Mackey Hitsman, *The Incredible War of 1812: A Military History*, 155, 172; and Hauptman and McLester, *Chief Daniel Bread*, 3–5.

5. HEA [Hope E. Allen] Notes, Oneida Commune Records, Box 40, File D, SU; Thomas Donaldson, comp., *The Six Nations of New York*, 25.

6. US Bureau of the Census, *The 8th Census of the United States, 1870* (Washington, DC, 1870).

7. HEA Notes, Oneida Commune Records, Box 40, File D, SU; Donaldson, *Six Nations of New York*, 25.

8. 7 *Stat.*, 15 (Oct. 22, 1784).

9. The three state treaties—at Fort Herkimer in 1785, at Fort Schuyler in 1788, and in Albany in 1795—can be found in the *Whipple Report*, 234–44. For an analysis, see three articles by Jack Campisi, "The Oneida Treaty Period, 1783–1838," in *Oneida Indian Experience*, edited by Campisi and Hauptman, 48–64; and his "New York–Oneida Treaty of 1795: A Finding of Fact." See also Barbara Graymont, "New York State Indian Policy after the American Revolution."

10. See, for instance, Section 4 of the Indian Trade and Intercourse Act of 1790 and 1793: 1 *Stat.*, 137–38 (July 22, 1790). For the continuing state violations of these federal acts, see Tiro, *People of the Standing Stone*, 91–114; and Philip Geier, "A Peculiar Status: A History of the Oneida Indian Treaties and Claims; Jurisdictional Conflict within the American Government, 1775–1920," 93–192. For the origins of Oneida land claims using the argument that New York State violated these acts, see George Shattuck, *The Oneida Land Claims: A Legal History*. Although the US Supreme Court continued to recognize the validity of this argument from 1974 to 2005, it nevertheless rejected efforts at redressing and compensating the Oneidas. *City of Sherrill v. Oneida Indian Nation*, 125 S.Ct., 1478 (2005).

11. For the market revolution, see Charles Sellers, *The Market Revolution: Jacksonian America, 1815–1846*; Charles Brooks, *Frontier Settlement and Market Revolution: The Holland Land Purchase*.

12. Tiro, *People of the Standing Stone*, 111–14; *Whipple Report*, 259–63.

13. *Whipple Report*, 263–323.

14. For greater detail, see Laurence M. Hauptman, *Conspiracy of Interests: Iroquois Dispossession and the Rise of New York State*, 1–97. See especially Nathan Miller, *The Enterprise of a Free People: Aspects of Economic Development in New York State during the Canal Era, 1792–1838*.

15. Blake McKelvey, "The Erie Canal: Mother of Cities"; W. Freeman Galpin, "The Genesis of Syracuse"; E. B. Tustin Jr., "The Development of the Salt Industry in New York"; Joseph Hawley Murphy, "The Salt Industry of Syracuse: A Brief Review." For textile development in Utica-Whitestown and New York mills, see Mary P. Ryan, *Cradle of the Middle Class: The Family in Oneida County, New York, 1790–1865*, 9–10, 46–49. See also Robert F. Berkhofer Jr., "The Industrial History of Oneida County, New York."

16. D. W. Meinig, "Geography of Expansion, 1785–1855" and "Elaboration and Change, 1850s–1960s," esp. 172–77; Luna M. Hammond, *History of Madison County, State of New York*, 127–34. The most comprehensive history with statistics of the canal era in New York State and its economic impact is still Noble E. Whitford, *History of the Canal System of the State of New York*. . . .

17. According to newspaper accounts, Scanandoah's fascination with these "iron horses" as a child was to spur his interest in mechanics. See, for example, "White Man's Navy Good to Lo': Oneida Indian Shenandoah to Serve Again," *New York Sun*, Jan. 3, 1903.

18. D. G. Beers, comp., *Atlas of Madison County, New York*, 56–57, 60–61; L. Hammond, *History of Madison County*, 134–37; Meinig, "Geography of Expansion, 1785–1855," 162–65; Meinig, "Elaboration and Change, 1850s–1960s," 172–77.

19. Treaty with the Six Nations, Jan. 15, 1838, 7 *Stat.*, 550; [Amended] Treaty with the Oneidas, Feb. 3, 1838, 7 *Stat.*, 566.

20. Jack Campisi, "Ethnic Identity and Boundary Maintenance in Three Oneida Communities," 403–7; *Laws of New York*, chap. 58 (Mar. 8, 1839); chap. 185 (Apr. 18, 1843); chap. 486 (Dec. 15, 1847).

21. Schoolcraft Population Census of Indian Reservations, 1845, Oneidas, NYSA; Henry Rowe Schoolcraft, *Notes on the Iroquois; or, Contributions to American History, Antiquities and General Ethnology*, 31–38, 75–87.

22. See ibid. For more on the controversial Schoolcraft and the 1845 census, see Richard G. Bremer, *Indian Agent and Wilderness Scholar: The Life of Henry Rowe Schoolcraft*, 271–83; Tiro, *People of the Standing Stone*, 173–79; Laurence M. Hauptman, "On Our Terms: The Tonawanda Seneca Indians, Lewis Henry Morgan, and Henry Rowe Schoolcraft."

23. L. Hammond, *History of Madison County*, 115–16.

24. Scanandoah to Keppler, Aug. 27, 1900, JKI MSS, Box 2, KL, CU.

25. "Full Military Honors Paid to Chief [Chapman] Schenandoah," *SPS*, Feb. 26, 1953; "Ritual of Pagans Missing at Funeral of [Albert Doc] Schanandoah," *SPS*, Jan. 15, 1934; Hampton Institute's newsletter noted his bilingual abilities: "Chapman Scanandoah," *T&T* (Nov. 1898): 3, HUA.

26. Tiro, *People of the Standing Stone*, 179–86.

27. [Hope E. Allen] Oneida Community MSS, Box 40, File D, SU; Mansion House, Oneida, NY. According to Allen, the following Oneida women worked at Mansion House: Anna Doxtator Johnson Scanandoah, Lydia Doxtator, Susie Chrisjohn, and Sally Johnson. Laurence M. Hauptman, interview of Anthony Wonderley, Jan. 29, 2015.

28. *Whipple Report*, 508; Campisi, "Ethnic Identity and Boundary Maintenance," 411–15; Tiro, *People of the Standing Stone*, 179–86.

29. Anthony Wonderley, "The Most Utopian Industry: Making Oneida Animal Traps, 1852–1925." For more on the economic activity of the Oneida Community, see Constance Noyes Robertson, ed., *Oneida Community: An Autobiography, 1851–1876*; and Maren Lockwood Carden, *Oneida: Utopian Community to Modern Corporation*.

30. Beers, *Atlas of Madison County*, 27, 29; "Town of Lenox, Madison County, New York," http://www.rootsweb.ancestry.com/~nymadiso/bit-of-past/borg/lenox.htm. See also John E. Smith, *Our County and Its People: A Descriptive and Biographical Record of Madison County, New York*.

31. "Solvay Takes Up Indian's Discovery," *SHJ*, June 27, 1931; "Indian's Find May Restore Lake's Beauty: Schanandoah Discovers Use for Waste Piled Up about Onondaga [Lake]," *SPS*, Sept. 27, 1931, "Indian Inventor's Death Revives Interest in Waste Problem of Solvay Firm," *SH*, Jan. 14, 1934; "Nedrow Indian Turns Solvay Waste to Use," unidentified

newspaper, newsclipping folder, Vertical Files: Indians—Onondaga [Reservation] individuals, Schanandoah, Albert, OHA.

32. William Skenandore to W. K. Harrison, Mar. 5, 1926, copy found in BIA, NYIAR, 1938–1949, Box 3, Folder 067: Tribal Relations: Oneidas, RG 75, FRC. In Wisconsin the name Scanandoah became Skenandore. William Skenandore, known as "Willie Fat," became a prominent advocate of Oneida sovereignty, treaty rights, and land claims. See Francis Skanandore, "William Skenandore," in *Oneida Indian Experience*, edited by Campisi and Hauptman, 126–30; and Laurence M. Hauptman, *The Iroquois and the New Deal*, 77, 20nn24–27. According to the correspondence cited above, Daniel Scanandoa Sr., born in New York and died in Wisconsin in 1880, was William Skenandore's grandfather. Importantly, he was also Chapman Scanandoah's grandfather. George, "Oneida Renaissance Man."

33. *ARCIA*, 1871, 684; Hope E. Allen Oneida Community MSS, Box 40, File D, SU.

34. W. J. Peacock (federal Indian agent), "Census of the "Oneidas" and "Census of the "Oneidas on the Onondaga Reservation," July 30, 1886, on CD *Heritage Books Archives: New York Indian Census* (Berwyn Heights, MD: Heritage Books, 2001), vol. 1, *1886–1899*; G. H. Ansley (federal Indian agent), "Oneidas on the Oneida Reservation," June 30, 1916, on ibid., vol. 3, *1913–1924* (National Archives Publication M95 New York Indian Censuses).

35. Chapman Scanandoah–Bertha Crouse marriage certificate, Apr. 29, 1905, *New York City Marriage Indexes*, New York City Department of Records, New York City Municipal Archives, http://www.ancestry.com.

36. Keith H. Basso, *Wisdom Sits in Places: Landscape and Language among the Western Apache*, 34–35.

37. Laurence M. Hauptman and George Hamell, "George Catlin: The Origins of His Indian Portrait Gallery"; Susan Fenimore Cooper, *Rural Hours*; Laurence M. Hauptman, L. Gordon McLester III, and Judy Hawk, "Another Leatherstocking Tale: Susan Fenimore Cooper, the Episcopal Church and the Oneida Indians."

38. See, for instance, Hope E. Allen, "An Oneida Tale." Allen's field notes are at Hamilton College's Burke Library and at Syracuse University's Bird Library.

39. Ibid.; Wonderley, *Oneida Iroquois Folklore, Myth, and History*, 1–14, 24–31. See also Charles A. Huguenin, "The Sacred Stone of the Oneidas"; Jeremy Belknap and Jedidiah Morse, *Report on the Oneida, Stockbridge and Brothertown Indians* (1796), reprinted in *Notes and Monographs*, no. 54 (New York: Heye Foundation/Museum of the American Indian, 1955).

40. J. H. French, comp., *Gazetteer of the State of New York*, 469n4.

41. L. Hammond, *History of Madison County*, 118.

2. Growing Up Oneida

1. Chapman Scanandoah's Oneida name is listed with his photographic portrait: Chapman Scanandoah, 1907. Photograph by Delancey W. Gill, BAE GN0096806208200. Credit line: National Anthropological Archives, Smithsonian Institution.

2. Lake Mohonk Conference of Friends of the Indian, *Proceedings, 1892*, 39–42.

3. Campisi, "Ethnic Identity and Boundary Maintenance," 413.

4. Ibid., 410–15. The Indian agent resumed giving the Oneidas treaty annuities in 1864, an action that showed a continuing federal recognition of the Oneida Nation. This distribution was to aid the Oneida arguments in the *Boylan* case. *ARCIA*, 1864, 432.

5. Wonderley, *Oneida Iroquois Folklore, Myth, and History*, 195.

6. HEA [Hope E. Allen] Indian Notes, Box 40, Folder D, Mar. 5, 1918, Hamilton College, Clinton, NY.

7. *Whipple Report*, 508–9; Wonderley, *Oneida Iroquois Folklore, Myth, and History*, 195.

8. *Whipple Report*, 46.

9. New York State Superintendent of Public Instruction, *Annual Report* (1888), 30. Until 1975 New York educational policies were largely assimilationist, denying Native Americans the opportunity to learn about their history and culture. New York State, Regents of the Univ. of the State of New York, *Position Paper No. 22: Native American Education*.

10. Ibid., 30–32. For more on Draper and his educational ideas, see Lake Mohonk Conference of Friends of the Indian, *Proceedings, 1888*, 25, 84, 87–88, 93, 98, 102–3; *Proceedings, 1889*, 77, 110; *Proceedings, 1891*, 57, 78, 95, 108; and Ronald M. Johnson, "Schooling the 'Savage': Andrew S. Draper and Indian Education."

11. *Official Record of Indian Conference Called to Determine the Status of the Indians of the Six Nations on the Indian Reservations of the State of New York and Their Relations to the Federal and State Governments*, 45–46, 57.

12. Abraham [Abram] Elm Pension Record, invalid application #983742, certificate #771598, Civil War Pension Records, NA; Laurence M. Hauptman, interviews of Ray Elm, May 6, 1990, and June 13, 1991, Onondaga Indian Reservation. The late Ray Elm, an Oneida elder, was Abram Elm's grandson.

13. *U.S. v. Elm*, 25 *Fed Case*, 1006 (1877), reprinted in *Whipple Report*, 385–90.

14. Ibid.

15. *Whipple Report*, 45–46.

16. Donaldson, *Six Nations of New York*, 25.

17. See, for example, Daniel Sherman to Commissioner of Indian Affairs, Aug. 31, 1880, *ARCIA*, 136. See also *ARCIA*, 1897, 206.

18. See chap. 4.

19. Campisi, "Ethnic Identity and Boundary Maintenance," 414–15, 413.

20. William Honyoust Rockwell to George Decker, Dec. 14, 1909, GPD MSS, Correspondence Folder 12-14-09, SJF.

3. An Oneida in an African American World

1. The best account of Native Americans at Hampton is Jon Brudvig, "Bridging the Cultural Divide: Hampton Institute's Experiment in American Indian Education, 1876–1923." Brudvig's dissertation is more balanced and more thorough than the following: Donal F. Lindsey, *Indians at Hampton Institute, 1877–1923*; Joseph W. Tingey, "Indians and Blacks

Together: An Experiment in Biracial Education at Hampton Institute, 1878–1923"; and Robert F. Engs, *Educating the Disenfranchised and Disinherited: Samuel Chapman Armstrong and Hampton Institute, 1839–1893*. For more on this interracial "experiment," see David Wallace Adams, "Education in Hues: Red and Black at Hampton Institute, 1878–1893"; and Wilbert H. Ahern, "'The Returned Indians': Hampton Institute and Its Indian Alumni, 1879–1983."

2. David Wallace Adams, *Education for Extinction: American Indians and the Boarding School Experience, 1875–1928*, 45.

3. Brudvig, "Bridging the Cultural Divide," 347.

4. *SW* (May 1878): 36. For the best treatment of the Carlisle Indian Industrial School, see Genevieve Bell's dissertation, "Telling Stories Out of School: Remembering the Carlisle Indian Industrial School." For the educational philosophy of its founder, see Richard Henry Pratt, *Battlefield and Classroom: Four Decades with the American Indians, 1867–1904*. For Wisconsin Oneidas at Carlisle, see Laurence M. Hauptman, "From Carlisle to Carnegie Hall: The Musical Career of Dennison Wheelock," in *The Oneida Indians in the Age of Allotment, 1860–1920*, edited by Hauptman and L. Gordon McLester III, 112–38.

5. Brudvig, "Bridging the Cultural Divide," appendix listing of students who attended; and Brudvig's website on Hampton's Indians, http://www.twofrog.com/hampton.html. Because of privacy concerns, the chart does not include disciplinary actions such as suspensions or dismissals brought against specific Oneidas.

6. See note 2; Frederick E. Hoxie, *A Final Promise: The Campaign to Assimilate the Indians, 1880–1920*; and Marilyn Holt, *Indian Orphanages*.

7. Brudvig states that health care at the school vastly improved after 1890 ("Bridging the Cultural Divide," 85–86). See also Helen Ludlow, ed., *Twenty-Two Years at Hampton, Virginia: Records of Negro and Indian Graduates*, 193 passim.

8. Charles Doxon, "Industrial Education for the Indians," *SW* (Aug. 1907). Other information about Doxon can be found in Lucinda George, "Indian Day, 1900," in "First Person Accounts as Written by American Indian Students at Hampton Institute, 1878–1923," compiled and edited by Jon L. Brudvig, http://www.twofrog.com/hamptonstories4.html.

9. "At the age of fifteen, Schenandoah could neither read nor write, but had a natural talent for mechanics" ("An Indian in the Navy," *Newport News Press*, Apr. 14, 1901). Chapman Scanandoah, "The Bear and the Fox," fragment, *T&T*, 1890, HUA. See chap. 2.

10. For Albert Scanandoah, see "Medicine Man Helps Doctor," *SPS*, July 1, 1928; "Ritual of Pagans Missing at Funeral of [Albert] Schanandoah," *SPS*, Jan. 15, 1934; "Indian Inventor's Death Revives Interest in Waste Problem of Solvay Firm," *SH*, Jan. 14, 1934; "Indian Dies with Secret for New Limestone Use," *NYT*, Jan. 12, 1934; and "Nedrow Indian Turns Solvay Waste to Use," unidentified newspaper, newsclipping folder, Vertical Files: Indians—Onondaga [Reservation] individuals, Schanandoah, Albert, OHA.

11. See note 8. See also Brudvig, "Bridging the Cultural Divide," 119–20.

12. See Laurence M. Hauptman, *The Iroquois in the Civil War: From Battlefield to Reservation*, 67–84.

13. Lake Mohonk Conference of Friends of the Indian, *Proceedings, 1892,* 39–40. For more, see *SW* 21 (Nov. 1892): 161–65, 171–74.

14. Ibid. For more on Clara M. Snow's visits to reservations in New York and her recruitment efforts and methods, see Snow, "A Visit to the New York Reservations," *SW* 21 (Nov. 1892): 169–71; and her "Glimpses of New York Reservations Life," *SW* (Aug. 1897): 155.

15. Lake Mohonk Conference of Friends of the Indian, *Proceedings, 1892,* 41–42. When Scanandoah had taken leave to earn money for tuition, he was missed by his fellow students who hoped that he would return: "Indian Incidents," *SW* 19 (Dec. 1890): 126. He had received no help from the government, but returned in November 1891. See "Indian Incidents," *SW* (Dec. 1891): 260.

16. Brudvig, "Bridging the Cultural Divide," 123–25. For the "Outing" system, see Robert A. Trennert, "From Carlisle to Phoenix: The Rise and Fall of the Outing System, 1878–1930"; Pratt, *Battlefield and Classroom,* 194.

17. Hollis Burke Frissell report to the Commissioner of Indian Affairs, Aug. 23, 1894, in *ARCIA,* 1894, 415–17.

18. Adams, *Education for Extinction,* 175.

19. See note 24.

20. Adams, "Education in Hues," 159–76.

21. Eric Foner, "Liberated and Unfree," review of Douglas R. Egerton, *The Wars of Reconstruction, NYT Book Review,* Feb. 2, 2014.

22. *SW* 9 (Nov. 1880): 114–15; Adams, "Education in Hues," 164–71; Engs, *Educating the Disenfranchised and Disinherited.*

23. Lezlie Cross, "Making Citizens of Savages: Columbia's Roll Call at the Hampton Institute."

24. Brudvig, "Bridging the Cultural Divide," 136–54. Each student on his or her entry form examined listed the student's religion. Hampton Univ. Student Files, HUA.

25. For the full list of the New York and Wisconsin Oneidas who attended Hampton, see Hauptman and McLester, *Oneidas in the Age of Allotment,* 292–94. For Lavinia Cornelius, see "The Oneida Hospital, and Its Nurse," *T&T* (Oct. 1898): 1–2, HUA; Julia A. Bloomfield, *The Oneidas,* 351–52; and [F. W. Merrill], *Oneida, the People of the Stone: The Church's Mission to the Oneidas* (Oneida Indian Reservation, 1899), 45–46.

26. George, "Indian Day, 1900."

27. *T&T* (Jan. 1896): 4–5, HUA.

28. Booker T. Washington initially opposed increased admission of Indian students to Hampton. Later, he supported the Indian program and fought to save it. Adams, *Education for Extinction,* 326–28.

29. Brudvig, "Bridging the Cultural Divide," 273–333; Lindsey, *Indians at Hampton Institute,* 156–70.

30. Lindsey, *Indians at Hampton Institute,* 170.

31. Brudvig, "Bridging the Cultural Divide," 319–31.

32. Chapman Scanandoah letter, *SW* 23 (Sept. 1894): 162–63.

33. Scanandoah to Keppler, Feb. 19, 1911, JKI MSS, Box 2, KL, CU. See chap. 4.

34. See the following in *T&T*: (Nov. 1894): 1, 3; (Sept. 1894): 3; (Mar. 1895): 5; (Jan. 1896): 4–5; (Nov. 1898): 1, 3; (Apr. 1899): 2; (June 1900): 3–4; (Nov. 1900): 3, HUA. See the following in the *SW*: 26 (Oct. 1897): 201–2; 27 (July 1898): 140; 27 (Dec. 1898): 247; 28 (Mar. 1899): 109; 29 (Dec. 1899); 29 (Feb. 1900]: 83; 40 (Jan. 1911): 62; 42 (Apr. 1913); 252; 50 (Feb. 1921): 96.

35. GE Employee Register, 1889–1895, #2583: "Shanandoah," Building #9, Sept. 4, 1894–Apr. 29, 1895, MiSci. These registers also clearly show the company's extensive use of teen-age labor. Julia Kirk Blackwelder, *Electric City: General Electric in Schenectady*, 4–14; David E. Nye, *Image Worlds: Corporate Identities at General Electric, 1890–1930*, 10–16.

36. GE Employee Register, 1889–1895, #2583: "Shanandoah," Building #9, Sept. 4, 1894–Apr. 29, 1895; G. E. Emmons, "Recollections of G. E. Emmons," MiSci.

37. *T&T* (Sept. 1894): 3; (Mar. 1895): 5; (Jan. 1896); 4–5; (Nov. 1898): 1, 3, HUA; *SW* 26 (Oct. 1897): 201–2. For the depression that began in 1893 and continued throughout much of the decade, see Douglas Steeples and David O. Whitten, *Democracy in Desperation: The Depression of 1893*.

38. See the following in the *SW*: 26 (Oct. 1897): 201; 27 (Dec. 1898): 247; 28 (Mar. 1899): 109; 28 (Dec. 1899): 499; (Feb. 1900): 83; 40 (Jan. 1911): 62; 42 (Apr. 1913): 252.

39. "Indian Education: Does It Pay?," *SW* 29 (Feb. 1900): 83.

40. "A Visit to the Flagship New York," *T&T* (June 1900): 3–4, HUA.

41. For example, Chapman Scanandoah, "Indian Incidents," *SW* 28 (Mar. 1899): 109; Scanandoah letter in *SW* (July 1898); Scanandoah letter, "A Letter from Cuba," *T&T* (Dec. 1898); 3; Scanandoah letter aboard the USS *Raleigh* in *T&T* (Apr. 1904); 3–4, HUA. See chap. 3.

42. *SW* 29 (Dec. 1899): 499; *Hampton Student* (Nov. 1910), HUA; *SW* 40 (Jan. 1911): 62.

43. George, "Indian Day, 1900."

44. "Indian Enlists in Navy: Chapman Shenandoah, an Oneida, Accepted by Engineer Matthews," *Chicago Chronicle*, Aug. 15, 1897.

4. A Global Education

1. "Indian Enlists in Navy, Chapman Shenandoah, an Oneida, Accepted by Engineer Matthews," *Chicago Chronicle*, Aug. 15, 1897.

2. Chapman Scanandoah's Naval Service Record, #1070186, NPRC, NA, St. Louis; Chapman Scanandoah, enlistment, Aug. 6, 1897, machinist second class, New York State Adjutant General's Office; abstracts of Spanish-American War Military and Naval Service Records, 1898–1902, Series #80809, NYSA.

3. "Chapman Shenandoah," *Hartford (CT) Courant*, Jan. 6, 1903.

4. See note 1; and "Great Orator Chief's Descendant, Only Indian Sailor in United States Navy," Mar. 10, 1901, unidentified newspaper, newsclipping folder, Vertical Files: Indians—Onondaga [Reservation] individuals, Schanandoah, Chapman, OHA.

5. "Indian Education: Does It Pay?," *SW* 29 (Feb. 1900}: 260. See also *SW* 28 (Dec. 1899): 499; *T&T* (Nov. 1900): 3, HUA; *SW* 42 (Apr. 1913): 252; "Only Indian in Navy an Expert Machinist; Schenandoah Is Now on Cruiser *Atlanta*—He Hails from Oneida, New York," *New York World*, Mar. 25, 1901; "Indian Sailor Boy: Descendant of the Great Chief Skenandoah," unidentified newspaper, Jan. 1903, newsclipping folder, Vertical Files: Indians—Onondaga [Reservation] individuals, OHA; Schanandoah, enlistment, Aug. 6, 1897, machinist second class, New York State Adjutant General's Office; and abstracts of Spanish-American War Military and Naval Service Records, 1898–1902, Series #80809, NYSA.

6. For the rise of the "new navy," see Kenneth J. Hagan, *This People's Navy: The Making of American Seapower*, 167–227; and Walter R. Herrick Jr., *The American Naval Revolution*.

7. For the inaccurate claims that he participated in the Battle of Manila Bay, see "Full Military Honors Paid to Chief Schenandoah," *SPS*, Feb. 26, 1953; George, "Oneida Renaissance Man"; "Spanish American War: Oneidas' Legacy to Freedom," http://oneidaindian nation.com. Scanandoah's name does not appear as having received the Dewey Medal that each crew member in the six-vessel fleet was later awarded for service at the Battle of Manila Bay. "Dewey Medal, Battle of Manila Bay," US Department of the Navy, Naval Historical Center, Naval History and Heritage Center website. For a concise analysis of the battle, see John B. Hattendorf, "The Battle of Manila Bay," in *Great American Naval Battles*, edited by Jack Sweetman, 175–97.

8. For a description of the *USS Marietta*, see *DANFS*, 6:310–11.

9. Chapman Scanandoah, "Letter from Cuba" (to Hampton), May 12, 1898, *T&T* (July 1898): 2–3, HUA; *SW* 27 (July 1898): 140; *SW* 27 (Dec. 1898), 247. For the horrendous conditions in the boiler rooms on these ships where Scanandoah worked during the Spanish-American War, see George W. Robinson Diary (fireman working in boiler room aboard the *USS Oregon*), Spanish-American War Centennial website.

10. See note 8; David F. Trask, "The Battle of Santiago," in *Great American Naval Battles*, edited by Sweetman, 198–218; and Trask, *The War with Spain in 1898*, 257–69, 286–335.

11. "Indian as Jack Tar," *Philadelphia Times*, May 10, 1901.

12. "Indian Incidents," *SW* 28 (Mar. 1899): 109; "The Heroes Come . . . Spanish Prize Ships," *Semi-Weekly Messenger* (Wilmington, NC), Dec. 16, 1898.

13. Schanandoah, "A Letter from Cuba" (to Hampton), *T&T* (Dec. 1898): 2–3, HUA. The epidemics were yellow fever, malaria, and dysentery. Trask, *War with Spain*, 324–25.

14. Chapman Scanandoah's US Naval Service Record #1070186, NPRC, NA, St. Louis; Schanandoah, enlistment, Aug. 6, 1897, machinist second class, New York State Adjutant General's Office; abstracts of Spanish-American War Military and Naval Service Records, 1898–1902, Series #80809, NYSA. He also served in the Philippines at the time of two insurrections while assigned to the cruiser USS *Raleigh* and the transport USS *Sherman*. "Army Transport Sails for the Philippines," *San Francisco Call*, July 26, 1906.

15. This exaggerated claim was repeated word for word in articles published throughout the United States. "Full-Blood Indian in Navy," *St. Louis Republic*, Mar. 10, 1901; "Indian

as Jack Tar"; "Full Blood Indian in United States Navy," *Minneapolis Journal*, May 31, 1901; "An Indian Sailor Boy," *Semi-Weekly Union* (Madison County, NY), Sept. 10, 1898; "Chapman Shenandoah," *Hartford (CT) Courant*, Jan. 6, 1903; "Quit His Ship in Far South," *SPS*, Jan. 1904. See also the series of articles in the *Washington Bee*: May 11 and 25 and June and 29, 1901. "Great Orator Chief's Descendant, Only Indian Sailor in United States Navy," Mar. 10, 1901, "Homesick for Sea: Old Schanadoah's Descendant Returns to the Navy," unidentified newspapers, newsclipping folder, Vertical Files: Indians—Onondaga [Reservation] individuals, Schanandoah, Chapman, OHA. Please note there were several more Native Americans serving in the Spanish-American War, such as Abel Davis, a Cherokee. See "War Brings 2 Old Seadogs Together after 43 Years," *SHJ*, Jan. 1, 1942.

16. "An Indian Sailor: One of the Crew of the *Atlanta* Is Member of the Oneida Tribe," *Utica (NY) Globe*, Mar. 9, 1901.

17. Scanandoah to Keppler, July 1 and Aug. 12, 1899; Scanandoah to Converse, Dec. 24, 1899; Scanandoah to Keppler, May 20, 1901, JKI MSS, Box 2, KL, CU.

18. Scanandoah to Keppler, Aug. 26, 1906, ibid.; "Army Transport Sails for the Philippines," *San Francisco Call*, July 26, 1906.

19. Scanandoah to Keppler, autumn 1906, JKI MSS, Box 2, KL, CU.

20. Scanandoah to Converse, Dec. 24, 1899, Feb. 20, Aug. 13, 1901, ibid.

21. Scanandoah's Naval Service Record, #107186, NPRC, NA, St. Louis; Scanandoah to Keppler, May 30, 1909, JKI MSS, Box 2, KL, CU.

22. Scanandoah to Converse, Nov. 19, 1900; Scanandoah to Keppler, Aug. 29, 1900, ibid.

23. Scanandoah to Converse, Jan. ? and Feb. 10, 1900, ibid.; Joseph Henker [USS *New York*] Memorandum, Aug. 1, 1900; Samuel C. Lemly [Judge Advocate General's Office] Memorandum to US Navy Bureau of Navigation, Mar. 6, 1900, Scanandoah's Naval Service Record #1070186, NPRC, NA, St. Louis; Scanandoah to Keppler, Sept. 4, 1900, JKI MSS, Box 2, KL, CU.

24. Scanandoah to Converse, Aug. 13, 1901, JKI MSS, Box 2, KL, CU.

25. Scanandoah to Keppler, Sept. 4, 1900, and May 20, 1901; Scanandoah to Converse, Aug. 13, 1901, ibid.

26. Quoted in "Chapman Shenandoah," *Hartford (CT) Courant*, Jan. 6, 1903. See also "Quit His Ship in Far South," *SPS*, Jan. 1904.

27. Converse to Keppler, Jan. 15, 1903, JKI MSS, MR 1; Scanandoah to Keppler, Dec. 19, 1903, JKI MSS, Box 2, KL, CU.

28. "White Man's Navy Good to Lo': Oneida Indian Shenandoah May Serve Again," *New York Sun*, Jan. 3, 1903; "Oneida Indian's Sentence Remitted: Shenandoah Ordered to Report for Duty aboard the *Raleigh*," *Washington Times*, Jan. ?, 1903, HUA; "Indian Sailor Boy; Descendant of the Great Chief Skenandoah," Jan. ? 1903, unidentified newspaper, newsclipping folder, Vertical Files: Indians—Onondaga [Reservation] individuals, Schanandoah, Chapman, OHA.

29. Although Keppler in his biting political cartoons was at times quite critical of Roosevelt, they were friends and socialized with each other. Keppler to Theodore Roosevelt, Jan. 29, 1903, Series 1, MR 32; Roosevelt to Keppler, Jan. 30, 1903, Series 2, MR 330, Roosevelt

Papers, Library of Congress. On March 28, 1908, Roosevelt praised Keppler's magazine: "*Puck* has no respect for business, big or little, that is not honest business." Roosevelt MSS, Series 2, MR 348, Library of Congress.

30. Samuel C. Lemly Memorandum to Commandant of the Washington Navy Yard, Dec. 22, 1902; C. H. Darling [Acting Secretary of the Navy] to Commanding Officer of *USS Raleigh*, Mar. 31, 1903, Scanandoah's Naval Service Record, #1070186, NPRC, NA, St. Louis; Scanandoah to Keppler, Dec. 19, 1903, JKI MSS, Box 2, KL, CU.

31. Scanandoah to Keppler, Sept. 4, 1900, May 20, 1901, Dec. 15, 1903, and Dec. 8 and May 12, 1909, JKI MSS, Box 2, KL, CU.

32. Scanandoah spent time working at improving his weak English writing abilities even before his enlistment in the navy in 1897. In 1890 Scanandoah started writing for Hampton's publications. His article "Letter from an Oneida Boy," *T&T* (Mar. 1890), HUA, reveals that he struggled with English. By 1894 his writing had vastly improved, and he actually submitted a well-written short story and a report on his class trip to visit John Brown's farmhouse and grave site: "The Sand Story," *T&T* (Apr. 1894): 3, HUA; "Indian Department," *SW* 23 (1894): 162–63.

33. "USS *Raleigh*," in *DANFS*, 6:18–20.

34. Scanandoah to Keppler, Sept. 20, 1903, JKI MSS, Box 2, KL, CU.

35. Ibid., June 20, 1903.

36. Scanandoah, letter to Hampton, *T&T* (Apr. 1904): 3–4, HUA.

37. Ibid.

38. See note 34.

39. See note 36.

40. Ibid.

41. See notes 34 and 36.

42. See note 34.

43. US Navy, *DANFS*, 6:310–11.

44. Scanandoah to Keppler, Dec. 20, 1908, JKI MSS, Box 2, KL, CU.

45. Ibid., May 24, 1910.

46. Ibid.

47. Scanandoah to Hampton, *SW* 28 (Mar. 1899): 83.

48. Scanandoah to Keppler, Mar. 21, 1910, JKI MSS, Box 2, KL, CU.

49. Scanandoah to Converse, July 11, 1900, with enclosed article dated July 8, 1900, JKI MSS, Box 2, KL, CU.

50. Scanandoah to Keppler, Feb. 19, 1911, JKI MSS, Box 2, KL, CU.

51. Chapman Scanandoah–Bertha Crouse marriage certificate, Apr. 29, 1905, *New York City Marriage Indexes*, New York City Department of Records, New York City Municipal Archives, http://www.ancestry.com.

52. His concern for what was happening on the thirty-two acres is reflected in Scanandoah to Keppler, Apr. 24, 1907, Jan. 7, Aug. 13, 1908, Dec. 4, 8, Aug. 20, 1909, and Mar. 21, 1910; Bertha Scanandoah to Keppler, May 12, 1909, JKI MSS, Box 2, KL, CU.

53. Wonderley, *Oneida Iroquois Folklore, Myth, and History*, 199.

54. See chap. 5.

55. Scanandoah to Keppler, Feb. 19, 1911, JKI MSS, Box 2, KL, CU.

56. For Scanandoah's later efforts to reenlist, see chap. 5. Adolphus Andrews [Chief of Naval Bureau of Navigation] to Scanandoah, June 3, 1937, Scanandoah's Naval Service Record, #107186, NPRC, NA, St. Louis; Chapman Schanandoah [*sic*] Pension File, Records of the United States Navy, pension application #1493032, certificate #124399 NY, Dec. 20, 1923.

57. *Marine Electrical Apparatus*, GE publication #1025, Jan. 19, 1900, in Publications: General Electric Co., Schenectady, Pamphlet Series, GE Historical File L: 4527, MiSci. Around 1912 the USS *Jupiter* was one of the first to be installed with GE turbines.

5. Saving the Thirty-Two Acres in the White Man's Courts

1. Rockwell, autobiographical sketch, Vertical Files: Rockwell, William, MCHS. See chap. 4.

2. Scanandoah to Keppler, Aug. 29, 1900, Dec. 12, 1905, and Dec. 8, 1909; W. J. McCluskey to Scanandoah, Dec. 15, 1905, JKI MSS, Box 2, KL, CU.

3. See, for example, Scanandoah to Keppler, Jan. 7, 1907, and Dec. 8, 1909, JKI MSS Box 2, KL CU.

4. Wonderley, *Iroquois Folklore, Myth, and History*, 199–200; "Indians Plead for Their Land: Seven Oneidas and Two Onondagas Testify at Federal Trial," *SPS*, July 28, 1916.

5. Scanandoah to Keppler, Dec. 8, 1909, JKI MSS, Box 2, KL, CU.

6. Ibid., July 10, 1909.

7. See note 1.

8. Rockwell to Decker, Dec. 14, 1909, Correspondence Folder 9-8-13, GPD MSS, SJF.

9. Chief Rockwell testified as the Oneida spokesman at nearly every federal and state hearing for three decades from the 1920s through 1950. Chapman Scanandoah was usually at his side. For typical stories about Rockwell, see "Oneida Chief Rockwell Notes His 86th Birthday," *SHJ*, May 11, 1956; "Chief Says Uncle Sam's Cloth Shrinks," *SHJ*, Aug. 8, 1951; photograph and caption in "Oneida-Indian Way," *SHJ*, July 20, 1955.

10. Scanandoah to Keppler, Dec. 18, 1903, JKI MSS, Box 2, KL, CU.

11. 7 *Stat.*, 550 (Jan. 15, 1838).

12. Geier, "Peculiar Status," 223–24. For more on the dispossession of Indians in Kansas, see H. Craig Miner and William Unrau, *The End of Indian Kansas: A Study of Cultural Revolution, 1854–1871.*

13. *ARCIA* (1857), 8.

14. E. L. Terry to Commissioner of Indian Affairs William Dole, Aug. 18, 1862, OIA, NYIAR, M234, MR 590, RG 75, NA; *ARCIA* (1862), 43.

15. *New York Indians v. United States*, 170 US 1 (Apr. 11, 1898). For an excellent treatment on the "loss" of these Kansas lands, see Geier, "Peculiar Status," 220–37.

16. For the end of US-Indian treaty making, see Francis Paul Prucha, *American Indian Treaties: The History of an American Anomaly*, 334–58. See also Colin Calloway, *Pen and Ink Witchcraft: Treaties and Treaty-Making in American Indian History*.

17. Bowman Act, 27 *Stat.*, 426 (Jan. 28, 1883).

18. *New York Indians v. United States*, 30 Ct. Cl. 413 (1895).

19. 170 US 1 (1898).

20. 33 Ct. Cl. 510 (1898).

21. 170 US 464 (1899).

22. 31 *Stat.*, 27 (Feb. 9, 1900).

23. E. A. Hitchcock [Secretary of the Interior] to Commissioner of Indian Affairs, Mar. 17, 1904, with undated attached report by Special Agent Guion Miller, BIA, SC29: KCNYIR, Box 3: Seneca, RG 75, NA20; B. B. Weber to Commissioner of Indian Affairs, Aug. 26, 1906; Reports of Special Agent Guion Miller, 1903–1905: Lists of Names of Applicants for Shares of the New York Indian Money Awarded by the Court of Claims, OIA, SC29: KCNYIR, Box 3, RG 75, NA.

24. New York Indians [Applications] Rejected Records Relating to Kansas Claims of New York Indians, BIA, SC29, KCNYIR, Box 3, RG 75, NA.

25. Geier, "Peculiar Status," 224.

26. Campisi states that every eligible Oneida received $179.33 ("Ethnic Identity and Boundary Maintenance," 307).

27. William Hanyoust Rockwell, "Rockwell Tells the Story of Lawyer Jenkins," ca. 1953, Rockwell Vertical File, MCHS.

28. As late as 1947, Superintendent William Benge of the New York Indian Agency stated, "They [Oneidas] have no reservation in New York." Transcript of William Benge Talk before Eastern Regional Conference of the National Fellowship of Indian Workers at the Rochester Museum and Science Center, BIA, NYIAR, 1938–1949, Box 3, Folder 071: Indian Customs, Conventions, Conferences, RG 75, FRC, reprinted in "Proposed Federal Legislation and New York Indians," *National Fellowship of Indian Workers Newsletter*, no. 34 (Winter 1947–48): 4–5; Charles Berry [Superintendent of New York Indian Agency] to Mary Winder, May 14, 1943; Walter Woehlke [BIA Assistant Commissioner, Land Division] to Winder, May 11, 1943; T. W. Wheat [BIA Land Division Claims] to Benge, Aug. 2, 1948; Benge to Commissioner of Indian Affairs, Aug. 10, 1948; Benge to Winder, Aug. 26, 1948, BIA, NYIAR, 1938–1949, Box 3, Folder 071: Indian Customs, Conventions, Conferences, RG 75, FRC.

29. Campisi, "Ethnic Identity and Boundary Maintenance," 436.

30. Bertha Scanandoah to Charles Berry, Feb. 13, 1941; undated, List of Canadian Indians at Onondaga, BIA, NYIAR, 1938–1949, Box 3, Folder 069: Relations with Canadian Indians, RG 75, FRC. The list states that Wilson's Cornelius first arrived in 1895. His daughters, Mary Cornelius Winder (born in 1897) and Delia (Dolly) Cornelius Winder (born in 1900), are not listed as "Canadian Indians." The two sisters are listed in the census taken of Oneida

Indians at Onondaga by B. B. Weber as early as 1906. Weber [Special Federal Indian Agent], June 30, 1906, in *Federal Indian Census: New York, 1906.*

31. See note 30.

32. Geier, "Peculiar Status," 239–51, 271–74. See chap. 6. The Treaty with the Six Nations, 7 *Stat.*, 44 (Nov. 11, 1794); the Treaty with the Oneidas, etc., 7 *Stat.*, 47 (Dec. 2, 1794).

33. Wonderley, *Oneida Iroquois Folklore, Myth, and History*, 195–96.

34. Rockwell to Decker, Dec. 14, 1909, Folder 9-8-13, GPD MSS, SJF.

35. Wonderley, *Oneida Iroquois Folklore, Myth, and History*, 196–202.

36. Ibid.

37. Ibid.; [Oneida] Petition to the Governor, the Honorable Governor Charles Evans Hughes, Oct. 15, 1907, Records of the New York State Governor, Series AO 531–78, Investigation Files, Relating to Petition of Oneida Indian Chiefs' Land, Box 27, Folder 4, NYSA; Robert Fuller [Secretary to the Governor] to Chief W. H. Rockwell, Sept. 24, Oct. 18, 22, Nov. 5, 1909, Correspondence Folder 9-8-13, GPD MSS, SJF; "Indians Appeal to Governor: Delegation of Oneida Chiefs Yesterday Sought His Protection," *Albany Argus*, Oct. 16, 1907.

38. Decker to Mr. Samson, Oct. 28, 1907, enclosing Decker's report (although signed by Jackson) to Governor C. E. Hughes, transmitted by Attorney General William Jackson, "Oneida Indians: Treaties with the State—Their Rights to Their Land, Albany, 1907," Ayer MSS, N. A. 641, Newberry Library (reproduced in DHI MR 49).

39. Charles Evans Hughes to William Schuyler Jackson, Oct. 29, 1907; Jackson to Hughes, Aug. 24, 1908. An Oneida Tribal Council meeting at Windfall later passed a resolution thanking Governor Hughes for his "fair treatment." Rockwell to Hughes, Jan. 24, 1908, Records of New York State Governors, Series AO 531–78, Investigation Files, Relating to Petition of Oneida Indian Chiefs' Land, Box 27, Folder 4, NYSA.

40. For more on this remarkable attorney, see Reitz, "Decker and the Oneida Indians"; "G. P. Decker, 74, Lawyer, Friend of the Indian," *Rochester Democrat and Chronicle*, Feb. 25, 1936; and "Noted Lawyer, Historian, Dead: Death Takes G. P. Decker," *Rochester Times Union*, Feb. 24, 1936. See also Hauptman, *Seven Generations of Iroquois Leadership*, 117–42. Decker hoped to get the Democratic Party's nomination for Congress, secure a federal judgeship, or be appointed to the Federal Power Commission. Undoubtedly because he was a strong advocate of both public power and Indian treaty rights, his friends, which included Franklin Delano Roosevelt, tried but failed to secure these positions for him. See, for example, Roosevelt to Franklin K. Lane [Secretary of the Interior], Mar. 25, 1918, Correspondence Folder #9-8-23, GPD MSS, SJF.

41. Wonderley, *Oneida Iroquois Folklore, Myth, and History*, 196–202.

42. Edward O'Malley to Hughes, June 17, 1909, and the Oneida response by Chiefs William Hanyoust Rockwell, Baptist Day, and Simeon Elm to Attorney General O'Malley's opinion, Nov. 4, 1909, Records of the New York State Governor, Series AO 531–78, Investigation Files, Relating to Petition of Oneida Indian Chiefs, Box 27, Folder 4, NYSA.

43. *Boylan v. George, et al.*, 133 AD 514 (June 24, 1909): "The Oneida Indian Case: *Boylan vs George et al.* Decision," *Oneida (NY) Dispatch*, Dec. 3, 1909.

44. Rockwell quoted in Wonderley, *Oneida Iroquois Folklore, Myth, and History*, 50. See also "William Hanyoust and Sister Dispossessed: Oneida Indian Carried Out of His Home by Force and His Effect as Placed in the Street by Madison County Deputy Sheriff and a Posse," *SPS*, Dec. 1, 1909.

45. Scanandoah to Keppler, Dec. 4, 8, 1909, JKI MSS, Box 2, KL, CU; 1910 AD 70, Memorial of a Band of Oneida Indians presented by their attorney George Decker, June 11, 1910, Correspondence Folder 9-8-14, GPD MSS, SJF.

46. Wonderley, *Oneida Iroquois Folklore, Myth, and History*, 204–6.

47. Decker, fragment of letter, Apr. 18, 1913, Correspondence Folder 9-8-17, GPD MSS, SJF.

48. Decker to Rockwell, Nov. 11, 1913; Decker to Charles V. Hooper [New York Secretary of State], Oct. 28, 1913; Hooper to Decker, Oct. 30, 1913, Correspondence Folder 9-8-18; Decker to Attorney General, July 11, 1912, and Acting Attorney General of the United States to Decker, Sept. 28, 1912, Correspondence Folder 9-8-16, GPD MSS, SJF.

49. Decker had asked Elihu Root to speak to the US attorney general about the Oneida case. Decker to Root, Mar. 15, 1920 [fragment]; Root to Decker, July 8, 1912, GPD MSS Folder 9-8-27. Root was pessimistic of the Oneida chances to get justice in federal courts. Root to Decker, Apr. 19, 1912, GPD MSS.

50. Decker to Peter G. Ten Eyck, Jan. 13, 1915, GPD MSS, Folder 9-8-20, SJF. Because Decker had won a reputation as a leading advocate of public power, Decker hoped to get a nomination to run for Congress, a judgeship, an appointment to head the Federal Water Power Commission, or a position in the Interior Department, all of which did not materialize, undoubtedly because of his growing criticism of the Office of Indian Affairs. Edward H. Hall [former secretary of the Association for the Protection of the Adirondacks] to President Woodrow Wilson, Mar. 19, 1918, Correspondence Folder 9-8-23, GPD MSS, SJF.

51. "Indians Plead for Their Land," *SPS*, July 28, 1916.

52. *United States v. Boylan, et al.*, 256 F. 468 (Mar. 3, 1919). "Oneida Land Must Be Returned, to the Indians," *Oneida (NY) Dispatch*, Mar. 7, 1919.

53. *United States v. Boylan, et al.*, 265 F. 165 (Mar. 3, 1920). See also "Court Gives Land Back to the Indians" and "Judge Ray's Decision Upheld," *Oneida (NY) Dispatch*, Mar. 12, 1920; "Indians Win Long War for Oneida Lands," *SH*, Apr. 19, 1922.

54. *United States v. Boylan, et al.*, 256 F. 468 (Mar. 3, 1919).

55. Hauptman, interviews of Reitz.

56. US Bureau of the Census, *14th Census of the United States* (Washington, DC, 1920). His daughter Louella was born five years later.

57. Campisi, "Ethnic Identity and Boundary Maintenance," 436.

58. [Everett], *Report of the New York State Indian Commission to Investigate the Status of the American Indian Residing in the State of New York,* transmitted to the New York State Legislature, Mar. 17, 1922, copy on file in New York State Library.

59. Ibid.

60. Ibid., 67–69. For Johnson's testimony the next day, see ibid., 99–102.

61. Ibid., 70.

62. Ibid., 91–94.

63. Ibid., 95–98, 104.

64. Ibid., 304–5.

65. For a description of the ceremony and list of attendees who participated in the ceremony, see "Ceremony in Honor of the Revertal [*sic*] of Land to the Indians; Case of *U.S. v. Boylan and Moyer*, Windfall Reservation, Lots 317 and #19, Town of Lenox, Madison County, New York, August 19, 1922," LS MSS, Box 1, Folder 1, NYSL.

66. See chap. 7.

6. A Native American Inventor in the Age of Edison

1. *T&T* (Sept. 1894); *T&T* (Jan. 1896), HUA.

2. The lake was on the federal superfund list because the company dumped six million pounds of toxic waste over the years. "Onondaga Lake—the Most Polluted Lake in America," Onondaga Nation website; "Onondaga Lake Natural Resource Damage Assessment," US Fish and Wildlife United States Service website. The Onondagas brought a suit into federal court. Kirk Semple, "Tribe Seeks Syracuse, but a Cleanup May Do," *NYT*, Mar. 12, 2005. A later Onondaga suit failed. Glenn Coin, "Onondaga Seek Public Support in Land Claim—Nation Concedes the Appeal It Files Today Likely Will Be Dismissed," *SPS*, Feb. 28, 2012. The appeal was heard by the Federal Court of Appeals, 2nd Circuit (New York City), in the early fall of 2012 but rejected. The Onondagas' next appeal was rejected by the US Supreme Court in October 2013.

3. "Solvay Takes Up Indian's Discovery," *SHJ*, June 27, 1931; "Indian's Find May Restore Lake's Beauty: Schanandoah Discovers Use for Waste Piled Up about Onondaga [Lake]," *SPS*, Sept. 27, 1931; "Nedrow Indian Turns Solvay Waste to Use," unidentified newspaper, newsclipping folder, Vertical Files: Indians—Onondaga [Reservation] individuals, Schanandoah, Albert, OHA; "Indian Inventor's Death Revives Interest in Waste Problem of Solvay Firm," *SH*, Jan. 14, 1934; "Indian Dies with Secret for New Limestone Use," *NYT*, Jan. 12, 1934.

4. Doc was an expert on Indian medical lore and displayed herbal medicines at the New York State Fair. He lectured against eating too much sugar and refined foods. He insisted that it "would be better if the doctors were paid for keeping people well, rather than making us well after we become sick." Quoted in "Medicine Man Helps Doctor," *SPS*, July 1, 1928. See also "Indian Village to Have Field," Apr. 23, 1929, unidentified newspaper clipping, WMB Scrapbooks, 38:139, NYSL.

5. "Only Indian in the Navy an Expert Machinist: Schenandoah Is Now on Cruiser *Atlanta*—He Hails from Oneida, New York," *New York World*, Mar. 28, 1901.

6. Scanandoah to Keppler, Feb. 24, 1904, JKI MSS, Box 2, KL, CU.

7. *SW* (Apr. 1913); *Carlisle Arrow* (Jan. 17, 1913).

8. US Patent Office, *Official Gazette* (1913); Chapman Scanandoah: Megaphone, application filed, Norfolk, VA, Dec. 19, 1911, serial #666,739, patent #1040775, patented Oct. 8, 1912, US Patent Office, *Index of Patents for the Year 1912* (Washington, DC: USGPO, 1913), 475.

9. "Chief Schanandoah of Oneidas Tribe Notes 82d Birthday," *SPS*, May 16, 1952; Blackwelder, *Electric City*, 86–105.

10. Scanandoah to Navy Bureau of Navigation, Nov. 7, 1916; M. S. Brown to Navy Recruiting Officer in Syracuse, Nov. 13, 1916; Brown to Navy Recruiting Officer in Buffalo, Nov. 24, 1916; D. C. Palmer [Chief, Navy Bureau of Navigation] to Congressman Walter W. Magee, Dec. 16, 1916; Scanandoah to Josephus Daniels [Secretary of the Navy], Jan. 1, 1917; Navy Bureau of Navigation Memorandum, Mar. 23, 1920; Scanandoah's Naval Service Record, #107186, NPRC, NA, St. Louis. He continued to try to reenlist at least until 1920. For his work back in Syracuse, see "Chief Schanandoah of Oneidas Tribe Notes 82d Birthday."

11. G. I. Brown, *The Big Bang: A History of Explosives*, 151–63; A. P. Fairchild, *Naval Ordnance*, 49–52.

12. Gerald J. Fitzgerald, "Chemical Warfare and Medical Response during World War I," 611, 612–15. See also Ludwig Fritz Haber, *The Poisonous Cloud: Chemical Warfare in the First World War*.

13. Alfred D. Chandler Jr. and Stephen Salsbury, *Pierre S. DuPont and the Making of the Modern Corporation*, 360, 381.

14. Quoted in "Indian Invents New Explosive," *SH*, Aug. 8, 1926. See also "Another Test; Oneida Indian to Try Out New Explosive Again Tomorrow," *SH*, Aug. 16, 1916; "Indian Inventor, Shenandoah Here—Descendant of Great Chief, Discovers New Powerful Explosive," *SPS*, July 7, 1916.

15. Scanandoah to Keppler, Nov. 17, 1917, JKI MSS, Box 2, KL, CU.

16. "Awards Made in Eight Classes," *SH*, Nov. 22, 1917, JKI MSS, CU; Scanandoah to Keppler, Nov. 25, 1917, JKI MSS, Box 2, CU.

17. "Indian Inventor, Shenandoah Here."

18. Schanandoah to Keppler, Feb. 24, 1918, JKI MSS, Box 2, KL, CU. For more on the history of the Frankford Arsenal, see James J. Farley, *Making Arms in the Machine Age: Philadelphia's Frankford Arsenal, 1816–1870*; and the earlier James Zupan, *Tools, Targets and Troopers: The History of the Frankford Arsenal*.

19. Schanandoah to Keppler, Sept. 23, 1923, JKI MSS, Box 2, KL, CU.

20. "Schanandite: Oneida Indian Invents New Explosive Which Is Safe to Handle," *Oneida (NY) Democratic Union*, Nov. 19, 1925; "Shenendite Moves Tons of Solid Rock," unidentified newsclipping, Aug. 24, 1926, Vertical Files: Indians—Onondaga [Reservation] individuals, Schanandoah, Chapman, OHA. See also "Indian Chieftain Granted Patent on Metal Press," Mar. 1, 1926, unidentified newspaper, newsclipping folder, Vertical Files: Indians—Onondaga [Reservation] individuals, Schanandoah, Chapman, OHA. See also "Indian Invents New Explosive," *SH*, Aug. 8, 1926; "Onondaga Chief's Explosive Meets Test: Shenendite Moves Tons of Solid Rock in Test," *SPS*, Aug. 24, 1926.

21. US Patent Office, *Official Gazette* (1927); Chapman Schanandoah: Method of Condensing Metals, application filed, Nedrow, NY, Feb. 2, 1925, serial #19.902, patent #US 1571737A, Feb. 2, 1926, US Patent Office, *Index of Patents for the Year 1926* (Washington, DC: USGPO, 1926), 577.

22. See note 20.

23. E. N. Brandt, *Growth Company: Dow Chemical's First Century*, 101–4; David A. Hounshell and John Kealy Smith Jr., *Science and Corporate Strategy: DuPont, R&D, 1902–1980*, 119–32.

24. US Bureau of the Census, *15th Census of the United States* (1930).

25. William N. Fenton to Schanandoah, Jan. 14, 1936; Schanandoah to Fenton, Dec. 6, 1936, William N. Fenton MSS, Coll. #20, Series I, Correspondence, APS.

26. "Indian Farm Society Formed," *SH*, June 1, 1917; "Indians to Organize Farm Society at Reservation," *SPS*, May 22, 1917; "Indian Crops Will Be Shown at State Fair," *SPS*, July 26, 1917; Erl [*sic*] Bates to Albert Schanandoah, Feb. 21, 1921, EB MSS, Box 1, Folder 6; "Indian Farmers Meet: Two Chiefs Will Speak," *Jamestown Post*, undated newsclipping, EB MSS, Box 1, Folder 29; mimeographs of Cornell Indian Board actions, Folder 23, EB MSS, Box 1, Folder 23, CU; "Reservation Indians Are Good Cooperators: Winter Course Students Take Active Part in Agricultural Societies," *Cornell Extension Service News* 5 (May 1921). On April 23, 1921, Chapman Scanandoah is listed as chairman of the Tractor Committee of the Six Nations Agricultural Society in Box 1, Folder 8, EB MSS, CU. Scanandoah also wrote to an Albany official asking that Bates be invited to testify before it. Chapman to Mr. Crosby, Aug. 9, 1920, Box 1, Folder 3, EB MSS, CU.

27. "Indian Village Work Starts," *SPS*, Apr. 6, 1929; "Indian Village Fair Feature," *SH*, Apr. 6, 1929. With little cultural sensitivity, the *Syracuse Post-Standard* carried the caption of a photograph of the Indian Village, labeling it "Primitive Iroquois Settlement at Fairgrounds Takes Place" in "Indian Village Takes Shape," *SPS*, July 21, 1929.

28. See the brochure that lists the founders of the Indian Village: New York State Department of Agriculture and Markets, *The 168th New York State Fair, August 21–September 1, 2014*. Friday, August 29, of that year was "Indian Day," a time when Native Americans are admitted free to the state fairgrounds. The founders of the Indian Village included four Oneida Chiefs—Chapman and Albert Scanandoah, William Hanyoust Rockwell, and Alex Burning. For Chapman Scanandoah's giant ear of corn, see "New York Keeps Its Word, Worth $1.41," *SPS*, Aug. 29, 1997.

29. There is a real need for a scholarly history of the New York State Fair and the Indian Village. For a brief (two-page) overview, see Henry M. Schramm, *Empire Showcase: A History of the New York State Fair*, 93–94. For early demeaning portrayals of the state fair's Indian Village, see caption for illustration, "Primitive Iroquois Settlement at Fairgrounds," *SPS*, July 29, 1929. Over the years, this portrayal changed for the better. I have been at events where the Hodinöhsö:ni´ talked about preparations for and the planned events at the New York State Fair. Hauptman, interviews of Elm.

30. "Six Nations Will Convene at State Fair; Iroquois Chieftains Will Meet at Exposition's Indian Village," *SH*, June 21, 1937; "Indian Village Dedicated," *NYT*, July 19, 1950.

7. An Outsider at Onondaga

1. "Oneida Indians to Hold Condolences Dance for Dead Chiefs Saturday: Night of New Moon Time for Paying Tribute to Leaders in Past Centuries—Women to Name Three New Chiefs," *SPS*, Mar. 14, 1920. Chapman Scanandoah is mentioned as one of the chiefs.

2. The Oneida census of 1922 was conducted by Chief Alex Burning. New York Indian Census Rolls, 1922; Hauptman, interviews of Reitz and Elm.

3. As early as July 23, 1902, an Onondaga petition requesting the removal of "foreign Indians" from the reservation was circulating at Onondaga. William Barnum to Jarius [Jairus] Pierce, Jarius Pierce MSS, OHA. Federal concerns about Canadian Indians resident there continued through the 1940s: Bertha Scanandoah to Charles H. Berry [Federal Indian Superintendent of the New York Agency], Feb. 13, 1941, with list of Canadian Indians at Onondaga, Feb. 10, 1941; William B. Benge [Federal Indian Superintendent of the New York Agency] to Commissioner of Indian Affairs, Feb. 16, 1948, Benge to Commissioner of Indian Affairs, Aug. 16, 1948; Scanandoah to Benge, Apr. 12, 1948. According to Benge, Mary Winder acted as spokeswoman voicing the concerns of these Canadian Oneidas. Aug. 10, 1948, BIA, NYIAR, 1938–1949, Box 3, Folder 069: Relations with Canadian Indians, RG 75, FRC.

4. "Chief Says U.S. Adopted Indian Laws Testifies in Action to Determine Six Nations Ruler," *SH*, Aug. 26, 1928; "Chief Says Bill Treaty Violation," *SPS*, Aug. 16, 1950; "Onondaga Chief's [actually story about Oneida Chief Chapman Scanandoah] Tribal Land Defense Quoted in Text Book," *SPS*, Sept. 12, 1948.

5. "Oneida Chiefs Declare War against the Huns," *SPS*, Sept. 28, 1918.

6. Oneida Chiefs [including Chief Chapman Scanandoah] to Governor Nathan L. Miller, Feb. 6, 1922, Records of New York State's Governors: Governor Nathan L. Miller Subject Files, Box 14, NYSA.

7. Ibid.

8. Decker to Miller, Apr. 24, 1922, ibid.

9. Ibid.; Miller to Charles C. Newton [NYS Attorney General], Feb. 9, 1922; Adelbert F. Jenks [NYS Deputy Attorney General] to William G. McCarthy [Acting Secretary to the NYS Governor], May 12, 1922; C. J. Stagg [of NYS Conservation Commission] to Miller, May 23, 1922, ibid.

10. Scanandoah to Keppler, Oct. 16, 1922, JKI MSS, Box 2, KL, CU.

11. See my fuller treatment of Deskaheh in my *Seven Generations of Iroquois Leadership*, 117–20, 124–42.

12. Gerald F. Reid, "'Illegal Alien'? The Immigration Case of Paul K. Diabo."

13. For examples of Oneida petitions to New York State officials about their larger claims to land, see 1872 SD 75 (Apr. 5, 1872); 1874 SD 79 (Mar. 24, 1874); and 1884 AD 63 (Feb. 7, 1884). For one of the most disputed state treaties, see Jack Campisi, "New York–Oneida Treaty of 1795: A Finding of Fact."

14. For a good treatment of Wilson K. Cornelius, see Geier, "Peculiar Status," 239–53, 271–74.

15. New York State Census Rolls, 1905 and 1906. B. B. Weber, the special federal Indian agent, and the local Oneida census taker (Phoebe George) attempted to remove Canadian Oneidas from the census count. Weber to US Commissioner of Indian Affairs, June 30, 1906, in New York State Census Roll, 1906.

16. Both Mary Winder and later, after Mary's death, her sister, Delia Waterman, kept the land claim alive. Hauptman, interviews of Jacob Thompson, Richard Chrisjohn, and Gloria Halbritter. The late Richard Chrisjohn was Winder's son-in-law, and the late Mary Winder was Gloria Halbritter's mother. For more on Mary Winder, see "Indians Prepare Legal Battle to Regain Sites of Two Villages," *SPS*, Aug. 17, 1947; Mary Winder to Charles Berry [Federal Indian Superintendent, New York Indian Agency], Apr. 15, 1943; Winder to William Benge [Federal Indian Superintendent, New York Indian Agency], Aug. 27, 28, 1948, Mar. 25, and Aug. 24. 1949; Winder to Theodore Haas [BIA Chief Counsel], June 7, 1948, BIA, NYIAR, 1938–1949, Box 3, Folder 067 Tribal Relations: Oneida, RG 75, FRC.

17. *Deere, et al. v. State of New York, et al.*, 22 F.2d 851 (1927); *Oneida (NY) Dispatch*, June 28, 1906.

18. For a more favorable examination of Minnie Kellogg and her writings and political views, see the new edition of Laura M. Kellogg, *Our Democracy and the American Indian*, 1–62. See also Kristina Ackley, "Renewing Haudenosaunee Ties: Laura Cornelius Kellogg and the Idea of Unity in the Oneida Claim." For more critical views, see Douglas Kiel, "Competing Visions of Empowerment: Oneida Progressive-Era Politics and Writing Tribal Histories," 434; and Hauptman, *Seven Generations of Iroquois Leadership*, 143–64.

19. Hazel W. Hertzberg, *The Search for an American Indian Identity: Modern Pan-Indian Movements*, 36, 60–61, 65, 97; William A. DePuy, "Looking for an Indian Booker T. Washington to Lead Their People," *New York Tribune*, Aug. 27, 1911.

20. Kellogg, *Our Democracy and the American Indian*, 63 passim; Ramona Herdman, "A New Six Nations; Laura Cornelius Kellogg Sees the Old Iroquois Confederacy Re-established on a Modern Basis," *SH*, Nov. 6, 1927.

21. "Thousands Will See Chiefs of Oneidas Sworn," *Appleton (WI) Post-Crescent*, Oct. 9, 1925; "What Has Become of the Investigators," *Tulsa Daily World*, Oct. 5, 1913; "Alleged Swindlers of Indian Caught," *Tulsa Daily World*, Oct. 12, 1913; "Police Jail Indian Princess Known in Denver; Charged with Impersonating an Officer," unidentified Colorado news-clipping, Oct. 1913, John Archiquette MSS, Box 2, Folder 62; "Verdict Expected in Indian Case This Afternoon," *Montreal Gazette*, Oct. 13, 1927; "Trio in Indian Case Found Not Guilty by Jury," *Montreal Gazette*, Oct. 14, 1927.

22. F. G. Tranberger to [Commissioner of Indian Affairs] Charles Burke, with attached memorandum, Nov. 2, 1927 (date received), BIA, CCF, 1907–1939, #9788-1923-260, NY, RG 75, NA.

23. I interviewed approximately twenty Oneidas in New York, Wisconsin, and Canada over the past forty years, and few had positive things to say about Minnie Kellogg. For example, well-respected artist Richard Chrisjohn, married to W. K. Cornelius's granddaughter, indicated to me that his family at the Oneida Reserve in Canada lost everything by giving money to the Kelloggs. Noted Wisconsin Oneida political figure and linguist Oscar Archiquette claimed that the Kelloggs swindled sixty thousand dollars from the Oneidas, and J. N. B. Hewitt, the prominent Smithsonian anthropologist of Tuscarora ancestry, claimed she solicited eighty thousand dollars from people at the Six Nations reserve in Canada. Robert W. Venables, interview with Archiquette, July 9, 1970, Shell Lake, WI, copy on file at Oneida Indian Historical Society, Oneida, WI; J. N. B. Hewitt to W. M. Stirling, June 25, 1932, Bureau of American Ethnology. Letters Received, 1909–1950, Box 45: J. N. B. Hewitt, 1929–1937, Smithsonian Institution, NAA.

24. See notes 17 and 22. For illustrations of these Kellogg tax receipts, see Hauptman, *Iroquois and the New Deal*, 75.

25. Kiel, "Competing Visions of Empowerment," 437.

26. Stillman was an unpaid advisor to the Iroquois Confederacy for three decades after the *Everett Report*. Laurence M. Hauptman, interview with Chief Ernest Benedict, Sept. 11, 1982, Akwesasne Mohawk Reservation. Her photograph hangs in the Akwesasne Cultural Center on the Akwesasne Mohawk Reservation. Her activism in support of Hodinöhsö:ni´ sovereignty was made clear in her correspondence: Lulu Stillman to Attorney General Tom Clark, Mar. 8, May 9, 1950; Stillman to John Nichols [Commissioner of Indian Affairs], Feb. 7, 1950, BIA Central Classified Files, 1940–1952, #28860-1947-013 (N.Y.), Part 3B, Box 1055 (New York), RG 75, NA; Stillman to US Attorney General for Public Lands, May 1, 1949, BIA, CCF, 1940–1952, #28853-1947-013 (N.Y.), Part 3B, Box 1055, RG 75, NA. Stillman strongly resented Minnie Kellogg, in part because the Oneida was the only Hodinöhsö:ni´ not to pay back loans for travel expenses used to attend the Everett Committee's hearings. Kellogg had borrowed three hundred dollars. Undated payment note on traveling expenses to Everett Committee hearing, LS MSS, Box 1, NYSL. After the Everett Commission report, the Hodinöhsö:ni´ attempted to hire Stillman to research the boundaries of Iroquoia at the conclusion of the Treaty at Fort Stanwix (1784). Rockwell to Stillman, Nov. 21, 1922, LS MSS, Box 1; Contract, Aug. 21, 1922, LS MSS, Box 5; "Agreement between Six Nations Confederacy and Lulu G. Stillman," 1922, Box 1, Folder 1; Contract, Aug. 21, 1922, LS MSS, Box 5, NYSL.

27. For illustrations of these Kellogg tax receipts, see Kellogg, *Our Democracy and the American Indian*, 50; and Hauptman, *Iroquois and the New Deal*, 75.

28. "Woman Is Boss of Indian Tribes," *SPS*, Mar. 1, 1928; "Chief Says U.S. Adopted Indian Laws Testifies in Action to Determine Six Nations Ruler," *SH*, Aug. 26, 1928; "Fighting Squaw Defends Rights of Oneida Tribe as Members of the Six Nations; Mrs. Laura Kellogg Denounces Attempt to Oust George Thomas as Head Chief, but Remains Away from

Onondagas' Council," *SH*, Mar. 14, 1924; "Indians Elect Feud Continues: 'Old Guard' Onondaga Council Meets; Rebels Convene," *SHJ*, Jan. 5, 1926. The feud could be followed in the extensive news coverage: William M. Beauchamp Scrapbooks, Boxes 38–39, WMB MSS, NYSL; and Warren H. Norton Scrapbooks, "Indians, 1916–1927," OHA, 88–265.

29. See note 27. See also "Who's Chief of Iroquois: Dispute Up to [Judge Frank] Cooper," *Syracuse American*, Oct. 10, 1926; "Iroquois Divided on Which Chief Rules," *SPS*, Oct. 10, 1926; "Court to Name Ruling Faction of Six Nations," *SPS*, Feb. 23, 1928; "Court Told of Chief's Fall," *SHJ*, Mar. 1, 1928. For the claims of Joshua Jones and George Thomas to be "head chief," see also US Congress, Senate Subcommittee on Indian Affairs, *Hearings on S.79, S. Res. 308, and S. Res. 263: Survey of Conditions of the Indians in the United States*, pt. 12, New York Indians 71st Cong., 2nd sess., 9 (Washington, DC: USGPO, 1931), pt. 12, 5007 passim (Jones) and 5025 passim (Thomas).

30. "Joshua Jones, Chief of Chiefs of Six Nations Dead," *SPS*, July 25, 1938.

31. "Indian Factions to Clash Again in Sand Hearing," *SH*, Mar. 7, 1927; "Indian Woman Wins 2-Year Dispute," *SHJ*, Mar. 11, 1927; "Chiefs Lose Legal War over Sand Pit," *SHJ*, Mar. 11, 1927; *Onondaga Nation of Indians v. Plaintiff v. Minnie Scanandoah, Bertha Scanandoah, John F. Lowery, James P. Lowry, and Thomas C. Lowery*, US District Court, Northern District of New York, Mar. 23, 1927—not reported but court opinion in US Congress, House of Representatives, Committee on Indian Affairs, *Hearings on H.R. 9720: Indians of New York*, 149–50. For Bertha Scanandoah's prominence, see "New York Keeps Its Word, Worth $1.41," *SPS*, Aug. 29, 1997; "Chiefs Issue Treaty Cloth," *SPS*, Sept. 21, 1950.

32. *Deere, et al. v. State of New York, et al.*, 22 F.2d 851 (1927); "$2,000,000,000 Suit of Indians Rejected," *NYT*, Oct. 25, 1927; Helen Upton, *The Everett Report in Historical Perspective: The Indians of New York*, 114–29.

33. Venables, interview of Archiquette.

34. Lewis Meriam et al., *The Problem of Indian Administration*; US Congress, Senate Subcommittee on Indian Affairs, *Hearings on S.79, S. Res. 308, and S. Res. 263*, pt. 12. See "Six Nations to Carry Land Fight to U.S. Senate," *SH*, Feb. 10, 1929.

35. US Congress, Senate Subcommittee on Indian Affairs, *Hearings on S.79, S. Res. 308, and S. Res. 263*, pt. 12, 4857–82, 4882–5035.

36. Ibid., 5046–67.

37. Ibid., 5071–72.

38. "Indians to Oppose Bill to Transfer Power to the States," *SPS*, Mar. 5, 1926; "Onondagas Preparing to Visit Capital," *Syracuse American*, Mar. 23, 1930; "Protests Made by Onondaga [*sic*] Tribe" (includes Oneida Chief Chapman Shenandoah who accompanied delegation to Washington), *Syracuse Journal*, Apr. 15, 1930. Scanandoah was referred to incorrectly as an Onondaga chief.

39. US Congress, House of Representatives, Committee on Indian Affairs, *Hearings on H.R. 9720*, 26–35, 147–54, 148.

8. The Wise Tribal Elder Tends His Garden

1. The earlier victory was the Tonawandas' US Supreme Court case of 1857: *Joseph Fellows, Survivor of Robert Kendle, Plaintiff in Error v. Susan Blacksmith and Ely S. Parker, Administrators of the Estate of John Blacksmith, Deceased*, 60 US 366 (Mar. 5, 1857). For more on this case, see Laurence M. Hauptman, *The Tonawanda Senecas' Heroic Battle against Removal: Conservative Activist Indians*, 87–114.

2. See the following articles in the *SPS*: "Indians Keep Alive Tradition in Receiving Cloth," Dec. 20, 1940; "Indian Chief Marks 150th Anniversary of Treaty with U.S.," Nov. 12, 1944; "Oneida Chief, Hale Hearty on 77th Birthday," May 19, 1947; "Chief Says Bill Treaty Violation," Aug. 16, 1950; and "Chief Schanandoah of Oneida Tribe Notes 82nd Birthday," May 16, 1952. On several occasions, he is identified as an Onondaga because he resided there. See, for example, "Onondaga Chief's [actually story about Oneida Chief Chapman Scanandoah] Tribal Land Defense Quoted in Text Book," Sept. 12, 1948.

3. Official List of Tribal Officials, Sept. 1943; Rockwell to Berry, Sept. 18, 1940, BIA, NYIAR, Box 1, Folder: Tribal Relations General (New York Indians), RG 75, FRC; "Indians Keep Alive Traditions in Receiving Cloth from U.S.," *SPS*, Dec. 20, 1940; "Chiefs Issue Treaty Cloth," *SPS*, Sept. 21, 1950.

4. See the following articles in the *SPS*: "Indians Formed One of First Democracies, Schanandoah, Student of People, Points Out," Sept. 22, 1940; "Chief Schanandoah of Oneidas, 80, Now Recalls Indian History," June 25, 1950; and "Indians Keep Alive Traditions in Receiving Cloth from U.S.," Dec. 20, 1940.

5. "Three Dead in Motor Accidents" (two in Scanandoah's automobile accident), *SH*, Oct. 20, 1931.

6. Scanandoah to Keppler, ca. early in 1932 and Dec. 19, 1933, JKI MSS, Box 2, KL, CU. He continued to struggle for several more years. Ibid., Dec. 21, 1935.

7. "Indian Inventor's Death, Revives Interest in Waste Problem of Solvay Firm," *SH*, Jan. 11, 1934; "Ritual of Pagan Missing at Funeral of Scanandoah," *SPS*, Jan. 15, 1934.

8. Scanandoah to Keppler, Dec. 30, 1937, Box 2, JKI MSS, KL, CU.

9. Federal Census of 1910, 1920, and 1930; *Federal Indian Census*, 1907–24.

10. New York State Legislature, Joint Legislative Committee on Indian Affairs, *Public Hearing Held at Nedrow, New York, Onondaga Reservation, in Schoolhouse, September 30th, 1943*, 21; "It's in My Blood, Declares Indian as He Joins Navy," *SHJ*, Dec. 11, 1941, "C. M. Shenandoah Here on Furlough," *SPS*, July 24, 1929. He served from 1927 to 1933 on the USS *Texas* and USS *Vega*.

11. For Six Nations opposition to the draft, see *Ex Parte Green* 123 F.2d 862 (1941); *United States v. Claus*, 63 F. Supp. 433 (1944); *Albany v. United States*, 152 F.2d 267 (1945). "Indian Loses Fight for Draft, Federal Appeals Court Rules against Warren E. Green a Citizen," *SHJ*, Nov. 25, 1941.

12. For a summary treatment of termination policies, see Francis Paul Prucha, *The Great Father: The United States Government and the American Indians*, 2:1013 passim. See also Donald L. Fixico, *Termination and Relocation: Federal Indian Policy, 1945–1960*. For an excellent analysis of the congressional origins of termination policies, see R. Warren Metcalf, *Termination's Legacy: The Discarded Indians of Utah*. For one Hodinöhsö:ni´ community affected by a pork-barrel hydropower–flood control project during the era of termination policies, see Laurence M. Hauptman, *In the Shadow of Kinzua: The Seneca Nation of Indians since World War II*, 21–103.

13. See note 12.

14. *United States v. Forness*, 125 Fed. Rep. 2d, 928 (1942).

15. New York State Legislature, Joint Legislative Committee on Indian Affairs, *Public Hearing Held at Nedrow*. For Leighton Wade and the operations of this committee, see Laurence M. Hauptman, *The Iroquois Struggle for Survival: World War II to Red Power*, 34–41, 52, 59–64, 192–93.

16. New York State Legislature, Joint Legislative Committee on Indian Affairs, *Public Hearing Held at Nedrow*, 19–27.

17. Ibid.

18. Ibid., 22–23.

19. Ibid., 23–27.

20. Berry to William Zimmerman Jr. [Assistant Commissioner of Indian Affairs], Nov. 25, 1943; Zimmerman to William H. Mackenzie, Dec. 11, 1943, BIA CCF, 1940–1952, Box 1055, File #22649-1940-013 (New York), RG 75, NA.

21. New York State Legislature, Joint Legislative Committee on Indian Affairs, *Report, 1944* (Albany, 1944).

22. "Indian Chief Marks 150th Anniversary of Treaty with U.S.," *SPS*, Nov. 12, 1944.

23. 60 *Stat.*, 1049–56 (Aug. 13, 1946).

24. Winder to Berry, Apr. 15, 1943, BIA, NYIAR, 1938–1949, 067 Tribal Relations: Oneida, Box 3, RG 75, FRC; Berry to Zimmerman [Assistant Commissioner of Indian Affairs], Nov. 25, 1943; Zimmerman to Mackenzie, Dec. 11, 1943, BIA CCF, 1940–1952, Box 1055, File #22649-1940-013 (New York), RG 75, NA; Hauptman, interview with Halbritter.

25. See note 23.

26. Fixico, *Termination and Relocation*, 21–44. See also US Indian Claims Commission, *Final Report*; Harvey Rosenthal, *Their Day in Court: A History of the United States Indian Claims Commission*.

27. "Indians Lay Claims to Lands along Oneida Lake," *SPS*, Aug. 15, 1947; "Indians Prepare Legal Battle to Regain Sites of Two Villages," *SPS*, Aug. 17, 1947.

28. Hauptman, interviews of Elm. Elm was one of the mainstays at the Indian Village at the New York State Fair for a half century.

29. Scanandoah to Benge, Apr. 12, 1948; Benge to Scanandoah, Aug. 8, 1948, BIA, NYIAR, Box 3, Folder: Tribal Relations: Oneida, RG 75, FRC.

30. T. W. Wheat to Benge, Aug. 2, 1948. See also Benge to Commissioner of Indian Affairs, Aug. 10, 1948; Benge to Winder, Aug. 22, 1948, BIA, NYIAR, 1938–1949, Box 3, Folder: Tribal Relations: Oneida, RG 75, FRC.

31. William A. Brophy to Kenneth B. Disher, Sept. 20, 1946, Brophy MSS, Box 2, Chron. File, Sept. 1946, Harry Truman Presidential Library.

32. US Congress, Senate Committee on the Post Office and Civil Service, *Hearings on S. Res. 41: Officers and Employees of the Federal Government*, pt. 3, 547.

33. Bess Furman, "Campaign Pushed to Free Indians," *NYT*, July 22, 1947. For more on Reed and Butler, see Hauptman, *Iroquois Struggle for Survival*, 48–64.

34. "Onondaga Chief's [actually story about Oneida Chief Chapman Scanandoah] Tribal Land Defense Quoted in Text Book," *SPS*, Sept. 12, 1948. "Chief Says Bill Treaty Violation," *SPS*, Aug. 16, 1950. See the overwhelming Hodinöhsö:ni´ testimony against jurisdictional transfer in US Congress, Senate Subcommittee on Interior and Insular Affairs, *Hearings on S. 1683, S. 1686, S. 1687: New York Indians*. Although some voiced support, the media wrongly presented the Hodinöhsö:ni´ leadership as severely divided over the merits of the bills. "Indians Split on Wisdom of New Legislation," *Buffalo Courier Express*, Mar. 11, 1948; "Indians Disagree over State Control," *NYT*, June 12, 1949.

35. 62 *Stat.*, 1224 (July 2, 1948).

36. *Report of the Committee on Indian Affairs to the [Hoover] Commission on Organization of the Executive Branch of Government*, Philleo Nash MSS, Box 44, Truman Presidential Library.

37. 64 *Stat.*, 845 (Sept. 13, 1950).

38. Lulu Stillman worked closely with Chapman Scanandoah in the fight against the imposition of New York State jurisdiction and its implications for the Hodinöhsö:ni´. See Stillman to George A. Thomas [*Tadodaho*], Nov. 23, 1949, Stillman MSS, Box 5, NYSL; Stillman to Senator Zales Ecton, Feb. 25 and Mar. 12, 1952; Ecton to Scanandoah, Oct. 23, 1951. Scanandoah and Ecton had earlier corresponded in place of Stillman because she had had an accident. Stillman MSS, Box 2, NYSL.

39. Stillman to Ecton, Mar. 12, 1952.

40. "Chief Skenandoah of Oneida Indians Dies at Syracuse Hospital," *Oneida (NY) Democratic Union*, Feb. 26, 1953; "Chief in Indian Tribe, 82, Dies," *NYT*, Feb. 23, 1953; "Chief Schanandoah Dies: Circled Globe with Navy," *SPS*, Feb. 23, 1953; "Full Military Honors Paid to Chief Schenandoah," *SPS*, Feb. 26, 1953; Schanandoah Tombstone, Onondaga Valley Cemetery, Nedrow, NY.

41. 67 *Stat.*, 588–90 (Aug. 15, 1953).

42. Jacob Thompson to President Lyndon Johnson, Jan. 19 and Feb. 12, 1968, Johnson MSS, White House Central Files, Box 3, IN/A–Z; Thompson to Johnson, Nov. 26, 1968; Thompson, Elm, and Ruth Burr to Johnson, Mar. 26, 1968, Johnson, White House Central Files, Box 101, Name File: Thompson, Ja, Johnson Presidential Library, Austin, TX. Thompson to Congressman James Hanley, Jan. 23, 1968, Hanley MSS, File 270, Hartwick College.

Copies of Oneida petitions sent to Albany can be found in Johnson MSS, White House Central Files, Box 3, IN/A–Z, Johnson Presidential Library. Hauptman, interviews of Thompson and George Shattuck, Aug. 25, 1983. For more on this case, see Shattuck, *Oneida Land Claims*, 4–38.

43. *Oneida Indian Nation of New York, et al. v. County of Oneida, New York, et al.*, 94 S.Ct. 772 (Jan. 21, 1974). See also Shattuck, *Oneida Land Claims*. Nations that benefited by the US Supreme Court's Oneida decision in 1974 include the Catawbas, the Mashantucket Pequots, the Mohegans, the Narragansetts, and the Passamaquoddys.

9. Conclusion

1. Joseph Mitchell, "The Mohawks in High Steel," in *Apologies to the Iroquois [with a Study of the Mohawks in High Steel by Joseph Mitchell]*, by Edmund Wilson, 1–36.

2. Richard Severo, "Joseph Mitchell, Chronicler of the Unsung and the Unconventional, Dies at 87," *NYT*, May 25, 1996.

3. See note 1.

4. Walter D. Edmonds, *Drums along the Mohawk* (1936; reprint, Syracuse: Syracuse Univ. Press, 1997).

5. The motion picture *Drums along the Mohawk* was produced by Darryl Zanuck for Twentieth Century Fox and costarred Edna May Oliver and Ward Bond.

6. Wilson, *Apologies to the Iroquois*.

7. Ibid., 172; William N. Fenton to Walter Taylor, Jan. 28, 1965, Taylor MSS, MR 14, Wisconsin Historical Society. Much of the scholarly literature on Six Nations peoples' ability to adapt to change focuses on the Senecas. See, for example, Anthony F. C. Wallace, *The Death and Rebirth of the Seneca*; and Hauptman, *In the Shadow of Kinzua*.

8. Lewis Henry Morgan to Ely S. Parker, Dec. 14, 1848, Parker MSS, APS; William H. Armstrong, *Warrior in Two Camps: Ely S. Parker, Union General and Seneca Chief*, 41–42, 59, 62–64.

9. http://www.oneidaindiannation.com. Gale Courey Toensing had reported earlier that 13,004 acres were put into trust. "Oneida Indian Nation Gets Trust Lands," *Indian Country Today*, June 5, 2014.

Bibliography

Archival Records and Manuscripts

American Philosophical Society, Philadelphia
    Fenton, William N.
    Parker, Ely S.
    Speck, Frank G.
    Wallace, Anthony F. C.

Buffalo History Museum (formerly the Buffalo and Erie Historical Society)
    Bryant, William, MSS
    Gansworth, Howard, MSS
    Indian Collection
    Parker, Ely S., MSS
    Photographic Collection

Chemung County Historical Society, Elmira, NY
    Converse, Harriet Maxwell, Vertical File
    Maxwell Family Vertical File

Columbia Univ., Butler Library, New York City
    Lehman, Herbert, MSS
    Poletti, Charles, MSS

Cornell Univ., Kroch Library, Ithaca, NY
    Bates, Erl, MSS
    Keppler, Joseph, Jr.—Iroquois MSS

Erie Canal Village, Rome, NY
    Benjamin Wright Journal, 1816 (copy in New York State Museum)

Federal Records Center, National Archives, New York City
    RG 75, Records of the New York Agency, 1938–1949

Hamilton College, Burke Library, Clinton, NY
    Allen, Hope E., MSS

Kirkland, Samuel, MSS
Historical Society of Pennsylvania, Philadelphia
    Indian Rights Association
Indiana Univ., William Hammond Mathers Museum of World Cultures, Bloomington
    Wanamaker Collection [Joseph Dixon MSS]
Library of Congress, Washington, DC
    Roosevelt, Theodore, MSS
    Schoolcraft, Henry Rowe, MSS
Madison County Historical Society, Oneida, NY
    Native American Collection, 1795–1993
    Oneidas on Onondaga Reservation Roll, 1922
    Oneida Tribal Census, 1886–1887
    Rockwell, William Hanyoust, autobiographical sketch
    Vertical Files on New York Oneidas
Miscellaneous Manuscript Collections
    Indian Claims Commission, Expert Testimony on Dockets No. 342 A, B, C, E, F, 368, 368 A (microfiche)
    Jennings, Francis, et al., eds. *Iroquois Indians: A Documentary History of the Six Nations and Their League.* Microfilm Reels #49–50. Woodbridge, CT: Research Publications, 1985.
    The Papers of Carlos Montezuma, M.D. Edited by John Larner. Wilmington, DE: Scholarly Resources, 1983. 9 microfilm reels.
    The Papers of the Indian Rights Association. Glen Rock, NJ: Microfilm Corporation of America, 1975.
    The Papers of the Society of American Indians. Edited by John Larner. Wilmington, DE: Scholarly Resources, 1987. 10 microfilm reels.
Museum of Innovation and Science, Schenectady, NY
    Ford, Bacon, and Davis Report: "Full Value of Real Property at [General Electric] Schenectady Works, 1944" (1945)
    General Electric Employee Registers, 1889–95
    General Electric Pamphlet Series
    General Electric Photographic Collection
    Recollections [of General Electric] by G. E. Emmons in Hammond Historical File, Parts K–L
National Archives, Washington, DC
    BIA Central Classified Files, 1881–1936

[New York Indian] Census Rolls, 1885–1940

Correspondence of the Office of Indian Affairs, Letters Received, 1824–1881, M234, RG 75

Green Bay Agency, 1824–1880
Microfilm Reels #315–36

Neosho Agency, 1831–1875
Microfilm Reels #530–37

Records of the New York Agency, 1829–1880
Microfilm Reels #583–96

Records of the New York Agency Emigration, 1829–1851
Microfilm Reel #597

Records of the Office of the Secretary of United States Navy, RG 45

Records Relating to Indian Treaties
Documents Relating to the Negotiation of Ratified and Unratified Treaties . . . , 1801–1869, T494, Microfilm Reels #1, 2, 4, 6, 8
Ratified Indian Treaties, 1722–1869, M668, Microfilm Reels #2, 3, 9, 12

Seneca Agency in New York, 1824–1832
Microfilm Reel #808

Six Nations Agency, 1824–1834
Microfilm Reel #832

Special Case File #29: Records Relating to the New York Indians, the Treaty of 1838 and the Kansas Claims

National Archives II, College Park, MD
Cartographic Records
Records of the Indian Claims Commission, RG 279
Records of the Secretary of the Interior, RG 48

National Personnel Records Center, National Archives, St. Louis
Chapman Scanandoah United States Naval Service Record #1070186 (and related documents)

Newberry Library, Chicago
Ayers Collection

New-York Historical Society, New York City
Keppler, Joseph, Family MSS

New York Public Library
Morse, Jedidiah, MSS
Moses, Robert, MSS
Schuyler, Philip, MSS

New York State Archives, Albany

    Indian Annuity Records

    Records of the New York State Canals Records of Indian Deeds and Treaties, 1748–1847

    Records of the New York State Comptroller's Indian Annuity Claims, Receipts and Related Documents, 1796–1925

    Records of the New York State Department of State
        Population Census of Indian Reservations, 1915

    Records of the New York State Governors, 1870–1954
        Charles Evans Hughes [Investigative Case Files, 1907–10]
        Governor Al Smith
        Governor Nathan Miller

    Records of the New York State Legislature, Assembly Papers, Indian Affairs

    Records of the New York State Surveyor-General, Land Office, Series I and II

    Records of the Thomas Indian School

    Records of the War of 1812—Certificates of Claims by War of 1812 Veterans

    Schoolcraft Population Census of Indian Reservations, 1845

New York State Bureau of Land Management, Albany

    Minutes of the New York State Board of Land Commissioners—Nineteenth-Century Minute Books

New York State Library, Manuscript Division, New York City

    Beauchamp, William, MSS

    Holland Land Company MSS

    Hough, Franklin Benjamin, MSS

    Hutchinson, Holmes, MSS

    New York State Legislature, [Everett Report] Assembly, *Report of the Indian Commission to Investigate the Status of the American Indian Residing in the State of New York . . .* , Mar. 17, 1922

    Ogden Land Company Record Book, 1811–82

    Parker, Arthur C., MSS

    Seymour, Horatio, MSS

    Stillman, Lulu, MSS

    Watson, Elkanah, MSS

    Wright, Benjamin, MSS

Oneida Nation of Indians of Wisconsin, Oneida, WI

    WPA Oneida Folklore and Language Project Stories

Onondaga Historical Association, Syracuse

Beauchamp, William, MSS

New York State Comptroller Records [Albany Papers]

Norton, William H. Norton Scrapbooks

Onondaga Census, 1896–1905

Pierce, Jarius [Jairus], MSS

Vertical Files

    Newsclipping Folders

        Inventors

        Oneida Indians

    Newsclipping Folders of Onondaga [Residents] of Note

        Scanandoah, Albert

        Scanandoah, Chapman

[Franklin D.] Roosevelt Presidential Library, Hyde Park, NY

    Franklin D. Roosevelt OF [Official] Files series

Smithsonian Institution, National Anthropological Archives

    Bureau of American Ethnology

    J. N. B. Hewitt MSS

St. John Fisher College, Lavery Library, East Rochester, NY

    Decker, George P., MSS

State Univ. of New York, College at Buffalo

    Reilly, Paul G.—Indian Claims Commission MSS

Syracuse Univ., Bird Library

    Harriman, Averill, MSS

    Moses, Robert, MSS

    Oneida Community MSS [Hope E. Allen MSS]

[Harry S.] Truman Presidential Library, Independence, MO

    Brophy, William A., MSS

    Chapman, Oscar A., MSS

    Myer, Dillon S., MSS

    Nash, Philleo, MSS

    Oral Histories

        Myer, Dillon

    Truman, Harry S., Records as President

        White House Official Files, 1945–1953

Univ. of Rochester, Rush Rhees Library

    Dewey, Thomas, MSS

    Morgan, Lewis Henry, MSS

Parker, Arthur C., MSS

Parker, Ely S., MSS

Wisconsin Historical Society, Madison

Draper, Lyman C.

McLaughlin, James, MSS

Yale Univ., Beinecke Library, New Haven, CT

Archiquette, John, MSS

Cooper, Susan Fenimore, MSS, "History of the Oneida Indians," in James Fenimore Cooper Collection

Pratt, Richard Henry, MSS

Government Publications

American State Papers: Documents, Legislative and Executive of the Congress of the United States. 38 vols. [Class 2: Indian Affairs. 2 vols. 1832–34.] Washington, DC: Gales & Seaton, 1832–61.

The Balloting Book and Other Documents Relating to Military Bounty Lands in the State of New York. Albany: Packard & Van Benthuysen, 1825.

Cohen, Felix S. *Handbook of Federal Indian Law.* Washington, DC: US Department of the Interior, 1942. Reprint, Albuquerque: Univ. of New Mexico Press, 1971.

Donaldson, Thomas, comp. *The Six Nations of New York.* Extra Census Bulletin of the 11th Census [1890] of the United States. Washington, DC: US Census Printing Office, 1892.

Hough, Franklin Benjamin, comp. *Proceedings of the Commissioners of Indian Affairs Appointed by Law for the Extinguishment of Indian Titles in the State of New York.* 2 vols. Albany: Munsell, 1861.

Kappler, Charles J., comp. *Indian Affairs: Laws and Treaties.* 5 vols. Washington, DC, 1904–41. Vol. 2 reprinted as *Indian Treaties, 1778–1883.* New York: Interland, 1972.

Morse, Jedidiah. *A Report to the Secretary of War of the United States on Indian Affairs, Comprising a Narrative of a Tour Performed in the Summer of 1820. . . .* New Haven, CT: S. Converse, 1822.

New York State. Regents of the Univ. of the State of New York. *Position Paper No. 22: Native American Education.* Albany: New York State Education Department, 1975.

New York State Adjutant General's Office. *Index of Awards: Soldiers of the War of 1812.* Baltimore: Genealogical Publishing, 1969.

New York State Board of Canal Commissioners. *Annual Report* [1811–78].

New York State Board of Land Commissioners. *Proceedings of the Commissioners for 1924*. Albany: J. B. Lyon, 1924.

New York State Department of Agriculture and Markets. *The 168th New York State Fair, August 21–September 1, 2014*. Syracuse, 2014 (brochure).

New York State Governor. *Public Papers of Thomas E. Dewey*. 12 vols. Albany, 1944–57.

New York State Legislature. Assembly, Document No. 51. *Report of the Special Committee to Investigate the Indian Problem of the State of New York*. Appointed by the Assembly of 1888. 2 vols. Albany: Troy Press, 1889. [Popularly known as the *Whipple Report*.]

———. *Assembly Journal*.

———. *Laws (Statutes) of the State of New York*.

———. *Senate Journal*.

New York State Legislature. Joint Legislative Committee on Indian Affairs. *Public Hearing Held at Nedrow, New York, Onondaga Schoolhouse, September 30th, 1943*. Albany, 1943 [transcript on file in New York State Library].

———. *Report, 1944–1954*. Albany, 1944–59.

New York State Secretary of State. *Census of the State of New York, 1825–1915*.

New York State Superintendent of Public Instruction. *Annual Reports, 1870–1890*. Albany, 1871–91.

Richardson, James D., comp. *A Compilation of the Messages & Papers of the Presidents, 1789–1897*. 10 vols. Washington, DC: USGPO, 1896–99.

Royce, Charles C., comp. *Indian Land Cessions in the United States*. 18th Annual Report of the Bureau of American Ethnology, 1896–97. Pt. 2. Washington, DC: USGPO, 1899.

US Board of Indian Commissioners. *Annual Reports, 1883–1916*.

US Bureau of the Census. 1st (1790)–15th (1930) Censuses.

US Congress. *Congressional Record, 1870–1953*.

US Congress. House of Representatives. Committee on Indian Affairs. *Hearings on H.R. 1198 and 1341: Creation of the Indian Claims Commission*. 79th Cong., 1st sess. Washington, DC: USGPO, 1945.

———. *Hearings on H.R. 3680, H.R. 3681 and H.R. 3710: Removal of Restrictions on Indian Property and for the Emancipation of Indians*. 79th Cong., 2nd sess. Washington, DC: USGPO, 1946.

———. *Hearings on H.R. 9720: Indians of New York*. 71st Cong., 2nd sess. Washington, DC: USGPO, 1931.

US Congress. House of Representatives. Committee on Public Lands. *Report No. 2355: Conferring Jurisdiction on State of New York with Respect to Offenses Committed on Indian Reservations with Such State.* Washington, DC: USGPO, 1948.

———. *Report No. 2720: Conferring Jurisdiction on Court of New York with Respect to Civil Actions between Indians or to Which Indians Are Parties.* Washington, DC, 1950.

US Congress. House of Representatives. Subcommittee on Indian Affairs of the Committee on Public Lands. *Hearings on H.R. 2958, H.R. 2165 and H.R. 1113: Emancipation of Indians.* 80th Cong., 1st sess. Washington, DC: USGPO, 1947.

US Congress. Senate Committee on Indian Affairs. *Hearings on S. 1093 and S. 1194: Removal of Restrictions on Property of Indians Who Served in the Armed Forces.* 79th Cong., 2nd sess. Washington, DC: USGPO, 1946.

US Congress. Senate Committee on Interior and Insular Affairs. *Report No. 1139: Commuting Annuities, Seneca and Six Nations of New York.* Washington, DC, 1948.

———. *Report No. 1489: Conferring Jurisdiction on Courts of New York over Offenses Committed by Indians.* Washington, DC, 1948.

———. *Report No. 1836: Conferring Jurisdiction on Courts of New York with Respect to Civil Actions between Indians or to Which Indians Are Parties.* Washington, DC, 1950.

US Congress. Senate Committee on the Post Office and Civil Service. *Hearings on S. Res. 41: Officers and Employees of the Federal Government.* 80th Cong., 1st sess. Washington, DC: USGPO, 1947.

US Congress. Senate Subcommittee on Indian Affairs. *Hearings on S.79, S. Res. 308, and S. Res 263: Survey of Conditions of the Indians in the United States.* 71st–76th Cong. Washington, DC: USGPO, 1928–43.

US Congress. Senate Subcommittee on Interior and Insular Affairs. *Hearings on S. 1683, S. 1686, S. 1687: New York Indians.* Washington, DC: USGPO, 1948.

US Department of the Interior, Commissioner of Indian Affairs. *Annual Reports* [1849–1953].

US Department of the Interior, Secretary of the Interior. *Annual Reports* [1849–1953].

US Department of the Navy. *Dictionary of American Fighting Ships.* 8 vols. Washington, DC: Division of Naval History/Naval Historical Center, 1976–91.

US Indian Claims Commission. *Decisions of the Indian Claims Commission.* Microfiche ed. New York: Clearwater, 1973–78.

———. *Final Report.* Aug. 13, 1946–Sept. 30, 1978. Washington, DC: USGPO, 1979.

US Patent Office. *Index of Patents* [for the years 1912–26]. Washington, DC: USGPO, 1913–27.

Whitford, Noble E., *History of the Canal System of the State of New York.* . . . 2 vols. Albany: Brandon Printing [supplement to the *Annual Report* of the State Engineer and Surveyor of the State of New York], 1906.

Interviews

Conducted by Laurence M. Hauptman

Chief Ernest Benedict, Sept. 10–11, 1982, and July 30, 1983, Akwesasne Mohawk Indian Reservation

Louis R. Bruce Jr., Dec. 11, 1980, and June 30, 1982, Washington, DC

Richard Chrisjohn, Sept. 4, 1985, Hunter Mountain, NY

Chief Edison [Perry] Mt. Pleasant, Oct. 20–21, Fort Stanwix National Historic Site, Rome, NY

Ray Elm, Oct. 20, 1984, Fort Stanwix National Historic Site, Rome, NY; May 6, 1990, Onondaga Indian Reservation; Apr. 21, 1985; June 13, 1991, Syracuse

William N. Fenton, Sept. 28, 1977, June 28, 1978, and May 18, 1983, Albany

Gloria Halbritter, Apr. 21, 1985, Rensselaerville, NY

Ray Halbritter, Oct. 20, 1984, Fort Stanwix National Historic Site, Rome, NY

W. David Owl, July 28, 1977, Cattaraugus Indian Reservation

Chief Irving Powless Jr., Oct. 21, 1984, Fort Stanwix National Historic Site, Rome, NY

Chief Irving Powless Sr., May 15, 1979, Onondaga Indian Reservation

Keith Reitz, May 2–4, 1982, New Paltz, NY; July 21, 1982, and June 8, 1984, Rochester, NY

Pauline Lay Seneca, June 14, 1978, and July 15–17, 1982, Cattaraugus Indian Reservation

George Shattuck, Aug. 25, 1983, Syracuse

Chief Leon Shenandoah, May 15, 1979, Onondaga Indian Reservation

Chief Corbett Sundown, May 22, 1980, Tonawanda Indian Reservation

Jacob Thompson, Apr. 15, 1972, and May 6, 1976, New Paltz, NY

Lincoln White, July 1, 1982, Washington, DC

Conducted by Robert W. Venables

Oscar Archiquette, July 8, 1970, Shell Lake, WI

Court Cases

Albany v. United States, 152 F.2d 767 (1945)

Boylan v. George, et al., 133 AD 514 (1909)

Cherokee Nation v. Georgia, 30 US 1 (1831)

City of Sherrill v. Oneida Indian Nation, 125 S.Ct. 1478 (2005)

County of Oneida, et al. v. Oneida Indian Nation of New York, 414 US 226 (1985)

Deere, et al. v. State of New York, et al., 22 F.2d 851 (1927)

Ex Parte Green, 123 F.2d 862 (1941)

Lonewolf v. Hitchcock, 187 US 553 (1903).

New York Indians v. United States, 30 Ct. Cl. 413 (1895)

New York Indians v. United States, 33 Ct. Cl. 510 (1898)

New York Indians v. United States, 170 US 464 (1899)

Oneida Indian Nation of New York v. County of Oneida, et al., 94 S.Ct. 772 (1974)

Six Nations, et al. v. United States, 12 Ind. Cl. Comm. 86 (1968)

United States v. Boylan, et al., 256 F. 468 (1919)

United States v. Boylan, et al., 265 F. 165 (1920)

United States v. Claus, 63 F. Supp. 433 (1944)

Newspapers and Magazines

Albany Argus

American Machinist

Appleton (WI) Post-Crescent

Buffalo Courier-Express

Buffalo Evening Times

Buffalo News

Carlisle (PA) Arrow

Cassier's Engineering Magazine (New York City)

Chicago Chronicle

Commercial Advertiser (Buffalo)

Cornell Extension Service News (Ithaca, NY)

Engineering Magazine (New York City)

General Electric Review (Schenectady, NY)

Green Bay Intelligencer

Green Bay Press-Gazette [formerly *Green Bay Gazette*]

Hampton (VA) Monitor

Hampton (VA) Student

Harrisburg (PA) Telegraph

Hartford (CT) Daily Courant

Indian Country Today (Oneida Nation of New York)

Indian Truth (Philadelphia)

Kaliwísaks (Oneida, WI)

Living Church (Chicago)

Minneapolis Journal

Montreal Gazette

New York Herald

New York Sun

New York Times

New York Tribune

New York World

Niles' Register (Baltimore)

Oneida (NY) Democratic Union

Oneida (NY) [Daily] Dispatch

Oneida (NY) Indian Nation News

Onondaga Standard (Syracuse)

Philadelphia Inquirer

Philadelphia Times

Red Man (Carlisle Institute)

Rochester Democrat and Chronicle

Rochester Post Express

San Francisco Call

Semi-Weekly Messenger (Wilmington, NC)

Semi-Weekly Union (Madison County, NY)

Southern Workman (Hampton Institute)

St. Louis Republic

Syracuse American

Syracuse Post-Standard

Syracuse Herald

Syracuse Herald American

Syracuse Herald-Journal

Syracuse Journal

Talks and Thoughts of the Hampton Indian Students

Towanda Daily Review (Bradford County, PA)

Tulsa Daily World

Utica (NY) Globe

Utica (NY) Intelligencer

Utica (NY) Patriot & Patrol

Washington Bee

Washington Post

Washington Times (older DC version)

Other Sources

Ackley, Kristina. "Haudenosaunee Genealogies: Conflict and Community in the Oneida Land Claim." *American Indian Quarterly* 33 (2009): 462–78.

———. "Renewing Haudenosaunee Ties: Laura Cornelius Kellogg and the Idea of Unity in the Oneida Land Claim." *American Indian Culture and Research Journal* 32 (2008): 57–81.

———. "'We Are Oneida Yet': Discourse in the Oneida Claim." PhD diss., SUNY Buffalo, 2005.

Adams, David Wallace. *Education for Extinction: American Indians and the Boarding School Experience, 1875–1928*. Lawrence: Univ. Press of Kansas, 1995.

———. "Education in Hues: Red and Black at Hampton Institute, 1878–1893." *South Atlantic Quarterly* 76 (Spring 1977): 159–76.

Ahern, Wilbert H. "'The Returned Indians': Hampton Institute and Its Indian Alumni, 1879–1893." *Journal of Ethnic Studies* 10 (Winter 1983): 263–304.

Allen, Hope E. "An Oneida Tale." *Journal of American Folklore* 57 (1944): 280–81.

Andrus, Carolyn W. *Hampton's Work for the Indians*. Hampton, VA: Hampton Institute Press, 1894.

Armstrong, Samuel Chapman. *Education for Life*. Hampton, VA: Hampton Institute Press, 1913.

Armstrong, William H. *Warrior in Two Camps: Ely S. Parker, Union General and Seneca Chief*. Syracuse: Syracuse Univ. Press, 1978.

Basehart, Harry S. "Historical Changes in the Kinship System of the Oneida Indians." PhD diss., Harvard Univ., 1952.

Basso, Keith. *Wisdom Sits in Places: Landscape and Language among the Western Apache*. Albuquerque: Univ. of New Mexico Press, 1996.

Beauchamp, William M. *A History of the New York Iroquois*. New York State Museum Bulletin 78. Albany, 1905.

Beers, D. G., comp. *Atlas of Madison County, New York*. Philadelphia: Pomeroy, Whitman, 1875.

Belknap, Jeremy, and Jedidiah Morse. *Journal of a Tour from Boston to Oneida, June 1796*. Edited by George Dexter. Cambridge, MA: John Wilson, 1882.

Bell, Genevieve. "Telling Stories Out of School: Remembering the Carlisle Indian Industrial School." PhD diss., Stanford Univ., 1998.

Benn, Carl. *The Iroquois in the War of 1812*. Toronto: Univ. of Toronto Press, 1998.

Berkhofer, Robert F., Jr. "The Industrial History of Oneida County, New York." Master's thesis, Cornell Univ., 1955.

———. *Salvation and the Savage: An Analysis of Protestant Missions and American Indian Response, 1787–1862*. Lexington: Univ. Press of Kentucky, 1965. Reprint, New York: Atheneum, 1976.

———. *The White Man's Indian: Images of the American Indian from Columbus to the Present*. New York: Random House, 1879.

Biographical Review: The Leading Citizens of Madison County, New York. Boston: Biographical Review, 1894.

Blackwelder, Julia Kirk. *Electric City: General Electric in Schenectady*. College Station: Texas A&M Press, 2014.

Bloomfield, Julia. *The Oneidas*. New York: Alden Bros., 1907.

Borchert, John R. "American Metropolitan Evolution." *Geographic Review* 57 (1967): 301–33.

Brandt, E. N. *Growth Company: Dow Chemical's First Century*. East Lansing: Michigan State Univ. Press, 1997.

Bremer, Richard G. *Indian Agent and Wilderness Scholar: The Life of Henry Rowe Schoolcraft*. Mt. Pleasant, MI: Clark Historical Library, 1987.

Britten, Thomas A. *American Indians in World War I: At Home and at War*. Albuquerque: Univ. of Mew Mexico Press, 1997.

Brooks, Charles E. *Frontier Settlement and Market Revolution: The Holland Land Purchase*. Ithaca, NY: Cornell Univ. Press, 1996.

Brown, G. I. *The Big Bang: A History of Explosives*. Stroud, UK: Sutton, 1998.

Brown, Robert H. *The Republic in Peril: 1812*. New York: Columbia Univ. Press, 1964.

Brudvig, Jon. "Bridging the Cultural Divide: Hampton Institute's Experiment in American Indian Education, 1876–1923." PhD diss., College of William and Mary, 1996.

Calloway, Colin. *The American Revolution in Indian Country: Crisis and Diversity in Native American Communities*. New York: Cambridge Univ. Press, 1995.

———. *Pen and Ink Witchcraft: Treaties and Treaty-Making in American Indian History*. New York: Oxford Univ. Press, 2014.

Campbell, William W., ed. *The Life and Writings of De Witt Clinton*. New York: Baker and Scribner, 1949.

Campisi, Jack. "Consequences of the Kansas Claims to Oneida Tribal Identity." In *Proceedings of the First Congress, Canadian Ethnology Society*, edited by Jerome H. Barkow, 35–47. Mercury Series 17. Ottawa: Canada National Museum of Man, Ethnology Division, 1974.

———. "Ethnic Identity and Boundary Maintenance in Three Oneida Communities." PhD diss., SUNY Albany, 1974.

———. "New York–Oneida Treaty of 1795: A Finding of Fact." *American Indian Law Review* 4 (Summer 1976): 71–82.

Campisi, Jack, Michael Foster, and Marianne Mithun, eds. *Extending the Rafters: Interdisciplinary Approaches to Iroquoian Studies*. Albany: SUNY Press, 1984.

Campisi, Jack, and Laurence M. Hauptman, eds. *The Oneida Indian Experience: Two Perspectives*. Syracuse: Syracuse Univ. Press, 1988.

Carden, Maren L. *Oneida: Utopian Community to Modern Corporation*. 1969. Reprint, Syracuse: Syracuse Univ. Press, 1998.

Catlin, George. *Letters and Notes on the North American Indians*. Edited by Michael M. Mooney. 1841. Reprint, New York: Clarkson N. Potter, 1975.

Chandler, Alfred D., Jr. *The Visible Hand: The Managerial Revolution in Business*. Cambridge, MA: Belknap Press of Harvard Univ. Press, 1993.

Chandler, Alfred D., Jr., and Stephen Salsbury. *Pierre S. DuPont and the Making of the Modern Corporation*. New York: Harper and Row, 1971.

Chazanof, William. *Joseph Ellicott and the Holland Land Company: The Opening of Western New York*. Syracuse: Syracuse Univ. Press, 1970.

Chester, Greg. *The Battle of Big Sandy*. Adams, NY: Historical Association of South Jefferson County, 1981.

Clark, Blue. *Lone Wolf v. Hitchcock: Treaty Rights at the End of the Nineteenth Century*. Lincoln: Univ. of Nebraska Press, 1994.

Clarke, T. Wood. *Utica: For a Century and a Half*. Utica, NY: Widtman Press, 1952.

Colles, Christopher. *Proposal for the Speedy Settlement of the Waste and Unappropriated Lands on the Western Frontiers of the State of New York, and for the Improvement of the Inland Navigation between Albany and Oswego.* New York: Samuel London, 1785.

———. *Proposal of a Design for the Promotion of the Interests of the United States of America, Extending Its Advantage to All Ranks and Conditions of Men . . . by Means of Inland Navigable Communication of a New Construction and Mode.* New York: Samuel Wood, 1808.

———. *A Survey of the Roads of the United States of America, 1783.* Edited by Walter W. Riston. Cambridge, MA: Harvard Univ. Press, 1961.

Conable, Mary. "A Steady Enemy: The Ogden Land Company and the Seneca Indians." PhD diss., Univ. of Rochester, 1995.

Converse, Harriet Maxwell. *Myths and Legends of the New York State Iroquois.* Edited by Arthur C. Parker. New York State Museum Bulletin 125. Albany: New York State Museum, 1908.

Cookingham, Henry J. *History of Oneida County, New York: From 1700 Present.* Vol. 1. Chicago: S. J. Clarke, 1912.

Cooper, Susan Fenimore. *Rural Hours.* 1850. Reprint, Syracuse Univ. Press, 1968.

Cornplanter, Jesse. *Legends of the Longhouse.* New York: Lippincott, 1938.

Christjohn, Amos, and Maria Hinton. *An Oneida Dictionary.* Edited by Clifford Abbott. Green Bay: Univ. of Wisconsin–Green Bay, 1996.

Cross, Lezlie. "Making Citizens of Savages: Columbia's Roll Call at the Hampton Institute." *Journal of American Drama and Theatre* 24 (Spring 2012): 33–48.

Cusick, David. *Sketches of Ancient History of the Six Nations . . . 1827.* 2nd ed. Lockport, NY: Cooley & Lothrop, 1828.

Davidson, John Nelson. "The Coming of the New York Indians to Wisconsin." In *Proceedings of the State Historical Society of Wisconsin 47,* 153–85. Madison: Democrat Printing, 1899.

Dearborn, Henry A. S. *Journals of Henry A. S. Dearborn.* Edited by Frank H. Severance. Buffalo Historical Society Publications 7. Buffalo: Buffalo Historical Society, 1904.

Deloria, Philip J. *Indians in Unexpected Places.* Lawrence: Univ. Press of Kansas, 2004.

———. *Playing Indian.* New Haven, CT: Yale Univ. Press, 1998.

Deloria, Vine, Jr., ed. *American Indian Policy in the Twentieth Century.* Norman: Univ. of Oklahoma Press, 1985.

Deloria, Vine, Jr., and Clifford M. Lytle. *American Indians, American Justice.* Austin: Univ. of Texas Press, 1983.

——. *The Nations Within: The Past and Future of American Indian Sovereignty.* New York: Pantheon, 1984.

Deloria, Vine, Jr., and David E. Wilkins. *Tribes, Treaties, and Constitutional Tribulations.* Austin: Univ. of Texas Press, 1999.

Disturnell, John. *A Gazetteer of the State of New-York.* Albany, 1842.

Draper, Lyman C. "Additional Notes on Eleazer Williams." *Wisconsin Historical Collections* 8 (1879): 353–69. Reprint, Madison: State Historical Society of Wisconsin, 1908.

Durrenberger, Joseph A. *Turnpikes: A Study of the Toll Road Movement in the Middle Atlantic States and Maryland.* Valdosta, GA: Southern Stationery, 1931.

Ellicott, Joseph. *Holland Land Company Papers: Reports of Joseph Ellicott.* Edited by Robert W. Bingham. 2 vols. Buffalo: Buffalo Historical Society, 1941.

Ellis, Albert G. "Fifty-Four Years' Recollections of Men and Events in Wisconsin." *Wisconsin Historical Collections* 7 (1876): 207–68. Reprint, Madison: State Historical Society of Wisconsin, 1908.

——. "Recollections of Rev. Eleazer Williams." *Wisconsin Historical Collections* 8 (1879): 322–52. Reprint, Madison: State Historical Society of Wisconsin, 1908.

——. "Some Account of the Advent of the New York Indians into Wisconsin." *State Historical Society of Wisconsin Collections* 2 (1856): 415–49.

——. "Some Accounts of the Advent of the New York Indians into Wisconsin." *Wisconsin Historical Collections* 2 (1856): 415–49.

Elm, Demus, and Harvey Antone. *The Oneida Creation Story.* Edited and translated by Floyd G. Lounsbury and Bryan Gick. Lincoln: Univ. of Nebraska Press, 2000.

Engs, Robert F. *Educating the Disenfranchised and Disinherited: Samuel Chapman Armstrong and Hampton Institute, 1839–1893.* Knoxville: Univ. of Tennessee Press, 1999.

——. *Freedom's First Generation: Black Hampton, Virginia, 1861–1890.* Philadelphia: Univ. of Pennsylvania Press, 1979.

Evans, Paul D. *The Holland Land Company.* Buffalo: Buffalo Historical Society, 1924.

Fairchild, A. P. *Naval Ordnance.* Baltimore: Lord Baltimore Press, 1921.

Farley, James J. *Making Arms in the Machine Age: Philadelphia's Frankford Arsenal, 1816–1870.* University Park: Pennsylvania State Univ. Press, 1994.

Fenton, William N. "Converse, Harriet Maxwell." In *Notable American Women, 1607–1950: A Biographical Dictionary,* edited by Edward T. James et al., 1:375–76. Cambridge, MA: Belknap Press of Harvard Univ. Press, 1971.

——. *The Great Law and the Longhouse: A Political History of the Iroquois Confederacy.* Norman: Univ. of Oklahoma Press, 1998.

————. "The Iroquois in History." In *North American Indians in Historical Perspective*, edited by Nancy O. Lurie and Eleanor Leacock. New York: Random House, 1971.

————. "Locality as a Basic Factor in the Development of Iroquois Social Structure." *Bureau of American Ethnology Bulletin* 149 (1951): 35–54.

————, ed. *Symposium on Local Diversity*. Bureau of American Ethnology Bulletin 149. Washington, DC, 1951.

————. "Toward the Gradual Civilization of the Indian Natives: The Missionary and Linguistic Work of Asher Wright (1803–1875) among the Senecas of Western New York." *Proceedings of the American Philosophical Society* 100 (1956): 567–81.

Fitzgerald, Gerald J. "Chemical Warfare and Medical Response during World War I." *American Journal of Public Health* 98 (July 2008): 611–25.

Fixico, Donald L. *Termination and Relocation: Federal Indian Policy, 1945–1960*. Albuquerque: Univ. of New Mexico Press, 1986.

Forbes, Jack. *Africans and Native Americans*. London: Blackwell, 1988.

Foreman, Grant. *The Last Trek of the Indians*. 1946. Reprint, New York: Russell & Russell, 1972.

Freilich, Morris. "Cultural Persistence among the Modern Iroquois." *Anthropos* 53 (1958): 473–83.

French, J. H., comp. *Gazetteer of the State of New York*. Syracuse: R. Pearsall Smith, 1860.

Frissell, Hollis Burke. *The Work and Influence of Hampton*. New York: Armstrong Association, 1904.

Galpin, W. Freeman. "The Genesis of Syracuse." *New York History* 30 (Jan. 1949): 19–32.

Geier, Philip Otto. "A Peculiar Status: A History of the Oneida Indian Treaties and Claims; Jurisdictional Conflict within the American Government, 1775–1920." PhD diss., Syracuse Univ., 1980.

George, Susan Hébert. "An Oneida Renaissance Man: Chapman Scanandoah." *Oneida* 10 (Mar.–Apr. 2008). http://wwww.oneidaindiannation.com.

Glatthaar, Joseph, and James Kirby Smith. *Forgotten Allies: The Oneida Indians and the American Revolution*. New York: Hill and Wang, 2006.

Goodrich, Carter, ed. *Canals and American Economic Development*. New York: Columbia Univ. Press, 1961.

————. *Government Promotion of American Canals and Railroads, 1800–1890*. New York: Columbia Univ. Press, 1960.

Graymont, Barbara, ed. *Fighting Tuscarora: The Autobiography of Chief Clinton Rickard*. Syracuse: Syracuse Univ. Press, 1973.

———. *The Iroquois in the American Revolution*. Syracuse: Syracuse Univ. Press, 1972.

———. "New York State Indian Policy after the Revolution." *New York History* 58 (Oct. 1976): 438–74.

Gunther, Gerald. "Governmental Power and New York Indian Lands: A Reassessment of a Persistent Problem of Federal-State Relations." *Buffalo Law Review* 7 (Fall 1958): 1–14.

Haber, Ludwig Fritz. *The Poisonous Cloud: Chemical Warfare in the First World War*. New York: Oxford Univ. Press, 1986.

Hagan, Kenneth J. *This People's Navy: The Making of American Seapower*. New York: Free Press/Macmillan, 1991.

Hagan, William T. *The Indian Rights Association: The Herbert Welsh Years, 1882–1904*. Tucson: Univ. of Arizona Press, 1985.

Hale, Horatio E. *The Iroquois Book of Rites*. 2 vols. Philadelphia: D. G. Brinton, 1883.

Hammond, Jabez D. *The History of Political Parties in the State of New York*. 2 vols. Albany: Charles Van Benthuysen, 1842.

Hammond, John Winthrop. *Men and Volts: The Story of General Electric*. Philadelphia: Lippincott, 1941.

Hammond, Luna M. *History of Madison County, State of New York*. Syracuse: Truair Smith, 1873.

Harlan, Louis R. *Booker T. Washington: The Making of a Black Leader*. New York: Oxford Univ. Press, 1972.

Hauptman, Laurence M. *Between Two Fires: American Indians in the Civil War*. New York: Free Press, 1995.

———. "Command Performance: Philip Schuyler and the New York State–Oneida 'Treaty' of 1795." In *The Oneida Indian Journey*, edited by Laurence M. Hauptman and L. Gordon McLester III, 19–37. Madison: Univ. of Wisconsin Press, 1999.

———. *Conspiracy of Interests: Iroquois Dispossession and the Rise of New York State*. Syracuse: Syracuse Univ. Press, 1999.

———. "How Native Americans Beat the British Navy." *New York Archives* 13 (Summer 2013): 30–33.

———. *In the Shadow of Kinzua: The Seneca Nation of Indians since World War II*. Syracuse: Syracuse Univ. Press, 2014.

———. *The Iroquois and the New Deal*. Syracuse: Syracuse Univ. Press, 1981.

——. "The Iroquois Count of 1845." *New York Archives* 11 (Fall 2011): 18–21.

——. "The Iroquois Indians and the Rise of the Empire State: Ditches, Defense, and Dispossession." *New York History* 89 (Oct. 1998): 325–58.

——. *The Iroquois in the Civil War: From Battlefield to Reservation.* Syracuse: Syracuse Univ. Press, 1993.

——. *The Iroquois Struggle for Survival: World War II to Red Power.* Syracuse: Syracuse Univ. Press, 1986.

——. "On Our Terms: The Tonawanda Seneca Indians, Lewis Henry Morgan, and Henry Rowe Schoolcraft." *New York History* 91 (Fall 2010): 315–36.

——. "Samuel George (1795–1873): A Study of Onondaga Indian Conservatism." *New York History* 70 (Jan. 1989): 4–22.

——. *The Tonawanda Senecas' Heroic Battle against Removal: Conservative Activist Indians.* Albany: SUNY Press, 2011.

——. *Tribes and Tribulations: Misconceptions about American Indians and Their Histories.* Albuquerque: Univ. of New Mexico Press, 1995.

Hauptman, Laurence M., and George Hamell. "George Catlin: The Origins of His Indian Portrait Gallery." *New York History* 54 (Spring 2003): 125–51.

Hauptman, Laurence M., and L. Gordon McLester III. "Captain John Archiquette: A Federal Indian Policeman in the Gilded Age." *Iroquoia* 1 (Autumn 2015): 25–60.

——. *Chief Daniel Bread and the Oneida Nation of Indians of Wisconsin.* Norman: Univ. of Oklahoma Press, 2002.

——, eds. *The Oneida Indian Journey: From New York to Wisconsin.* Madison: Univ. of Wisconsin Press, 1999.

——, eds. *The Oneida Indians in the Age of Allotment, 1860–1920.* Norman: Univ. of Oklahoma Press, 2006.

Hauptman, Laurence M., L. Gordon McLester III, and Judy Hawk. "Another Leatherstocking Tale: Susan Fenimore Cooper, the Oneida Indians, and the Episcopal Church." *New York History* 94 (Winter–Spring 2013): 9–39.

Haydon, Roger, ed. *Upstate Travels: British Views of Nineteenth-Century New York.* Syracuse: Syracuse Univ. Press, 1982.

Herrick, Walter R., Jr. *The American Naval Revolution.* Baton Rouge: Louisiana State Univ. Press, 1966.

Hertzberg, Hazel W. *The Search for an American Indian Identity: Modern Pan-Indian Movements.* Syracuse: Syracuse Univ. Press, 1971.

Hewitt, J. N. B. *Iroquois Cosmology.* Pt. 1. Bureau of American Ethnology, *21st Annual Report.* Washington, DC: USGPO, 1899–1900.

———. *Iroquoian Cosmology*. Pt. 2. Bureau of American Ethnology, *Annual Report*. Washington, DC: Bureau of American Ethnology, 1928.

Hickey, Donald R. *The War of 1812: A Forgotten Conflict*. Urbana: Univ. of Illinois Press, 1989.

Hitsman, J. Mackay. *The Incredible War of 1812: A Military History*. Toronto: Univ. of Toronto Press, 1965.

Hodge, Frederick Webb, ed. *Handbook of American Indians North of Mexico*. 2 vols. Washington, DC: USGPO, 1907–10.

Holm, Tom. *The Great Confusion in Indian Affairs: Native Americans and Whites in the Progressive Era*. Austin: Univ. of Texas Press, 2005.

Holmes, Oliver W. "The Turnpike Era." In *History of the State of New York*, edited by Alexander C. Flick, 257–93. New York: Columbia Univ. Press, 1934.

Holt, Marilyn. *Indian Orphanages*. Lawrence: Univ. Press of Kansas, 2001.

Hopkins, Vivian C. "De Witt Clinton and the Iroquois." Pts. 1–2. *Ethnohistory* 8 (Spring 1961): 113–43; (Summer 1961): 213–41.

Horsman, Reginald. "The Origins of Oneida Removal to Wisconsin, 1815–1822." In *An Anthology of Western Great Lakes Indian History*, edited by Donald Fixico, 203–32. Milwaukee: American Indian Studies Program of the Univ. of Wisconsin–Milwaukee, 1987.

Hough, Franklin B. *Notices of Peter Penet and His Operations among the Oneida Indians*. Lowville, NY: Albany Institute, 1866.

Hounshell, David A. *From the American System to Mass Production, 1860–1932: The Development of Manufacturing Technology in the United States*. Baltimore: Johns Hopkins Univ. Press, 1985.

Hounshell, David A., and John Kealy Smith Jr. *Science and Corporation Strategy: DuPont R&D, 1902–1980*. New York: Cambridge Univ. Press, 1988.

Hoxie, Frederick. *A Final Promise: The Campaign to Assimilate the Indians, 1880–1920*. Lincoln: Univ. of Nebraska Press, 1984.

———, ed. *Talking Back to Civilization: Indian Voices from the Progressive Era*. Boston: Bedford/St. Martin's, 2001.

Huguenin, Charles A. "The Sacred Stone of the Oneidas." *New York Folklore Quarterly* 8 (1957): 16–22.

Hulbert, Archer B. *Historic Highways of America*. Vol. 12, *Pioneer Roads and Experiences of Travelers*. Cleveland: Arthur H. Clark, 1904.

Hultgren, Mary Lou, and Paulette Fairbanks Molen. *To Learn and to Serve: American Indian Education at Hampton Institute, 1878–1923*. Virginia Beach: Virginia Foundation for the Humanities, 1989.

Hurt, R. Douglas. *Indian Agriculture: Prehistory to the Present*. Lawrence: Univ. Press of Kansas, 1987.

Iverson, Peter. *Carlos Montezuma and the Changing World of American Indians*. Albuquerque: Univ. of New Mexico Press, 1982.

Jennings, Francis, William N. Fenton, Mary A. Druke, and David R. Miller, eds. *The History and Culture of Iroquois Diplomacy: An Interdisciplinary Guide to the Treaties of the Six Nations and Their League*. Syracuse: Syracuse Univ. Press, 1985.

Johnson, Ronald M. "Schooling the 'Savage': Andrew S. Draper and Indian Education." *Phylon* 35 (1974): 74–82.

Keegan, John. *The First World War*. New York: Alfred A. Knopf, 1999.

Kellogg, Laura Cornelius. *Our Democracy and the American Indian*. [1920]. Reprint edited by Kristina Ackley and Cristina Stanciu. Syracuse: Syracuse Univ. Press, 2015.

Kiel, Douglas. "Competing Visions of Empowerment: Oneida Progressive-Era Politics and Writing Tribal Histories." *Ethnohistory* 61 (Summer 2014): 419–44.

———. "The Oneida Resurgence: Modern Indian Renewal in the Heart of America." PhD diss., Univ. of Wisconsin, 2012.

Klein, Daniel B., and John Majewski. "Plank Road Fever in Antebellum America: New York State Origins." *New York History* 75 (Jan. 1994): 39–65.

Krouse, Susan Applegate. *North American Indians in the Great War*. Lincoln: Univ. of Nebraska Press. 2007.

———. "Traditional Iroquois Socials: Maintaining Identity in the City." *American Indian Quarterly* 25 (Summer 2001): 400–408.

Kvasnicka, Robert, and Herman Viola, eds. *The Commissioners of Indian Affairs, 1824–1977*. Lincoln: Univ. of Nebraska Press, 1979.

Lafitau, Joseph François. *Customs of the American Indians* [1724]. 2 vols. Edited by William N. Fenton. Translated by Elizabeth Moore. Toronto: Champlain Society, 1974.

Lake Mohonk Conference of Friends of the Indian [after 1900 retitled Lake Mohonk Friends of the Indian and Other Dependent Peoples] *Proceedings, 1883–1916, 1929*. Lake Mohonk, NY, 1883–1929.

Lehman, J. David. "The End of the Iroquois Mystique: The Oneida Land Cession Treaties of the 1780s." *William and Mary Quarterly* 47 (Oct. 1990): 523–47.

Lender, Mark, and James Kirby Smith, eds. *Citizen Soldier: The Revolutionary War Journal of Joseph Bloomfield*. Newark: New Jersey Historical Society, 1982.

Lennox, H. J. *Samuel Kirkland's Mission to the Iroquois.* Chicago: Univ. of Chicago Libraries, 1935.

Leupp, Francis L. *The Indian and His Problem.* New York: Charles Scribner's Sons, 1910.

Lewis, Herbert, ed. *Oneida Lives: Long-Lost Voices of the Wisconsin Oneidas.* Lincoln: Univ. of Nebraska Press, 2005.

Liberty, Margot, ed. *American Indian Intellectuals.* St. Paul: American Ethnological Society, 1978.

Lindsey, Donal F. *Indians at Hampton Institute, 1877–1923.* Urbana: Univ. of Illinois Press, 1994.

Locklear, Arlinda. "The Buffalo Creek Treaty of 1838 and Its Legal Implications on Oneida Land Claims." In *The Oneida Indian Journey,* edited by Laurence M. Hauptman and L. Gordon McLester III, 85–104. Madison: Univ. of Wisconsin Press, 1999.

Ludlow, Helen, ed. *Twenty-Two Years' Work at the Hampton Normal and Agricultural Institute.* Hampton, VA: Hampton Institute Press, 1893.

Maddox, Lucy. *Citizen Indians: Native American Intellectuals, Race, and Reform.* Ithaca, NY: Cornell Univ. Press, 2005.

Manley, Henry S. "Buying Buffalo from the Indians." *New York History* 27 (July 1947): 313–29.

———. "Indian Reservation Ownership in New York." *New York State Bar Bulletin* 32 (Apr. 1960): 134–38.

———. *The Treaty of Fort Stanwix, 1784.* Rome, NY: Sentinel, 1932.

Mano, Jo Margaret. "Unmappimg the Iroquois: New York State Cartography, 1792–1845." In *The Oneida Indian Journey,* edited by Laurence M. Hauptman and L. Gordon McLester III, 171–95. Madison: Univ. of Wisconsin Press, 1999.

Martin, Albro. *Railroads Triumphant: The Growth, Rejection and Rebirth of a Vital American Force.* New York: Oxford Univ. Press, 1992.

Mau, Clayton, ed. *The Development of Central and Western New York.* New York: DuBois Press, 1944.

McDonnell, Janet. *The Dispossession of the American Indian, 1887–1934.* Bloomington: Indiana Univ. Press, 1991.

McKelvey, Blake. "The Erie Canal: Mother of Cities." *New-York Historical Society Quarterly* 30 (Jan. 1951): 54–71.

McLester, L. Gordon, III, and Laurence M. Hauptman, eds. *A Nation within a Nation: Voices of the Oneidas in Wisconsin.* Madison: Wisconsin Historical Society Press, 2010.

Meinig, D. W. "Elaboration and Change, 1850s–1960s." In *Geography of New York State*, edited by John H. Thompson, 172–99. Rev. ed. Syracuse: Syracuse Univ. Press, 1977.

———. "Geography of Expansion, 1785–1855." In *Geography of New York State*, edited by John H. Thompson, 140–71. Rev. ed. Syracuse: Syracuse Univ. Press, 1977.

———. *The Shaping of America: A Geographical Perspective on 500 Years of History.* 2 vols. New Haven, CT: Yale Univ. Press, 1986 and 1993.

Meriam, Lewis, et al. *The Problem of Indian Administration.* Baltimore: Johns Hopkins Univ. Press, 1928.

Metcalf, R. Warren. *Termination's Legacy: The Discarded Indians of Utah.* Lincoln: Univ. of Nebraska Press, 2002.

Miller, Nathan. *The Enterprise of a Free People: Aspects of Economic Development in New York State during the Canal Era, 1792–1838.* Ithaca, NY: Cornell Univ. Press, 1962.

———. "Private Enterprise in Inland Navigation: The Mohawk Route prior to the Erie Canal." *New York History* 31 (Oct. 1950): 398–413.

Miner, H. Craig, and William Unrau. *The End of Indian Kansas: A Study of Cultural Revolution, 1854–1871.* Lawrence: Regents Press of Kansas, 1978.

Montgomery, David. *The Fall of the House of Labor: The Workplace, the State, and American Labor Activism, 1865–1925.* New York: Cambridge Univ. Press, 1987.

Morgan, Lewis Henry. *League of the Ho-de-no-sau-nee, or Iroquois.* Rochester: Sage & Bros., 1851. Paperback reprint introduction by William N. Fenton. New York: Corinth Books, 1962.

Moses, L. George. *Wild West Shows and the Image of American Indians, 1883–1933.* Albuquerque: Univ. of New Mexico Press, 1996.

Murphy, Joseph Hawley. "The Salt Industry of Syracuse: A Brief Review." *New York History* 30 (July 1949): 304–15.

Noble, David F. *America by Design: Technology and the Rise of Corporate Capitalism.* New York: Alfred A. Knopf, 1977.

Norton, David J. *Rebellious Younger Brother: Oneida Leadership and Diplomacy, 1750–1800.* DeKalb: Univ. of Northern Illinois Press, 2009.

Nye, David E. *Image Worlds: Corporate Identities at General Electric, 1890–1930.* Cambridge, MA: MIT Press, 1985.

Oberg, Michael Leroy. *Professional Indian: The American Odyssey of Eleazer Williams.* Philadelphia: Univ. of Pennsylvania Press, 2015.

Official Record of Indian Conference Called to Determine the Status of the Indians of the Six Nations on the Indian Reservations of the State of New York and Their Relations to the Federal and State Governments. Syracuse: Onondaga Historical Association, 1919.

Parker, Arthur C. *The Life of General Ely S. Parker: Last Grand Sachem of the Iroquois and General Grant's Military Secretary.* Buffalo Historical Society Publications 23. Buffalo: Buffalo Historical Society, 1919.

———. *Parker on the Iroquois.* Edited by William N. Fenton. Syracuse: Syracuse Univ. Press, 1968.

Patrick, Christine. "Samuel Kirkland: Missionary to the Oneida Indians." PhD diss., SUNY Buffalo, 1992.

Peabody, Francis Greenwood. *Education for Life: The Story of Hampton Institute.* New York: Doubleday Page, 1918.

Pevar, Stephen L. *The Rights of Indians and Tribes.* 4th ed. New York: New York Univ. Press, 2012.

Philp, Kenneth R. *Termination Revisited: American Indians on the Trail to Self-Determination, 1933–1953.* Lincoln: Univ. of Nebraska Press, 1999.

Pilkington, Walter, ed. *The Journals of Samuel Kirkland.* Clinton, NY: Hamilton College, 1980.

Porter, Joy. *To Be Indian: The Life of Iroquois-Seneca Arthur Caswell Parker.* Norman: Univ. of Oklahoma Press, 2001.

Pound, Cuthbert W. "Nationals without a Nation: The New York State Tribal Indians." *Columbia Law Review* 22 (Feb. 1922): 97–102.

Pratt, Richard Henry. *Battlefield and Classroom: Four Decades with the American Indians, 1867–1904.* Edited by Robert Utley. New Haven, CT: Yale Univ. Press, 1964.

———. "The True Origin of the Indian Outing System at Hampton (Va.) Institute." *Red Man* (Sept.–Oct. 1885).

Prucha, Francis Paul. *American Indian Policy in Crisis: Christian Reformers and the Indian, 1880–1900.* Norman: Univ. of Oklahoma Press, 1976.

———. *American Indian Policy in the Formative Years: The Indian Trade and Intercourse Acts, 1790–1834.* Cambridge, MA: Harvard Univ. Press, 1962.

———. *American Indian Treaties: The History of an American Anomaly.* Berkeley: Univ. of California Press, 1994.

———, ed. *"Americanizing" the American Indians: Writings by the "Friends of the Indians," 1880–1900.* Cambridge, MA: Harvard Univ. Press, 1973.

————. *The Great Father: The United States Government and the American Indians.* 2 vols. Lincoln: Univ. of Nebraska Press, 1984.

Recht, Michael. "The Role of Fishing in the Iroquois Economy." *New York History* 76 (Jan. 1995): 5–30.

Reid, Gerald F. "'Illegal Alien'? The Immigration Case of Paul K. Diabo." *Proceedings of the American Philosophical Society* 151 (Mar. 2007): 61–78.

Reilly, John C., Jr., and Robert L. Schein. *American Battleships, 1886–1923: Predreadnought Design and Construction.* Annapolis, MD: Naval Institute Press, 1980.

Reitz, Keith. "George P. Decker and the Oneida Indians." *Iroquoian* 13 (Fall 1987): 28–33.

Ricciardi, Alan F. "The Adoption of White Agriculture by the Oneida Indians." *Ethnohistory* 10 (Fall 1963): 309–28.

Richards, Cara E. *The Oneida People.* Phoenix: Indian Tribal Series, 1974.

Richter, Daniel K. "War and Culture: The Iroquois Experience." *William and Mary Quarterly* (1983): 528–59.

Robertson, Constance Noyes, ed. *Oneida Community: An Autobiography, 1851–1876.* Kenwood, NY: Oneida Community Mansion House in association with Syracuse Univ. Press, 1970.

Rosen, Deborah A. *American Indians and State Law: Sovereignty, Race and Citizenship, 1790–1880.* Lincoln: Univ. of Nebraska Press, 2007.

Rosenthal, Harvey. *Their Day in Court: A History of the United States Indian Claims Commission.* New York: Garland, 1990.

Ryan, Mary P. *Cradle of the Middle Class: The Family in Oneida County, New York, 1790–1865.* Cambridge: Cambridge Univ. Press, 1981.

Satz, Ronald. *American Indian Policy in the Jacksonian Era.* Lincoln: Univ. of Nebraska Press, 1975.

Schein, Richard H. "A Historical Geography of Central New York: Patterns and Processes of Colonization on the New Military Tract, 1782–1820." PhD diss., Syracuse Univ., 1989.

Schoolcraft, Henry R. *Notes on the Iroquois; or, Contributions to American History, Antiquities and General Ethnology.* Albany: Erastus H. Pense, 1847.

Schramm, Henry M. *Empire Showcase: A History of the New York State Fair.* Utica, NY: North Country Books, 1985.

Sellers, Charles. *The Market Revolution: Jacksonian America, 1815–1846.* New York: Oxford Univ. Press, 1992.

Shattuck, George C. *The Oneida Land Claims: A Legal History.* Syracuse: Syracuse Univ. Press, 1991.

Shaw, Ronald E. *Canals for a Nation: The Canal Era in the United States, 1790–1860.* Lexington: Univ. Press of Kentucky, 1990.

———. *Erie Water West: A History of the Erie Canal, 1792–1854.* Lexington: Univ. Press of Kentucky, 1966.

Sheriff, Carol. *The Artificial River: The Erie Canal and the Paradox of Progress, 1817–1862.* New York: Hill & Wang, 1996.

Shoemaker, Nancy. "The Rise and Fall of Iroquois Women." *Journal of Women's History* 2 (Winter 1991): 39–57.

Smith, John E. *Our County and Its People: A Descriptive and Biographical Record of Madison County, New York.* 1899. Reprint, Markham, VA: Apple Manor Press, 2014.

Snyder, Charles M., ed. *Red and White on the New York Frontier . . . from the Papers of Erastus Granger, 1807–1819.* Harrison, NY: Harbor Hill Books, 1978.

Spafford, Horatio Gates. *A Gazetteer of the State of New-York.* Albany: B. D. Packard, 1824.

Stagg, J. C. A. *Mr. Madison's War.* Princeton, NJ: Princeton Univ. Press, 1983.

Stanciu, Cristina. "An Indian Woman of Many Hats: Laura Cornelius Kellogg's Embattled Search for an Indigenous Voice." *American Indian Quarterly* 37 (Fall 2013): 87–117.

Steeples, Douglas, and David O. Whitten. *Democracy in Desperation: The Depression of 1893.* Westport, CT: Praeger/Greenwood, 1998.

Sweetman, Jack, ed. *Great American Naval Battles.* Annapolis, MD: Naval Institute Press, 1998.

Talbot, Edith Armstrong. *Samuel Chapman Armstrong: A Biographical Study.* New York: Doubleday, 1904.

Tate, Michael L. "From Scout to Doughboys: The National Debate over Integrating American Indians into the Military, 1891–1918." *Western Historical Quarterly* 17 (1996): 417–37.

Taylor, Alan S. *Divided Ground: Indians, Settlers, and the Northern Borderlands of the American Revolution.* New York: Alfred A. Knopf, 2006.

———. *William Cooper's Town.* New York: Alfred A. Knopf, 1995.

Taylor, Frederick Winslow. *The Principles of Scientific Management.* New York: Harper and Brothers, 1912.

Taylor, George Rogers. *The Transportation Revolution, 1815–1860.* New York: Rinehart, 1951.

Thompson, John H., ed. *Geography of New York State.* Rev. ed. Syracuse: Syracuse Univ. Press, 1979.

Tingey, Joseph W. "Indians and Blacks Together: An Experiment in Biracial Education at Hampton Institute, 1878–1923." EdD diss., Teachers College, Columbia Univ., 1978.

Tiro, Karim. "A Civil War? Rethinking Iroquois Participation in the American Revolution." *Explorations in Early American Culture* 4 (2000): 148–65.

———. "James Dean in Iroquoia." *New York History* 80 (Oct. 1999): 391–422.

———. *The People of the Standing Stone: The Oneida Nation from the Revolution through the Era of Removal.* Amherst: Univ. of Massachusetts Press, 2011.

———. "'We Wish to Do You Good': The Quaker Mission to the Oneida Nation." *Journal of the Early Republic* 26 (Fall 2006): 353–76.

Tooker, Elisabeth. *The Iroquois Ceremonial of Midwinter.* Syracuse: Syracuse Univ. Press, 1970.

———. "The Iroquois White Dog Sacrifice in the Latter Part of the Eighteenth Century." *Ethnohistory* 12 (1965): 129–40.

———. "On the New Religion of Handsome Lake." *Anthropological Quarterly* 41 (1968): 187–200.

———. *Proceedings of the 1965 Conference on Iroquois Research.* Albany: New York State Museum and Science Service, 1967.

Trask, David F. *The War with Spain in 1898.* New York: Free Press/Macmillan, 1981.

Trennert, Robert A. "From Carlisle to Phoenix: The Rise and Fall of the Outing System, 1878–1930." *Pacific Historical Review* 52 (Aug. 1983): 267–91.

———. *The Phoenix Indian School: Forced Assimilation in Arizona, 1891–1935.* Norman: Univ. of Oklahoma Press, 1988.

Trigger, Bruce G., ed. *Handbook of North American Indians.* Vol. 15, *The Northeast.* Washington, DC: Smithsonian Institution, 1978.

Tustin, E. B., Jr. "The Development of the Salt Industry in New York." *New-York Historical Society Quarterly* 33 (1949): 40–46.

Upton, Helen M. *The Everett Report in Historical Perspective: The Indians of New York.* Albany: New York State American Revolution Bicentennial Commission, 1980.

Vecsey, Christopher, and William A. Starna, eds. *Iroquois Land Claims.* Syracuse: Syracuse Univ. Press, 1988.

Viola, Herman, J. *Diplomats in Buckskin: A History of Indian Delegations in Washington City.* Washington, DC: Smithsonian Institution Press, 1981.

Wallace, Anthony F. C. *The Death and Rebirth of the Seneca.* New York: Alfred A. Knopf, 1969.

Wilson, Edmund. *Apologies to the Iroquois [with a Study of the Mohawks in High Steel by Joseph Mitchell]*. New York: Farrar, Straus, & Giroux, 1960. Paperback reprint with introduction and letters by William N. Fenton. Syracuse: Syracuse Univ. Press, 1991.

Witmer, Linda F. *The Indian Industrial School, Carlisle, Pennsylvania, 1878–1918*. Carlisle, PA: Cumberland County Historical Society, 2002.

Wonderley, Anthony. *At the Font of the Marvelous: Exploring Oral Narrative and Mythic Imagery of the Iroquois and Their Neighbors*. Syracuse: Syracuse Univ. Press, 2009.

———. "The Most Utopian Industry: Making Oneida's Animal Traps, 1852–1925." *New York History* 19 (Summer 2010): 175–95.

———. "An Oneida Community in 1780: Study of an Inventory of Iroquois Property Losses during the American Revolutionary War." *Northeast Anthropology* 56 (1998): 19–41.

———. *Oneida Iroquois Folklore, Myth, and History: New York Oral Narrative from the Notes of H. E. Allen*. Syracuse: Syracuse Univ. Press, 2004.

Zupan, James. *Tools, Targets and Troopers: The History of the Frankford Arsenal*. Reprint, Mattituck, NY: Amereon, 1985.

Index

Laurence M. Hauptman is SUNY Distinguished Professor Emeritus of History at SUNY New Paltz, where he taught courses on Native American history, New York history, and Civil War history for forty years. In 2011 Dr. John B. King, Jr., then the New York State commissioner of education, awarded Hauptman the New York State Archives Lifetime Achievement Award for his research and publications on the Empire State. Hauptman is the author of numerous books and articles on the Hodinöhsö:ni´ and other Native Americans. His most recent book, *In the Shadow of Kinzua: The Seneca Nation of Indians since World War II*, was published by Syracuse University Press in 2014. Hauptman has testified as an expert witness before committees of both houses of Congress and in federal court and has served as a historical consultant for the Wisconsin Oneidas, the Cayugas, the Mashantucket Pequots, and the Senecas. He was twice the recipient of the Peter Doctor Memorial Indian Scholarship Foundation Award from the Six Nations and was honored by the Seneca Nation of Indians for his writings and applied work on behalf of Native Americans in eastern North America.